Collapse of Stout Party

The Decline and Fall of the Tories

JULIAN CRITCHLEY
& MORRISON HALCROW

VICTOR GOLLANCZ

LONDON

BIRKBECK
LIBRARY
COLLEGE

D0101547

First published in Great Britain 1997
by Victor Gollancz
An imprint of the Cassell group
Wellington House, 125 Strand, London WC2R 0BB

© Julian Critchley and Morrison Halcrow 1997

The right of Julian Critchley and Morrison Halcrow
to be identified as authors of this work has been
asserted by them in accordance with the Copyright,
Designs and Patents Act, 1988.

Lines from 'Godolphin Horne' from *Cautionary Verses* by
Hilaire Belloc, © The Estate of Hilaire Belloc, are reprinted
by permission of The Peters Fraser and Dunlop Group Limited
on behalf of the Estate of Hilaire Belloc.

A catalogue record for this book is
available from the British Library.

ISBN 0 575 06277 0

Typeset by Rowland Phototypesetting Ltd,
Bury St Edmunds, Suffolk
Printed in Great Britain by
St Edmundsbury Press Ltd, Bury St Edmunds, Suffolk

All rights reserved. No part of this publication may be
reproduced or transmitted in any form or by any means,
electronic or mechanical including photocopying,
recording or any information storage or retrieval system,
without prior permission in writing from the publishers.

This book is sold subject to the condition that it shall not,
by way of trade or otherwise, be lent, resold, hired out, or
otherwise circulated without the publisher's prior consent
in any form of binding or cover other than that in which it
is published and without a similar condition including this
condition being imposed on the subsequent purchaser.

97 98 99   5 4 3 2 1

Contents

Prologue

JULIAN CRITCHLEY

14 April 1997

I have observed this election campaign from a distance, dominated as it has been by irrelevancies such as sleaze and privatisation. Europe has been barely mentioned, and then only to be attacked.

Tory Eurosceptics, of course, have one eye on the future leadership of the Conservative Party. I cannot help feeling, too, that much of the rhetoric employed by the Eurosceptics suggests that their opposition is based on resistance to change and an inability to come to terms with economic and geopolitical realities which is hardly consistent with the aspiration to become 'the enterprise centre of a newly competitive Europe'. We should not be surprised if our European partners take us at our word. A refusal to enter economic and monetary union when we were qualified to do so would be the clearest possible signal that Britain was not committed to the goals of the European Union, giving credence to the view that we are determined to undermine it.

EMU is a major goal, a dynamic enterprise that is intended to take the European Union forward to a new level of economic and political integration; it is comparable with the projects to establish the original customs union, and later the single market. A partner that stands aside from such a project can hardly be expected to be treated as a full member of the club; and whatever the legal position, the psychological damage to Britain's standing and influence would be immense. This surely cannot be gainsaid. The reluctance to advocate a move that would so obviously enhance Britain's interest is the principal reason why, as a Tory of thirty-one years' standing, I shall not vote Conservative on 1 May. In fact, I shall not vote at all.

PART I

Downhill all the Way?

MORRISON HALCROW

Reaping the Whirlwind

The 1997 general election was the one where the British class system didn't work the way it is supposed to work. The Conservative Party, political wing of the middle classes, had its come-uppance.

It wasn't quite what John Major had in mind when he talked of the classless society. After six and a half years of Majorism, Britain was more of a middle-class nation than ever before. The sage of the Grantham grocer's shop had left her mark. The ethos of suburbia reigned from north to south. Wine shipping, once the profession of gentlemen, was now part of the Tesco and Safeway marketing programmes. Two-car families thronged the out-of-town shopping centres.

The bottom line in Conservative election-winning strategy has always been that people vote for governments which put money into their pockets. The other things politicians talk about, like abroad, and family values – at the end of the day the voters don't give a damn. At least, that had been the accepted wisdom. Until 1997.

In terms of money in pockets, the Conservatives had done the electorate proud. Average GDP per head rose by something like 15 per cent in real terms between 1979 and 1995 – not as much as in some countries, certainly, but quite a lot. Moreover, the Thatcher–Major years padded middle-class wallets as a matter of faith. The higher you were up the income scale, the more you benefited from tax cuts. At the bottom end of the scale, after eighteen years you were little better off; in some cases, worse off. Of course, the income-tax-paying classes would have liked more chopped off of the standard rate. But for the income-tax-paying classes to grumble about Britain under Thatcher and Major was like accusing the Brigade of Guards of not believing in discipline and spit-and-polish. The middle classes were given the chance to keep themselves in the manner to which they wished to become accustomed.

What defeated the Tories? The new 'feelgood factor', or lack of it, was evidently more important than the standard rate of tax. That was part of the story. New Labour, shamelessly wooing the middle classes, was another part of it. But there was more to it than that. Under John Major something had collapsed within the structure of the Conservative Party as we knew it.

*

Margaret Thatcher was always bound to be a hard act to follow. Until the day she left Downing Street in tears in 1990, Margaret herself believed, quite seriously, that the ideal solution would have been for her to 'go on and on'. When the news reached her in Downing Street that her Chancellor had won the succession, she rushed through the connecting door to his house at No. 11 and threw her arms round Norma. 'The future is assured,' she told Norma. 'It's everything I've dreamed of for such a long time.' 'Rejoice,' she might have added, but didn't.

She was fantasising, of course; unfortunately, she was not the last within her party to do so. Her praetorian guard certainly knew there was no assured future for Thatcherism under John, and made their arrangements for spending more time with their families, and with employers who could afford to pay them better. The moment that Norma Major found Margaret's arms around her that evening in 11 Downing Street marked the arrival of the post-Thatcher age. On television screens a tearful Margaret was seen being handed into her car outside No. 10, and strong men dabbed their eyes in saloon bars up and down the country. Some of us were more distressed than others.

Tears were one thing. Guilt was another. There were a lot of guilty men around the Palace of Westminster after Margaret drove out for the last time through the great gates that the IRA had made her build at the end of Downing Street. Even after a decade of the Resolute Approach, the typical Tory in 1990 still believed in being a gentleman. He still felt rotten about seeing a lady cry. The Tory party suffering from guilt feelings is not a pretty sight. To any shrewd social worker, had such a person been called in to advise the party on its guilt feelings at the end of 1990, the answer would have been clear: Go and get help. But from whom? Care in the Community was not, in the circumstances, an option. Instead, the post-Thatcher Conservative Party took refuge in the form of group therapy that Tories have always understood, based on nostalgia, mythology and selective memory.

If the mythology had been fact, John Major would been like one of those heirs to great industrial dynasties told, 'One day, son, all this will be yours,' as they gaze out over proud acres of industrial townscape alive with eager, happy workmen striding to their places at the workbench. In reality, what John needed to do during that first post-Thatcher winter was to draw up a balance sheet of the Thatcher years and decide which bits of his inheritance should be treasured, and which had to be reformed. The longer he put it off, the more difficult it became to fashion a party based on common sense rather than mythology.

The myth-makers were already hard at work. Their raw material was near at hand in countless pronouncements made by Margaret over the years. Only a few weeks before her downfall, for instance, she had been pouring scorn on one Labour critic for failing to appreciate 'the total industrial and commercial transformation that has taken place in this country'. Her critics, she declared, ignored 'the colossal increase of production' during the Thatcher period.

All politicians exaggerate. But problems arise when their disciples treat the small change of political banter as purest gold. The Authorised Version was that the Thatcher economics of the 1980s had achieved not just a bit more than the Callaghan government here, a bit more than Harold Macmillan there, a bit more than the French or the Germans or the Americans, but something literally on the scale of a Colossus, bestriding the elements, a symbol of hope and achievement, towering into the clear blue sky and visible on the far horizon to the mariners of lesser nations as they battled against the storms. 'Tory reforms', Margaret liked to say, 'have transformed a lame duck economy into a bulldog economy.' But the mythology of those in 1990 who wanted Thatcherism to go on and on went further than that.

The increase in GDP during the Thatcher years was genuine enough; but it wasn't the exponential growth – the unique kind of growth – which was basic to the mythology of the Thatcherite ultras.

British manufacturing output when Margaret left Downing Street was barely 6 per cent higher than when she arrived there – a modest rather than a 'colossal' achievement. Over the same period there was a 35 per cent increase in manufacturing output in the United States and a 58 per cent increase in Japan. The Italians were said to have over-taken the British in terms of GDP per head during the 1980s – but then, no sensible economist will stake his reputation on statistics that come out of Italy. More alarmingly, by the time Britain approached the 1997 election, economists were predicting that Ireland – blessed Ireland – would soon be richer per head than the UK. Ian Gilmour, one of the most intelligent members of the original Thatcher Cabinet, who might have improved the quality of the Thatcher revolution if both he and she had been more alert to what was really happening, sought to produce a balanced summing-up of the Thatcher years in his book *Dancing with Dogma*, in the course of which he argued that Britain's economic growth rate was actually lower during the Thatcher years than during any similar period since the Second World War.

Of course, the Gilmour statistics are debatable. All those GDP per head figures are debatable, as indeed is almost everything about the Thatcher years – but this is the point. During the Major years no Conservative *wanted* a serious party debate on the Thatcher record. Ministers in Major Cabinets enjoyed a freedom of discussion that hadn't been known for a decade. But there were limits. None of them would have dared stand up at a post-Thatcher party conference to challenge the mythology. It would have been like Mr Gladstone going to the newly widowed Queen Victoria and proposing an open-ended discussion on the merits of the late Prince Consort.

It was the mythology, too, that made Euroscepticism so nasty. To the age-old, often harmless, adage of British politics, 'We don't like foreigners,' were added much more harmful illusions about how foreigners don't know how to run their economies. It added up to a dangerous kind of chauvinism, which cries 'Traitor!' in the face of rational argument – and which successfully thwarted the rational restructuring of the Conservative Party.

Ironically, it was Labour who chose – who were bullied by Tony Blair into choosing – to enter into a serious debate on post-Thatcherism. Far more than they were prepared to admit in public, they took much of the Thatcherite revolution as the 'given' part of the proposition, and started from there. Only a few – admittedly a dangerous few – thought of putting the clock back on trade union reforms or privatisation. By contrast, the Conservatives after Thatcher seemed too often to be engaged in the kind of political posturing that comes naturally to professional politicians but puzzles ordinary voters. It was still puzzling them when they went to the polls in 1997.

The man in the street has a robust way of judging prime ministers. In 1945 he had no problems about cheering Churchill for winning the war but then deciding he was not right as a postwar premier. In 1990 he admired Margaret for doing to the unions what Churchill did to the Nazis. But that was not the same as a vote for Thatcherism.

*

John Major had been marked out as Margaret Thatcher's chosen successor when he was plucked from the background and made Foreign Secretary, and confirmed as heir apparent when, three months later (this being a period of high mortality rates among senior members of her Cabinet), he moved on to be Chancellor. He was the Thatcher trusty sent to the Foreign Office to replace the despised Geoffrey Howe and then moved on to the Treasury to take over from the wayward Nigel Lawson. But the Thatcherite mantle didn't really fit, then or later. Someone once told him his colleagues were puzzled about whether he was really a Thatcherite radical or an old-fashioned consensus man. He is said to have smiled, 'Oh good.'

When John became Prime Minister, Douglas Hurd remarked: 'We've got ourselves another Baldwin.' It was not entirely a compliment. Nevertheless the public in the early nineties gave John full marks for decency, in the way that middle England had warmed to Stanley Baldwin for trying to heal the class conflicts of the twenties and thirties. They heaved a sigh of relief when he quietly got rid of the poll tax without mentioning that it had been Margaret's 'flagship', and enough of them supported him in the 1992 election to win him his famous victory. The Thatcherite wing of the party were prepared to give him the benefit of the doubt. More importantly, they were prepared to put up with him because he was not Michael Heseltine.

But then, having won his victory in 1992, John began to take on another side of the Baldwin character. Some, as they watched him, remembered what they had read in the Churchill memoirs about the

celebrated Commons speech in which SB confessed why he had been
slow to rearm against Hitler. Supposing, he said, he had addressed
the country and told them honestly what was happening in Europe.
He would simply have lost the next general election. 'My position as
the leader of a great party was not altogether a comfortable one,' SB
told the House in that speech in 1936. John Major in the 1990s could
not have put it better. For him, as for Baldwin, a clock was ticking
in the continent of Europe. It made his position as leader of a great
party not at all comfortable.

Within a year of John Major becoming Prime Minister, the Maastricht negotiations loomed and the bloodletting started within the
Conservative Party. There was not much constructive debate about
the future of Conservatism. For those with a nose for sniffing the
political wind, there was more sinister significance in an article written
in the autumn of 1991 by a middle-ranking member of the opposition
team and published in, of all places, the magazine *Marxism Today*.

Tony Blair's *Marxism Today* article, closely argued and some would
say almost unreadable, was more influential in setting out the political
agenda for the 1990s than anything that was going on at that time
among the Tories, intellectually and emotionally exhausted after a
dozen years in office. Margaret herself was later to commend a significant part of the Blair philosophy, and no wonder. It wasn't just that
he condemned the Labour Party for being caught in a time warp of
nineteenth-century thinking. He enthused over the Thatcher style.
The Tories' big mistake, he was sure, had been to get rid of her: 'a
vital sense of direction (even if admittedly in the wrong direction) was
lost.'

John Smith's second and fatal heart attack on 12 May 1994, and his
succession by Tony Blair, constituted probably the most devastating of
the long list of misfortunes that beset an unlucky Prime Minister.
John Major, in his uncomfortable position as leader of an increasingly
unleadable party, found himself in competition with a leader who was
proving that it *was* possible to stand up against neanderthal colleagues.
Within months he had got rid of Clause Four and dared to say that
common sense was more important than political correctness in edu-
cating children. Comparisons are odious. Maybe the Tory right was
a more hopeless case than the Labour left. But the contrast in style
between the two party leaders left John Major looking like one of those

well-meaning schoolmasters who believe in freedom of expression in the classroom and then wonder why the children keep stabbing each other in the playground.

There had always been a left and a right wing to the Tory party, but many Conservatives, including some of the more interesting ones, were hard to slot into either. Was Winston Churchill, one-time lieutenant of Lloyd George, on the right or the left? How do you classify Rab Butler? What about Quintin Hailsham, or the monetarist Geoffrey Howe? The Conservative Party has its Whigs and Tories, but that is a useful distinction only up to a point. When the One Nation Group was established in the 1950s it was scarcely a left-wing conspiracy: it included Enoch Powell and Keith Joseph among its members. But by the mid-1990s Margaret was sneering at One Nation Europhiles, dubbing them No Nation Tories. By that time, the divide between the two Tory parties had emerged as a gulf of a different kind, and Margaret herself was the key. 'One Nation' had somehow come to embody a threat to the nation-state.

'Euroscepticism' wasn't invented under Major. The most distinguished Eurosceptic was Enoch Powell, in his prime years before John was an MP. Almost from the outset of the European project, Enoch opposed the Conservative strategy on what was then called the Common Market; and in 1974, honourably, he struck camp and left the party. But it was under Major's leadership that Euroscepticism came to serve as shorthand for all sorts of things that had always lurked beneath the surface in the Conservative Party. The issue of Europe has to be the starting point of the inquiry into the collapse of the party.

*

Robert Peel wrote the Tamworth Manifesto and changed the face of Conservatism. John Major will not go down as a great manifesto writer, but occasionally he found words which caught the precise flavour of what was going on in his party – reflecting its face, if not changing it. They were not always intended for publication. Late in the evening on 23 July 1993, he unclipped the microphone from his tie after an interview with ITN's political editor, Michael Brunson, after he had just – only just – got the better of his Eurosceptic critics in the last of the series of votes on Maastricht. He was pleased with himself. How was it, he wondered aloud to Brunson, that 'a complete wimp like me' could have got so far? Of course, he mused, he still had the problem of Eurosceptic critics inside the Cabinet itself, but he was content to leave them there – 'What's that Lyndon Johnson maxim?'

'You mean', said Brunson, 'that if you've got them by the balls, hearts and minds will follow?'

'No, no,' said John, 'although that's pretty good.' What he meant was that it was better to have your critics safely, and hygienically, inside the tent than to have 'three more of the bastards out there'.

This exchange on the political charm techniques of Lyndon Johnson didn't go out on the airwaves, but enough of the studio crew heard it to ensure that the Major view on the Maastricht bastards was around the corridors of Westminster within hours. The bastard factor at work in the Tory party had been identified. And, like the 'wets' during the Thatcher years, the 'bastards' wore their name with pride.

The central figure in the European story within the Conservative Party was Harold Macmillan, a leader whose methods – even more than Baldwin's, perhaps – repay study whenever the party seems determined to tear itself apart. In the 1990s the British had run into the buffers in Europe in a situation not entirely dissimilar to the one in which they found themselves after the Suez debacle of 1956. The skill of the Macmillan government then was to restore national self-confidence in a way which quietly but ruthlessly challenged the mythology of the Tory right about Britain's world role. If Harold, in the late 1950s, had tried to deal with his Suez rebels in the way John Major did in the 1990s when confronted with the Eurosceptic rebellion, Britain might have been bogged down in conflict in Africa for decades. But Harold, of course, had a working majority in the Commons.

The Major government knew it had a management problem, a whipping problem, over the Maastricht Treaty which was to set the structure of the next stage of the European Union's development. Negotiations took place before the 1992 election. Maastricht didn't loom large as a campaign issue in that election, but the whips sensibly made plans to ensure that the British team at Maastricht, where they had difficulties enough with the Europeans, wouldn't be shot from behind by their own troops back at Westminster. It was now a year since John had replaced Margaret, and Thatcherites who had given him the benefit of the doubt were getting restless.

Among these was the chairman of the back-bench Committee on European Affairs, Bill Cash. Bill, of the family whose name has been immortalised for generations of schoolchildren by the name tabs sewn on to their every item of clothing, was proud also to be a descendant of John Bright, the Anti-Corn-Law campaigner. The whips decided the time had come to replace him on the committee with a mainstream Tory; and nobody could be more mainstream than Norman Fowler, formerly a Cabinet minister and party chairman under Thatcher and now a back-bencher again and thus eligible to serve on a committee.

The choosing of office-bearers of back-bench committees is like the annual elections in undergraduate societies. Normally the process becomes a cosy carving up of the spoils among friends, but just occasionally it can be a pretext for a punch-up. The pre-Maastricht elections for the European Affairs Committee were organised by the whips with more zeal than subtlety. Committee Room 14 witnessed scenes which, had they taken place on the terracing of a football ground, would have had Conservative voters clamouring for the reintroduction of National Service. Voting irregularities were alleged as Bill Cash and like-minded colleagues were swept off the list of office-bearers. At one point, Norman Tebbit could be seen standing on the top of a table, expressing disapproval.

Thus heartened, the Prime Minister went off to negotiate at Maastricht.

By 1997 it was easy to forget the shape of the House of Commons which resulted from John Major's victory in 1992. He had a fair working majority, but there were forty fewer Tory MPs than there had been under Margaret. Moreover, the 1992 election had brought changes in the character as well as the numbers of the parliamentary Conservative Party. Demographics were at work. Altogether, fifty-six Tories had retired in 1992, including Margaret Thatcher, although she was soon to re-emerge in the Upper House. Also gone were Norman Tebbit, Peter Walker and Ian Gilmour. The changes were to have a significant effect on the rules of engagement during the battles over Europe. This explained the nature of John Major's problems, just as the demographic changes wrought in the 1997 election set the agenda for the next stage in the evolution of the Tory party.

In the 1992 election, in the austere words of David Butler and his colleagues in *The British General Election*: 'The youngest group of newcomers had been mere teenagers when Mrs Thatcher became party leader. The orthodoxies into which they were schooled were inevitably different from those of the Macmillan years. In this sense, the new Conservative intake of 1992 implied a drift to the right as 60-year-old One Nation Tories made way for 30-year-old free marketeers.'

An election majority of the size John Major had in 1992 meant that he could be relaxed about rebellions. On the second reading of the Bill to ratify the Maastricht Treaty, twenty-two Tories voted against the government and four more abstained. It was a major rebellion, but no threat to the administration's survival because Labour Party policy was to back the government on Maastricht. Rebellion is a luxury in that kind of situation: the Tory rebels could look tough without drawing blood. John, too, could afford to be scathing about the Euro-sceptics. They were defeatists – 'defeatists who make your flesh creep', he was reported as telling a Conservative dinner. 'They practise a sort of phantom grandeur, a clanking of unusable suits of armour, but they are running against the tide, a tide that will flow ever more strongly into the enlarged Community.' A 'flowing tide' didn't have the ring of a 'wind of change', but at that time – it seems a long time ago – John was determined to stand his ground.

The rebels took to the hills. It might have saved a lot of trouble if the party's mainstream forces had pursued them and hunted them down. In the event, the Euro-enthusiasts, the solid middle of the party, saved their powder and shot, as they had done too often before. The Europe debate, in so far as it happened at all, was largely conducted on the rebels' agenda and in terms of the rebels' mythology. For evil to triumph, all that is necessary is for good men to remain silent. Unchecked, Euroscepticism dropped any pretence about being a movement to improve the machinery of the European Union. It descended into unreconstructed Little Englandism.

At that stage, 1992–3, this was guerrilla warfare not so much between Europhobes and Europhiles as simply between rebels and whips. It was warfare of mutual recrimination and conspiracy politics. The sceptics were especially worked up because the Foreign Office minister responsible for piloting the Maastricht Bill through the

House was Tristan Garel-Jones, whose techniques in unarmed combat had been honed by long years, and long nights, in the whips' office. One of the sceptics' in-jokes was that the Prime Minister denied office to any back-bencher who didn't have his MOT certificate – Mate of Tristan. All these things ought to be remembered by whips on both sides as they try to marshal their forces for the new millennium.

Among those dropped from the Major government for not having a valid MOT was Michael Spicer. Michael's political life had begun on the Tory left when he helped to found the PEST Group at Cambridge and he was taken on by the Conservative Research Department under Ted Heath. Later he was to become a protégé of Cecil Parkinson and drifted rightwards. Between times he wrote political thrillers. He it was who now became a rebel leader by founding the Fresh Start Group.

The Eurosceptics had been muted by the approach of the general election, once it had been called for 9 April 1992. Having lost the Battle of Committee Room 14, however, they were determined not to lose the war. They organised themselves into a fighting group, taking their name from an early day motion calling on the government to draw back from the Maastricht Treaty and make a fresh start: a name with the merit of making it clear that on Europe they were much more than merely sceptical. The rebels were now moving the goalposts. 'Fresh start' had the pleasing connotation, for some, of putting the clock back, not just to before Maastricht but to before the Treaty of Rome. The Fresh Start rebels adopted the trappings of a party of their own, even boasting a couple of whips – Christopher Gill and James Cran, both former office-bearers of the European Affairs committee who been ousted in the Fowler *putsch*. To Christopher, a pork butcher by profession, went the credit for the wording of the rebels' collective comment when the news came through of the Danish referendum result rejecting Maastricht: 'The Danes', said Christopher, 'have saved our bacon.'

Fresh Start were not the only group giving the Prime Minister problems. Notable among others were the No Turning Back Group, who saw themselves as the vanguard of the continuing Thatcherite revolution. Like the Fresh Start Group, they were hostile to what they came to see as a Europe heading for federalism, and between them the two groups drew support from across right-wing and centre-right

Conservatism. Where this wide range of critics differed among themselves was on how far they would press their principles when there was a danger of splitting the party and letting Labour in. This was a dilemma – sharpened by the fact that they were operating in a parliamentary party with a small majority – which was to last right up to polling day in 1997. The Tory instinct is still that good Conservatives don't rock the boat.

The rebels were a mixed bunch. Teresa Gorman was a biology teacher turned businesswoman (she spotted the commercial possibilities of selling science teaching kits to schools), who shared with Margaret Thatcher the distinction of being one of the few women admired by Essex man. Launched on her career as a Eurosceptic, Teresa had never enjoyed herself so much since she discovered hormone replacement therapy. 'It was the first time', she wrote, 'I had joined a group of male colleagues who shared a common interest. For the first time since entering Parliament I began to appreciate the meaning of being one of the boys.' After a dozen years with their party in office, the rebels were discovering the joys of opposition. It was the kind of camaraderie you used to find, in the heyday of Old Labour, in a pub used by Tribune Groupers.

Teresa's colleagues contained names that were on the whips' list of usual suspects. George Gardiner, for instance: the Cliff Richard of right-wing journalism, bringing out new numbers for the grandchildren of his old fans. George earned his spurs in the right-wing media world back in the days when being right-wing meant backing Ian Smith in Rhodesia and muttering about the malign influence of the American anti-imperialist foreign policy. He ended up in the Goldsmith Referendum Party.

Among other important supporting players of the drama of the Major years was Teddy Taylor, a man possessed of impeccable anti-EEC credentials. A minister in the Heath government at the age of thirty-three, he resigned when Britain went into the European Community. He had strong views on a lot of things – in favour of hanging and flogging, but against alcohol (though a fairly enthusiastic smoker for most of his life) – as well as being an admirer of *The Thirty-Nine Steps* and president of the John Buchan Club.

A different kind of respectability was provided by the occasional involvement with the rebels of John Biffen, one of the nicest and cleverest members of the 1992–7 parliament, an old associate of Enoch Powell and a sceptic in the best sense of the term. His scepticism, not about Europe but about Thatcherism, had led to his being purged from the Thatcher Cabinet.

But none of these people had any doubts about who was the dominant personality driving the Eurosceptic guerrilla war.

Margaret Roberts had formed her prejudices about Europe as a girl growing up during the Second World War. Indeed, her views on Germans – which the Foreign Office of the 1980s found old-fashioned, to say the least – had been influenced even before the war, when she had a Austrian Jewish pen friend who found refuge in Grantham in 1938 through the good offices of the Roberts family. Hearing about Nazi atrocities at first hand had a lasting effect. When war came, the family gathered round the wireless in the living room in Grantham to listen to the broadcasts with the blackout curtains drawn; and thus began Margaret's admiration for 'Winston', as she would freely refer to him – to the great irritation of the Churchill family – once she had reached Downing Street.

Her admiration for the British soldier dated from the same time. As Prime Minister, one of her proudest moments was to visit the SAS team fresh from storming the terrorist-held Iranian embassy in 1980 and to be told by them: 'We never thought you'd let us do it.' She had to tear herself away from the SAS men to keep a dinner engagement with, of all people, the assembled permanent secretaries of the Whitehall departments. Never a natural mandarin lover, she made no attempt to hide her feelings about the relative merits of the two all-male groups she had found herself mixing with that evening. Britain's first woman Prime Minister had forthright notions of manhood. A military band could get her adrenalin moving, and bring the tears to her eyes, as was clear when she stood on the saluting base for the march-past of the victorious servicemen from the Falklands. As the 1980s progressed, Euro-watchers noted that the thrill supplied by the drums and brass of the British army contrasted starkly with the Prime Minister's emotions when she listened to the European anthem, as she had to do from time to time, standing beside the presidents and chancellors of Europe at some formal Community occasion. 'Last on her feet, and first to sit down on the final chord of the Beethoven,' one diplomat recorded.

If her hero Churchill had survived to the days of the European Union, the old warrior's instincts would have been touched, one suspects, by the sight of the leaders of France, Germany and Great Britain standing side by side in unity, although he would have been every bit as irritated as Margaret by the lunacies of Brussels bureaucracy. Winston's Europeanism was a matter of rhetoric rather than conviction politics, but there was a dimension, an historical dimension, of grand international design in Churchill's outlook which was lacking in Margaret.

Indeed, the European project, from its inception during the bleak postwar years, had always been a grand design. It was never a mere exercise in market economics or a job creation scheme for power-mad European civil servants. The rewriting of history by the Conservative Party of the 1980s involved ignoring not only the idealism of the Treaty of Rome but the fact that the founding fathers of the treaty really meant what they said about fulfilling the dreams of Europeans ashamed of the bloody way Europe had torn itself apart twice in the twentieth century. In the 1990s there were Tory MPs who ought to have known better professing that we had signed up to join no more than a free trade area. 'We agreed to a common market,' they would say. 'Nobody warned us about all this stuff from Brussels.' This might pass for wisdom in a saloon bar, but coming from supposedly serious politicians was less than ingenuous. When 'Europe' was debated in the 1975 referendum campaign, which showed a two-to-one majority for staying in the Community, the full extent of the founding fathers' dreams – a common foreign policy, an increased role for the European Parliament, a single currency – was clear for all to see in the small print.

And not just in the small print. The political platforms of the 1970s resounded with anti-European rhetoric. The sceptics of the 1990s sometimes gave the impression that they had invented national sovereignty as a Tory issue, but in the 1970s Enoch Powell had made it abundantly clear that when Ted Heath signed us up for Europe it meant a real transfer of political power across the Channel. That was why Enoch, at the February 1974 election, advised his supporters to vote Labour, arguing that the Labour Party of the time represented the best hope for preserving the integrity of the Westminster Parliament. Enoch's may have been a voice crying in the wilderness, but it was a loud and articulate voice. His intellectual vigour and rigour made the sceptics of the 1990s look almost insipid by comparison. He had plenty of articulate support, too – back in the 1970s – from the left, notably from Tony Benn. Both Tony and Enoch, it is fair to say, were to be more consistent in following their principles over the next quarter-century than some of their colleagues. Twenty years later, the Tories shouldn't have been allowed to get away with the pretence that their predecessors in the 1970s were like virginal school-girls setting out on a school trip to 'abroad' with nobody to warn them about the seductive charms of wicked foreigners.

Margaret herself, when Ted Heath took the decision to go into Europe, was but a newcomer to the Cabinet; no more, some said, than the statutory woman in the team. But by the time of the referendum – dreamed up by Harold Wilson to paper over the cracks in his party's European policy – Margaret was party leader. As such, she argued the Yes case vigorously and with all her characteristic distaste for caveats and saving clauses. At that stage she seemed to accept that the Community was much more than a free trade area. The paramount case for being inside the Community, she told one audience, was . . . what? Fighting Britain's corner? Not exactly. Selling British widgets in Dusseldorf? No: 'The paramount case for being in', she said, 'is the political case for peace and security.' Later, some of her supporters were to blame much of our European trouble on the famous Dean Acheson argument that Britain, having lost an empire, had to find a new role after Suez. But that argument seemed to make sense to Margaret during the 1975 referendum campaign. 'The Community', she told voters, 'opens windows on the world for us which since the war have been closing.' The Tories, she added, had been pursuing 'the European vision for almost as long as we have existed as a party'.

The claim that the Conservative Party was swept into Europe on a false prospectus was always a nonsense. If Britannia lost her virginity, it didn't happen at Maastricht. If loss of constitutional virginity is a sin, we committed it back in the 1970s.

Having campaigned on the Yes side in the 1975 referendum, Margaret largely allowed Europe to go on to the back burner for a decade. There was a Labour government in power, and there was too much happening within the United Kingdom in the late seventies and early eighties – inflation, trade union power, the effects of world recession

much attention to be directed across the Channel. A more
European-oriented Conservative leadership might have taken the view
that these problems would be tackled more realistically by working
with the grain of Europe, but Margaret was developing her own
agenda.

In the early years of her premiership her prejudices on European
matters were kept reasonably well in check, although it didn't always
seem like that to her European partners. For one thing, in the early
1980s she was still deferring to more experienced Cabinet colleagues.
Her first Foreign Secretary, Peter Carrington, was certainly no Little
Englander, while the two men most dominant in economic policy
during the 1980s, Geoffrey Howe and Nigel Lawson, were
Thatcherites but had no illusions about the importance of working
with Europe; and her agriculture minister, who had the job of holding
her coat-tails when she went into the battle over the Common Agricultural Policy, was the unThatcherite Peter Walker.

Moreover, Margaret *was* excited by one part of 'Europe': the single
market, the 'free trade area' part of the deal. One of her favourites,
an acquaintance from her days as a tax lawyer, Lord Cockfield, was
despatched to Brussels as European Commissioner to push it through.
A clever ploy, she thought: but it ended in tears. Arthur Cockfield
proved to be one of a string of committed Thatcherites who failed to
match her hopes when they came face to face with the realities of
Europe. Arthur, she complained sadly, 'went native' in Brussels. As
she put it magisterially in *The Downing Street Years*, he 'tended to
disregard the larger questions of politics – constitutional sovereignty,
national sentiments and the promptings of liberty . . . Alas, it was not
long before my old friend and I were at odds.' Leon Brittan – who
had shown his loyalty to Margaret by being persuaded to fall on his
sword as a blood offering after the Westland affair – was another who
went native when he became a Brussels Commissioner. In the
Thatcher years it tended to be the natives who were wrong.

If Margaret could say 'Alas' for her old friend Arthur, she was
less charitable to Geoffrey Howe. Geoffrey, one of the architects of
Thatcherism, also went native, not in Brussels but in the notoriously
dangerous corridors of the Foreign Office. When she made him
Foreign Secretary she seems to have been remarkably slow to appreciate that he might have his own views on Europe, or that they might

be worth listening to. When she came to sum him up in her memoirs, the resulting passage was more revealing about her than about him: 'To the extent that Geoffrey did have a cause to guide him in foreign affairs it was one on which the two of us were far apart, although I did not give this much thought at the time. For Geoffrey harboured an almost romantic longing for Britain to become part of some grandiose European consensus ... For him, this was a touchstone (along with liberal views on Home Office matters) of highmindedness and civilised values.' And, she added frankly: 'It was to bring us all no end of trouble.'

There was indeed no end of trouble towards the end of the 1980s – trouble with the natives, the highminded, and the exponents of civilised values. The full extent of the trouble was, however, masked until that traumatic afternoon in 1990 when the world listened, incredulous, to the Howe resignation statement.

Alongside Geoffrey as he delivered it was Nigel Lawson, who had already walked out on Margaret. By that time she had long since come to the conclusion that in an ideal world the only reliable way to save Britain from Europe was effectively to remove European economic policy from both the Treasury and the Foreign Office and bring it into No. 10. Nigel's resignation had been precipitated when the Prime Minister wanted to put him in double harness with Alan Walters as her No. 10 economic adviser. Walters swiftly and understandably withdrew from the situation, but there was another adviser at No. 10 whose influence worried more than one member of the Cabinet: Charles Powell. It was Powell to whom Margaret turned at the time of her tense confrontation with Geoffrey and Nigel in the autumn of 1989 prior to the Madrid summit, a confrontation culminating in what she later recalled as the 'nasty little meeting' where both her Chancellor and her Foreign Secretary said they would resign unless she was more forthcoming at Madrid on the question of European monetary union.

The resignations first of Nigel and then of Geoffrey bore witness to how far the traditional forms of Cabinet government had broken down in the last phase of the Thatcher administration, when Cabinet management, according to Nigel's memoirs, *The View from No. 11*, 'degenerated into increasingly complex attempts to divide and rule ... Her conduct at meetings became increasingly authoritarian.' It all ed to seal Margaret's fate in the leadership election which followed Geoffrey's resignation. The colleagues in Cabinet had had enough.

Within a couple of years of John Major taking over, it was clear that the Baldwinesque approach to squaring the circle of Tory policy on Europe would never have worked. Inertia worked in favour of the sceptics, and their net was spreading wider. Getting rid of Margaret was one thing. Finding a realistic new way to run the government, after an unprecedented eleven years of Thatcherism, was something else. The Tories resembled the tribes of Yugoslavia after the death of Tito.

The completely unreconstructed Thatcherites were in a minority in the early 1990s. If that had not been so, the party would never have got rid of Margaret. But the Lady failed to vanish. Loyalty, people used to say, is the Tories' secret weapon; but in the mid-1990s the electorate watched fascinated as conflicting Conservative loyalties were transformed into doubled-edged, occasionally treble-edged weapons: loyalty to the memory of Margaret, loyalty to the principle of being 'at the heart of Europe', to the principle of national sovereignty, to the importance of strong government . . . The Tory party, always a coalition, was laid open like the side of a mountain with an interesting geological history, the rich diversity of strands and strata exposed to the public gaze.

Meanwhile the electorate was able to watch something interesting happening in the Labour Party too.

*

Envisioned in the flickering black-and-white of a between-the-wars film, John Major looked like a Stan Laurel of a prime minister. There he would be, making his well-meaning way across the kitchen carrying a bucket of whitewash, when a banana skin would somehow appear under his feet.

Events had a way of letting him down. Even the sunny weather let him down at one point in the Major years and had voters queuing up with buckets at the stand-pipes: bad news for any government. People let him down – fat-cat businessmen; naughty back-benchers; distinguished men whom he appointed to investigate scandals and who dug up more than he had bargained for; and of course the Irish, as they have let down British prime ministers for a couple of centuries.

Mostly, it was not his fault. Many of his misfortunes had their roots in events long before he became Prime Minister. The origins of the 'mad cow' crisis, for example, were buried in the accepted wisdom of the agricultural establishment of the 1970s and 1980s. And he followed a lucky prime minister. Fortune had not been least generous in giving Margaret the right kind of enemies, from Arthur Scargill to General Galtieri. She was lucky, too, in her leaders of the opposition. Within months of losing the 1979 election to her, the Labour Party chose the charming bibliophile Michael Foot. The plot might have been written for her by a collaboration between Trollope and Kingsley Amis. Even this stroke of luck was almost surpassed when Labour replaced Foot with Neil Kinnock, with his knack of seizing defeat from the jaws of victory: 'Fifthly and penultimately, Mr Speaker, may I ask the Prime Minister to give a straight answer to this question . . .' If it had been Kinnock's successor, John Smith QC, and not the Welsh windbag who had been in charge of the attack on Margaret during the Westland crisis in 1986, the post-Thatcher era might have begun four years earlier.

The Labour Party let John Major down badly by picking Tony Blair as leader.

Bambi, he was called, though not for long. But the Bambi babyface, marking a new generation, was itself part of the danger facing the Major government. Until Tony Blair arrived on the scene, politics in the 1990s was run by people whose agenda had been set in the mid-1970s, when Thatcherism shifted the goalposts. In the mid-1970s, Tony Blair was at Oxford. He was there when the miners brought down the Ted Heath government, some pundits were predicting that assorted anarchists would soon be marching on Downing Street, and Keith Joseph discovered he had never been a Conservative. Yet these stirring events seem to have passed over his head. He took no part in politics during the nail-biting days when the Conservatives got rid of Ted and replaced him with Margaret. Tony attended the Oxford Union only once, when persuaded by a girlfriend that it would be fun to listen to a politician called Michael Heseltine. His major undergraduate ambition was to be accepted into the rock band Ugly Rumours. He had a talent, one colleague remembered, for 'giving it a bit of serious Mick Jagger'. His biographer John Rentoul describes how Blair *père*, going to pick up his son, met a long-haired undergraduate, shirt open to the navel, large ceramic cross round the neck and long, black synthetic skin coat open to reveal its red lining. 'I wondered who the hell it was. Then he said, "Hi, Dad!"' There is no record of Alderman Roberts ever having this kind of difficulty with his daughter at Oxford.

The ceramic cross was a clue. A fellow undergraduate had introduced the young Blair to the work of the Scottish philosopher of the 1930s John Macmurray, who combined Christian socialism with a contempt for fashionable 'liberalism'. (Blair *almost* met Macmurray in person. He and some friends, on a trip to Scotland, discovered that the great man was living in retirement in Edinburgh and drove up to his home, but decided at the last minute that only one of them should actually drop in. Blair stayed outside.)

The young Margaret Thatcher had come to her philosophy from a different direction. She was a voracious if not always discriminating reader and in her memoirs recalls the influence of a worthy magazine that came into the family home when she was a schoolgirl. It was rich in inspirational verses, one of which, by Ella Wheeler Wilcox, she was still quoting half a century later:

> One ship drives East, and another drives West,
> By the self-same gale that blows;
> 'Tis the set of the sail,
> And not the gale,
> That determines the way she goes.

It summed up Margaret's determination to make events happen the way she wanted them to happen. Tony Blair wouldn't have quarrelled with her over that. He always believed the Tory party was mad to get rid of Margaret and her talent for 'setting the sail'. As a young MP, in the heyday of Margaret's power, he sat in the House fascinated by her. She returned the compliment. She seemed happy to treat Tony as she treated the ex-Communists of eastern Europe. Both the leaders of the new Russia and the leader of New Labour she regarded as reformed sinners who were dismantling the ramshackle structure of socialism because they had seen the Thatcherite light.

If Tony admired the sail-setting skills of Margaret, he was less impressed by her successor. He knew how to underline the contrast, and never did it more brutally than one afternoon during Prime Minister's questions, on the day after the Euro-rebels had been allowed to take the Conservative whip once again – without giving any significant promises about their future behaviour. Labour gloated. John Major made the standard riposte across the despatch box: look at your side, he said – look at the Labour divisions over Europe. Tony Blair didn't bother to disagree. He just went for the jugular. There was a difference, he said cruelly. 'I lead my party. He follows his.'

By that time Tony could afford to be bullish. He had learned, like Margaret, that what matters is not how much bitching there is in the background among your back-benchers. The important thing is how much you can get away with. He had got away with ditching Clause Four. He got away with earning the faint praise of political opponents, like John Redwood, who dubbed him 'the thieving magpie of British politics – every political idea that glistens he takes into his own nest.' A decade of Thatcherism had moved the goalposts for Labour as well as for the Tories, with the result that by the mid-1990s the Labour Party, to the annoyance of Old Labour, was becoming seriously electable.

There was another lesson Blair had learned from Margaret Thatcher. She won the 1979 general election after making remarkably few specific pledges. As opposition leader in the late 1970s she put forward a colourful image of the kind of Britain she wanted. There were buzz-words aplenty – freedom of choice, enterprise, individual responsibility, monetary discipline. They seemed to add up to a coherent programme, but the number of specifics was actually small. Once she had arrived in Downing Street, the two most far-reaching actions of the Thatcher government in its first months were to abolish exchange controls and to alter the balance of the tax burden from income tax to VAT in Geoffrey Howe's first budget. Both these shifts in national policy were absolutely in tune with the pre-election rhetoric. But neither had been spelt out. Indeed, some members of the Cabinet knew nothing about either until they happened.

The Thatcherite rhetoric in the 1970s had been carefully honed, and the message conveyed carefully to key audiences – to small businessmen, to the upwardly mobile, to the moral majority. She knew, or her advisers knew, that there were some audiences not worth wooing. There was no point in wasting powder and shot on the liberal establishment. Many of the media commentators, she calculated, were lost cause – but it was well worth the effort to make friends with the *Sun* and with the *Jimmy Young Show*. The electorate got the overall picture.

The Blair team pored over the lessons of the pre-1979 Thatcher strategy. Their burden was clear: no hostages to fortune. As the 1997 election came nearer, one member of the shadow Cabinet was heard muttering about 'the sheer terror we feel at the prospect of office after eighteen years'. The prospect may have terrified some of his colleagues, but Tony himself strode into 1997 looking remarkably confident.

What lessons, meanwhile, were the Tories learning? Many were not in a learning mood. As a result, the Major government made at least three serious miscalculations in reacting to the Blair revolution in the Labour Party.

The first was simply to fail to realise that a revolution was taking place. The Tories were making the mistake that Labour made in 1979 of not believing that Margaret Thatcher actually meant what she said. By the time Labour woke up, it was too late. (Many Conservatives, too, took a long time to wake up to what Margaret was up to.)

Secondly, once the more intelligent Tory had recognised the historical significance of what was going on – the ditching of Clause Four; the repudiation of Marx, who had been hovering over the Labour Party for a century – the clever thing might have been to say, 'Well done, chaps, you're coming along nicely.' After all, the Conservatives had spent the best part of a century telling the electorate that socialists were economically illiterate and innumerate: they deserved at least one cheer for trying to educate themselves. It would have been the generous thing to say. It would also have been the patronising thing to say. But the Conservatives were no more in a generous mood than they were in a learning mood. They did not even seem shrewd enough to recognise that a compliment on abandoning Clause Four would embarrass the Blair leadership by infuriating the Old Labour left.

It was only gradually that the Tories realised that the Labour shift in the direction of common sense meant they had to work that much harder to sell themselves, to demonstrate that 'clear blue water' separated the two parties. Unfortunately the Tories chose the most shark-infested stretch of water they could find.

This was the third great miscalculation: to look to European policy for a vote-winner. The Conservative Party was never likely to speak with a single voice on Europe, any more than the Labour Party was. If there was unity on Europe in the Commons it was unity of a sort between the Tory left and the Labour right. The fact was that in the 1992–7 parliament there was a cross-party majority in the House of Commons on the basic principles of a British role in Europe, although the Conservative leadership eventually persuaded itself otherwise, and decided, like Tweedledum, to have a battle. In an ideal world it might just have been possible for the Tories to have reached an understanding with New Labour to separate the fundamentals of European unity from controversy over the details of the social chapter, the beef war, the single currency and all the rest of it. It might have suited Blair as much as Major to flush out the incorrigibles on both sides – the hard left and hard right who were not just 'sceptical' about Europe but wanted to get shot of the place.

If it could have worked out like that, the Tories could then have looked for clear blue water where they were genuinely united. But it was too late. The Tory incorrigibles had been allowed to get the bit between their teeth and the party leadership by the short hairs. Recent events (plus the continuing presence of Lady Thatcher and the old British incubus of foreigner-bashing) sent the party down the road to Little England. Many Conservatives truly felt this could carry the voters with them; but it needed more than that to send a thrill through middle England in the mid-1990s.

*

It was in the mid-1990s that the Feelgood Factor joined the Dow, the Nikkei and the Hang Seng as a serious index that could make rich men reach for their telephones and give orders to Buy or Sell. In Westminster, the Major team pored over the feelgood statistics like King Canute's courtiers studying the tide tables. 'Feelgood' became the buzz-word of the nineties, like yuppies in the eighties and swinging in the sixties.

In May 1996 the Gallup polling organisation carried out an exercise for the *Daily Telegraph* which proved, according to the *Telegraph*'s report of the results, that 'the British evidently think the country is going to the dogs so quickly that we shall soon all be living in kennels'.

p asked a sample of voters a series of questions which had origin-
been asked a generation earlier, in May 1968. Is the country
ng healthier? Happier? Better-behaved? The results were not
good news. By comparison with 1996 the mid-1960s, it seemed, must
have been like Merrie England, with happy peasants frolicking under
skies that were sunny and expected to get sunnier. In 1968, most
people told Gallup they believed the health of the nation was improving – and its intelligence likewise. This optimism had not survived.
Half the earlier Gallup sample believed standards of honesty were
deteriorating in 1968; but by 1996 that view was taken by three-
quarters. And almost everyone in the later sample believed there was
less 'peace of mind' now, and that 'standards of behaviour' were going
down the plug-hole.

To compare post-Thatcher Britain with 1968 was to tread on
dangerous ground, for 1968 had not been just any old year. It was
the heyday of Harold Wilson, and conservatives with either a capital
C or a small one muttered about the end of civilisation as sensible
people knew it. It was the great year of student revolt in Paris. Revolting students were, indeed, to be seen everywhere in the late sixties.
In London it was the year of the Grosvenor Square rioting. It was
the era of flower people. It was the time of the Rolling Stones, who,
with their middle-class groupies, had raised blood pressures and
caused lips to purse at Conservative conferences.

The next twenty-odd years saw the Conservatives presenting themselves as the party which would stop the rot. The Thatcher revolution
had been as much about social values as about market forces. And
yet, a generation later, here were the public saying that things were
going downhill even faster than in the days of pot and protest. It was
a sad picture and it carried a grim message for Conservatives.

'Feelgood' has always been taken seriously by Tories, who knew all
about it long before the newspapers invented it in the nineties. It was
what Baldwin was on about when he commended the strong, simple,
rustic virtues that shone forth from the works of his favourite novelist,
Mary Webb. The need to make people feel good was what drove
Churchill to spend many wartime hours crafting the phrases that
would equip the nation with morale when it wasn't equipped with
much else.

For the second half of his premiership John Major had to reflect, with growing frustration, on man's ingratitude, as the evidence piled up that voters refused to accept that they had never had it so good. Month after month, Downing Street would produce the latest statistical triumphs. Britain was at the top of the growth league table. John Major (in contrast to Margaret Thatcher) had actually licked inflation. Unemployment was going down – more people were in work in the UK than in any other major country in the European Union. That was the good news. The bad news came, month after month, from Gallup and MORI political polls.

The official line was that the statistics of success had to have time to 'work through the system'. The feelgood factor was solemnly discussed in the way the monetarists of the 1980s used to produce graphs of the M3 figures and show how a peak in the graph was reflected eighteen months later in the price of beans on the shelves in Tesco. Yet no great mathematical skill was needed to explain why the feelgood factor was absent. The electorate didn't dispute the evidence of economic growth. But by now they had a canny notion of what economists mean when they talk about 'growth'. Yes, it means more money in the system; but 'growth', in the economist's sense, also means that companies produce more at lower cost. Put bluntly, this often means they shed people.

The Thatcher years, and the post-Thatcher years, witnessed a revolution in the British employment market. The Thatcherite enterprise revolution meant de-manning. It meant 'flexibility' in the labour market. Jobs once done by full-time staff were handed over to part-timers – part-time shelf-packers in supermarkets at one end of the scale, self-employed 'consultants' at the other. The extent of the 'part-time' revolution was dramatised, to the embarrassment of Conservative spin doctors, by none other than Maurice Saatchi, who became one of John Major's 'working peers'. Apart from giving professional advice, on and off, to the Conservative Party, Maurice Saatchi had clients in commercial broadcasting, who wanted him to tell the world about the pulling power of television. His researchers searched hard for some striking statistic to demonstrate the massive coverage of a popular programme. They came up with this: the number of people who watch *Coronation Street* is greater than the number of people who work full-time.

The 1997 general election was the first fought in a Britain where the typical voter did not belong to a family supported by the traditional kind of breadwinner. In spring 1997 we may have been a prosperous nation, but it was a prosperity founded in a complicated mix of bits and pieces of earnings, bonuses, pensions and allowances. Work patterns had been revolutionised. No wonder the spin doctors found it hard to find the right messages for their election posters.

The voters knew, in their hearts, that Britain had needed a bomb to be put under its industrial infrastructure. They knew the damage that had been done by the trade unions and by the traditions that made it all but impossible to sack useless workers. They knew that all too many British managers had deserved to be sacked, but weren't. So they welcomed the Thatcher 'enterprise revolution' – with their heads; their hearts told them something else. The self-same radical forces which produced record productivity had also meant, for some, a bomb put under their own bottoms. 'Security' became another buzz-word. Statistically, the extent of job insecurity was probably exaggerated. Tables were produced which showed that the average length of time people stayed in their jobs had not changed much. Bar charts were generated on computer screens to demonstrate the extent of disposable wealth – more cars, more holidays abroad, more people able to afford to eat out. But, as every armchair psychologist knows, 'feelgood' has little to do with logic or statistics. The wind of change had swept away much of what had once been taken for granted, not least the cosy old assumption that, if you had a job, you had a good chance of still being in it this time next year. For a large proportion of the population, cosy assumptions had been connected, unfortunately, with trade unionism. The enterprise revolution put the boot into trade unionism. Many workers, freed from the restrictions of the closed shop, did find they could earn more, just as the Thatcherite zealots had predicted. Many did indeed end the 1980s in better jobs than they could once have hoped for – though some were poorer and many others were unemployed. Then, in the recession of the early nineties, a lot of the jobs of the eighties began to disappear.

Even more important was the transformation of the work culture. The image of the typical British worker as a married man supporting a wife and two-point-something children – the image once taken for granted both by both Old Labour and old Conservatives – was seemingly gone for ever. Women's liberation had been more effective than

some of its devotees would admit. Women were now holding the
economy together. Because women were typically more 'flexible' than
men, many employers, given the choice, tended to prefer women
workers. Harold Wilson's Britain provided jobs for over 15 million
men. John Major's Britain provided jobs for fewer than 11 million
men – who now accounted for only marginally over 50 per cent of
the workforce.

Overall, prosperity had increased, but it was no secret that this was
not evenly spread across the population. It wasn't supposed to be.
One aim of the enterprise revolution had been to 'restore differentials'.
Social patterns had changed. Margaret Thatcher meant them to
change. The success of the industrial shake-out under her government
was a direct cause of the failure of the feelgood factor under John
Major. Economics, which were supposed to work hand in hand with
the Conservative virtues of self-reliance and family values, often
seemed, in the short term, to be working against the ideal of the
nuclear family. Here was something else that had to be given time to
work through the system. It was John Major's misfortune that time
ran out on him.

*

In 1995 a book was published which turned out, rather unexpectedly,
to be a best-seller. Written by a *Guardian* journalist who then became
editor of the *Observer*, Will Hutton, *The State We're In* contained a
lot of old-fashioned left-wing analysis of the kind now supposed to
be politically incorrect. Yet *The State We're In* scored a trick when it
appeared, and among a far wider public than the typical *Guardian*-
reading classes.

The book looked at the issue of job security in a way which rang
true – not so much to the Cs and Ds of the social pyramid, who
probably knew all about insecurity already, but to the As and Bs.
Hutton described what he called the 30/30/40 society. The '40' were
those people who had clearly benefited from the changes since
1979: the 'privileged', he called them, and calculated that they made
up not much more than 40 per cent of the population. They weren't
all well-to-do by any means, but they included the people who
had done very nicely out of the changes of the Thatcher years. At
the other end of the spectrum were what Hutton described as the

'disadvantaged'. These, he calculated, made up 30 per cent of the population, if you threw in not just the unemployed total as measured by the official figures but also those outside the benefit network and those supporting themselves, and sometimes dependants, on 'scraps of part-time work'. These figures could be and were disputed, but the most interesting part of the Hutton analysis concerned what he identified as the middle 30 per cent of society, those who were neither 'privileged' nor 'disadvantaged'. Some of the middle '30' might have reasonable money incomes, but what characterised them, according to Hutton, was their lack of certainty about their future. They included people on short-term contracts, the self-employed, and skilled or semi-skilled workers whose security had once depended on strong trade unions and whose industries had now been largely de-unionised.

If the unions and the closed shop had been the only sacred cows slaughtered during the Thatcher years, the Tory party would have had fewer problems. But by the 1990s there were a lot of insecure people out there in middle England, people who regarded themselves as natural Conservative voters. Many in the middle classes had certainly done well out of the shake-out of the 1980s – and many had joined the middle class for the first time. But many others were only beginning to realise that Thatcherite market economics could be painful and that the pain was not suffered exclusively by the working classes.

For the working classes, certainty used to be knowing that you could probably get a boring job on an assembly line if you couldn't do any better, and that your trade union would see you all right; and you assumed, in the old days, that the government would protect your assembly line from 'unfair' competition from lesser breeds beyond the sea.

For the grammar-school-educated classes in the old days there had always been jobs in banks and insurance companies – as boring as an assembly line, perhaps, but providing a reasonably secure niche in the middle-class hierarchy. These were the jobs of the loyal white-collar foot soldiers of the Conservative Party.

The British middle classes have always been strongly in favour of market economics. In theory. In practice, many of their members, as every Conservative political manager knew, used to live and work in conditions comfortably insulated from the rigours of competition. The middle classes became adept, over the years, at constructing their own closed shops. Professional men had grown up in a world where it was ungentlemanly – indeed, often illegal – to advertise or market themselves, or undercut on fees. In industry and commerce the white-collar culture was largely rooted in the certainties of a business world where people joined a firm, advanced steadily through the white-collar ranks (assuming they weren't actually caught with their hands in the till) and finished up with a good pension. It was a world which spelt comfortable certainty for the middle classes, and for their children who would pass smoothly into the same world.

The feelgood factor – and its elusiveness – affected the Conservative Party, quite simply, because so many people were finding that unemployment isn't something that happens to other people. Maybe the evidence was anecdotal rather than statistically demonstrable. But elections are won or lost on anecdotes. By 1997 it was clear that unemployment could happen not just to other people's feckless, ill-educated children but to the young of the middle classes. During the 1980s the term 'redundant executive' had become part of the small change of the social revolution, and the middle managers of middle England found themselves as much at risk as screwdriver-wielders who lost their jobs to robots on the assembly line. Computers now did complex paperwork once done by senior pen-pushers. In 1977 a managing director relied on a network of well-salaried human information providers to provide him with the data he needed to make his decisions; his successor twenty years later in 1997 could sit at his desk calling up all the information he needed on a screen.

The fact that the redundant manager might soon get another job, often a better one, was not the point. The Thatcher revolution, however welcome in theory, cut the emotional ground from under people to whom certainty and respectability were everything. It was a convenient fiction in the Conservative Party that the backbone of the party consisted typically of 'businessmen' (and their lady wives). In fact a typical Tory grassroots committee of loyalists probably includes no more than one or two people who relish the cut and thrust of commercial risk-taking. For the majority, experience of excitement is more likely to have been gained negotiating the office politics of some white-collar hierarchy. Consequently, these loyalists were often baffled and confused by the new ground rules of the enterprise economy.

Then there was the housing market. For generations, owner-occupation had had a place in Britain's middle-class ethos unparalleled anywhere else in the developed world. Extension of owner-occupation was one of the triumphs of Thatcherism, and the rise in the owner-occupier vote was duly reflected in the results of the general elections of the 1980s. In the 1990s there were Tory voters, both in the leafy estates of five-bedroomed designer homes in Surrey and in the ex-council houses of the midlands, who found it hard to forgive the Tories when they discovered they had negative equity, or that their home was about to be repossessed by the building society. The Thatcher government had raised their hopes; the Major government was left with the job of disillusioning them.

The weak pound – as it was after Britain was forced out of the European exchange rate mechanism – was good news for exporters but had some irritating incidental effects on the well-being of the middle classes. It was no longer so easy to slip across the Channel for a long weekend; and as for the cost of the upkeep of the second home in the Dordogne ... Prosperity can be a drag.

Another pleasing 1980s dream went sour, too. The right of the property-owning middle classes to pass a modest patrimony on to their children was put at risk, for many, when the rules were changed to allow local authorities to seize the assets of the elderly – which meant, mainly, their houses – to pay for care in an eventide home. Middle-class aspirations could end in tears.

In retrospect, it is easy enough to see that the authors of the enterprise culture were overly simplistic. You only have to look at a celebrated speech that Keith Joseph made back in 1974 which formed the basis of the Thatcherite monetarist revolution. He was at pains to emphasise that fighting inflation didn't mean creating a pool of unemployed. Under monetarist discipline, Keith said, some industries would decline, yes; but in the better-ordered economy that would take shape, new opportunities would appear to create new jobs. Admittedly, he emphasised, 'this prescription will not be easy or enjoyable. But after a couple of years,' he insisted, giving up a brave hostage to fortune, 'we should be on to a sounder basis and be able to move forward again ... If I had to give a personal guess about the total time horizon of a successful anti-inflation policy, I would say three or four years.'

Politicians predict time-scales at their peril. When Keith and Margaret duly got into office in 1979 and applied their prescription, it didn't quite work like that. World conditions conspired against them; and there were entrenched problems too deep for monetarism to cure. When the time-scale ran out, it was not Margaret but her successor who had to cope with the consequences for the disgruntled middle classes.

The Thatcher–Joseph revolution was not just about monetarism. It was about what Margaret saw as middle-class values. Plenty of people rose to the challenge of the enterprise culture. Among them were executives who, having lost their jobs because the big, long-established companies where they worked were in trouble, decided to go it alone. New businesses grew by the hundred. Britain was seeing a new kind of middle-class businessman, hitherto more familiar in the United States, who wasn't ashamed to say he hoped to make a lot of money. Much of the work that used to be done within the structure of large companies was farmed out to businesses run by these people. New technology made it that much easier for small businesses to launch themselves. As big companies 'downsized' and the unemployment figures rose during the 1980s, the businesses set up by these new entrepreneurs often looked to be the only job creators on the scene. It was all very much part of the enterprise culture – but for some, in Keith Joseph's words, it was not a prescription that was easy or enjoyable.

Numerically, the new middle-class businessmen didn't add up to a lot of voters; but they were the bedrock of the new social class that came to be personified as Essex man, who served Margaret well in the elections of the 1980s. It was John Major who had to face up to him when things went wrong in Essex.

'Essex man' was to be found in the west midlands, in the new towns of southern England and indeed all over the country, but various special factors operated in Essex. Here he was sufficiently near the fleshpots of London to know that the middle classes had got things organised so as to enjoy the good things of life. Essex man approved of the Thatcherite policy of allowing him to keep more of his income. He believed in economic Darwinism and had little sympathy for

society's scroungers. If he was in a council house, he liked the idea
of buying it at a discount. He liked the idea of buying privatisation
shares that meant a quick buck. Half the shares in privatisation issues
were bought by the working classes, skilled and unskilled. The old
rules of thumb for defining the middle classes were never quite going
to apply again.

There was one specific range of opportunities for the new aspirant
middle class of Essex. Many of the young men and women from east
of London had always commuted to Liverpool Street to jobs in the
City. Now deregulation of the financial markets in the 'Big Bang' was
creating exciting new opportunities. The sharpest of the Essex men
became the traders who shifted millions of Eurodollars across their
desks in the City's glory days of the late 1980s. You saw them, wearing
suits that cost a lot of money but never quite seemed to fit, drinking
their designer lager in the wine bars of EC2. They worked hard. They
played hard. And they were among those who were soon to fall on
their faces hard when the City was rocked by the sound of bursting
bubbles at the end of the decade.

There are heart-rending stories of ambitious young Tories – well-
educated young men with robust views on crime and punishment,
immigration and the defence of the nation-state, and steeped in Hayek
and Maurice Cowling – who decided to learn about politics at the
grass roots by getting themselves invited to constituency suppers out
in Essex. They would arrive, with eager smiles on their faces, in halls
awash with suburban *décolletage* and loud, lusty east London banter;
but within minutes the colour could be seen draining from their faces.
These were young men accustomed to jolly rugby club jokes about
coons and poofters. But this was something else. The people around
these trestle tables were the nephews and nieces of the London dockers
who had once marched to Westminster in support of Enoch Powell's
call to keep out the blacks. The well-educated young men were known
to gulp down their Perrier water and make their excuses.

No one can fully understand the problems that beset John Major
without understanding Essex man. It was after 1987 that doubts began
to stir in Essex. The City's Big Bang had ceased to echo reassuringly
– and house prices plunged. Essex man never really took John Major
to his heart.

Margaret Thatcher was never in any doubt that Essex man was a vital part of her constituency. Essex man, and his counterpart in the rest of the country, did the Thatcher government proud. His father and grandfather had voted Labour because, in a them-and-us world, 'them' meant the Tory establishment. In the 1979 election, 45 per cent of Britain's skilled worker vote was still going to Labour. By 1987 the figure was down to 34 per cent – and the Tories were winning 36 per cent of the manual worker vote. There was a rough-and-ready rapport between the moral codes of the housing estates of Basildon and the corner shops of Grantham. The Lord looks after those who look after themselves. Despite the unfair jokes about the sexual mores of his sisters, Essex man thinks he belongs to the moral majority. You can see his morality at work if you visit an Essex night club. (Southend-on-Sea, surprisingly, claims to be the night-club capital of Europe.) Essex man sits at his little table with his woman at his side. He doesn't talk to her much. He doesn't even smile much. His eyes are constantly travelling round the hall checking that nobody else is eyeing his girl.

With the advice of her PR advisers, Margaret had seen, early on, that it was more important to get a good press in Essex man's daily paper, the *Sun*, than in *The Times*. By 1997 both these papers, and others, were doing few favours for Margaret's heir.

*

Sir David English, chairman of Associated Newspapers and a former editor of the *Daily Mail*, enjoyed recalling pleasant memories of socialising with Tony Blair. It had not always been thus when Labour leaders were invited to break bread with the men of the *Mail*. Neil Kinnock always declined their offers of lunch. Neil's successor, John Smith, accepted the call to the Second Empire dining room which had once been the office of the megalomaniac Northcliffe and which was moved bodily out of Fleet Street to the new *Mail* offices in Kensington; but, according to David English in an account he wrote for the *Spectator*, Smith was not at ease there. Mind you, English went on to say that John Major never seemed at ease when he came along to eat at the *Mail* offices either.

The New Labour leader was evidently something else. He took the *Mail* people in his stride, in ways that would have made Neil Kinnock's toes curl. In his *Spectator* article, English recalled one such episode.

'We all agree', he remembered Tony Blair telling the lunch party, 'that the welfare state has got to be radically reformed. Who's going to do it? You may find that I am the only one who has the will to do it.'

English recorded that around the lunch table 'a thoughtful silence followed'.

There was indeed a remarkable amount of thoughtful silence during the Major years about the relationship between the newspapers and the politicians. Once upon a time, newspaper politics used to be so simple. We knew the *Mirror* was solid, reliable Labour, with a bit of mischief thrown in. The old *Daily Herald*, if anyone could remember it, had been solid Labour too, but was so boring that it found itself being sold off for a song. Under a new name it was picked up by an Australian called Rupert Murdoch, but nobody paid much attention at the time because everybody knew that such a brash newcomer to Fleet Street couldn't last long.

The new name for the old *Herald* was the *Sun*. Thus was born a political force which summed up all too much of what was happening to England.

The Tory party had always thought it knew where it stood with the posher papers. Admittedly *The Times* could be unpredictable and had an occasionally tiresome conscience, but it was run by people who could be regarded as basically sound. Other papers could be awkward, too. But come a general election they knew where their duty lay. It was accepted wisdom that British newspaper proprietors were all Tories, even if a disproportionate number of the writers they employed were leftish liberals (or worse). Or so it seemed to the Conservative Party. In fact the Lord Coppers of Fleet Street always resented being taken for granted by the Tories. All the same, so far as their staff's politics were concerned, they always knew that the high-profile lefty scribes of the heyday of Fleet Street – the Michael Foots and the James Camerons – were adequately counterbalanced by loyal journalistic workhorses who tended to be conservative with both a small and a large C. In short, until the 1990s, there was a great deal of justification for the complaint of old-fashioned socialists, whenever they had to carry out yet another post-mortem on why they had lost an election, that 'We was beaten by the Tory press.'

When Margaret Thatcher became party leader in 1975 she was

cleverly advised on how to handle the press. It would be counterproductive, she was told, to go around browbeating editors or proprietors.
Moreover, it was explained to her, journalists on the posh papers, the
broadsheets, are a toffee-nosed lot, and wouldn't take kindly to a brash
arriviste party leader telling them what to do. Under guidance from
her advisers Margaret concentrated instead on the other end of the
market. Thus began the happy friendship between her and the
revamped *Sun* – which claimed to have swung the 1979 election for
Margaret with its front-page editorial telling its multi-million
readership to vote Tory. Thatcherism appealed to the anti-
establishment instincts of the *Sun*'s then editor, Larry (in due course
Sir Larry) Lamb, and it appealed to the instincts of Rupert Murdoch
(who made himself ineligible for knighthoods or higher honours
because his business interests necessitated American citizenship).

Margaret benefited from anti-establishment sentiments elsewhere,
too. It soon became clear that some of the best-known of those left-
wing scribes who had prospered in the old Fleet Street were rein-
venting themselves as Thatcherites. Paul Johnson was the outstanding
case, but there were others who changed their spots. They would have
claimed that it was not they but the politicians who had changed
their principles. The stock-in-trade of the old left-wingers had never
actually been socialism: what they were good at was knocking the
establishment. In the 1970s and 1980s they quickly recognised that
when it came to establishment-knocking, the first woman leader of
the Tory party was a sister under the skin.

By the late 1980s, much of the press was more or less singing from
the Thatcherite hymn sheet. There were important exceptions – not
least the reservations expressed by the *Financial Times*, which was
better placed than some others to assess how far monetarism was
working. The brave new *Independent* was dry on economics but wet
on other matters. Of course, newspaper proprietors, not least Rupert
Murdoch, had a lot to thank Margaret for. She did what generations
of them had never been able to do. She stood up to the greedy men
of the printing unions. The barbed wire and the police cordons around
Wapping displeased the politically correct, but they brought some
kind of realism to the economics of newspaper production.

On the whole, Margaret, after a stormy passage, could be satisfied
with her press. She took a very sensible attitude to newspapers, in

that she seldom wasted much time actually reading them. (Denis was the newspaper-reader of the family, and the habit led him to his considered view of journalists as 'reptiles'.) For Margaret it was enough to glance through the daily file of cuttings prepared for her at the crack of dawn by her press secretary, Bernard Ingham (another anti-establishment Labour supporter who fitted into the new regime as if slipping on a glove). Harold Wilson, and before him Anthony Eden, used to pore over the nuances of the editorial columns as if sucking on a rotten tooth. Not Margaret. She preferred making news to reading it.

All this was bound to change under her successor. John Major lacked Margaret's newsworthiness. To newspapers, right or left, broadsheet or tabloid, the politics of 'on the one hand ... on the other ...' were of limited interest; they preferred the knockabout style. 'Battling Maggie' was good for headlines. The same was true, as David English recognised, of Tony Blair when he was rude to the unions and unreconstructed Clause Four socialists. In media terms, John was too middle-of-the-road for his own good. Nor was Rupert Murdoch, welcome guest at Downing Street when he jetted in during the Thatcher years, likely to treat John as a fellow titan. Tycoons make their money by investing in success, not least in building up communications empires, and watch the market. Blair looked to be a more likely growth stock than Major.

The love affair, if that was what it was, between Tony Blair and the media was a stormy one. Relations with his feisty press adviser, Alastair Campbell, could be even stormier. Editors and producers of radio and television programmes with the bruises to show for their encounters with Margaret's press secretary were heard to remark how, in retrospect, they were aware of Bernard Ingham's quiet charm.

Relations between the press and John Major had their ups and downs too, but the general direction was down. As with the death of a marriage, you couldn't put your finger on precisely when things went wrong; but suddenly the couple are spitting at each other, and everyone is saying knowingly that it had always been bound to end in tears.

The *Express* stayed loyal to John longer than the *Mail*. The *Mail* – the paper taken by Tories, according to the old joke, for their lady wives to read – had its own quirky agenda on morality and family values and on Lord Mackay's sensible attempts to tidy up the divorce law. The *Daily Telegraph* was a special case. The *Telegraph* never really deserved its old title of the *Torygraph*, but it did have a special relationship with the Tory party. So some of the patronising things written, week in, week out, in the editorial columns of the *Telegraph* in the long run-up to the election hit many of the party faithful where it hurt. With the *Telegraph* and *Mail* behaving like this, the party rank and file felt as uneasy as Guards subalterns in a mess in the Peninsular campaign would have felt listening to their rowdier colleagues black-guarding the great Duke. Of course, as polling day approached, the *Telegraph* and *Mail* tidied up their act, but it all made for confusion.

By the mid-nineties the newspapers of the new generation of press lords were showing little loyalty to any politician, and in the face of this disengagement the politicians developed their own knee-jerk reaction, an all-purpose response to even the most reasonable and well-documented reports of this or that political skulduggery: 'It's all got up by the media.' A Tory split over Europe? Malicious gossip. Would Tony Blair be able to stand up to trade union pressure once he became Prime Minister? The splutterings of Alastair Campbell, in his role as Bernard-Ingham-in-Waiting, rivalled those of Brian Mawhinney.

A recurring politicians' grievance was that journalists spent too much time reporting rumours, but they didn't enthuse when the *Sunday Times* sought to establish facts behind the rumours – fairly wide-spread rumours – that there were MPs willing to ask parliamentary questions for cash. When a *Sunday Times* journalist posed as a businessman willing to pay £1,000 for such a service, two Members fell into the trap. (It was widely noted that among MPs there seemed to be at least as much anger at the *Sunday Times'* tactics as at their own colleagues.) Not a major disaster for parliamentary morality, perhaps; but it set in train a chain of events, as we shall see, which did the Conservative Party no favours when it came to polling day. Under the Major government it was not just the royal family that lost its footing on the slippery slopes of journalistic *lèse majesté*.

Decades earlier, the *Telegraph* had been a pioneer of what came to be called Thatcherism. It had preached monetarism back in the days when the term seemed no more than a label for mumbo-jumbo dreamed up on the far side of the University of Chicago campus. This

gave the *Telegraph* an impeccable pedigree in the eyes of the ultras of
the 1990s. Actually, though, the pedigree was more complicated than
that. In Ted Heath's time and even earlier, the *Telegraph* had also been
a vigorous pioneer of European unity. This tended to be forgotten in
Downing Street during the 1980s, but the *Telegraph* did manage to
distance itself in a mild way from the excesses of Thatcherite anti-
Europeanism. Then it changed ownership, and its new Canadian proprietor, Conrad Black, was no Europhile. His first appointment to
the editor's chair was Max Hastings, whose Conservatism tended to
be based on common sense, not doctrine, and on politics there was
always an uneasiness between editor and proprietor: in due course
Hastings went off to edit the *Evening Standard*, which then became
the nearest thing to a lone voice in the press for the kind of pragmatic
Toryism which, before Thatcher, was taken for granted. In Hastings'
place, Black appointed as editor of the *Telegraph* Charles Moore, who
did know his doctrine and had a clear view of Conservatism drawing
on a range of political thinkers from Burke through Lord Salisbury
to Enoch Powell and Thatcher. This was the kind of Conservatism
that believes in a special interpretation of the role of the nation-state;
it was a far cry from Harold Macmillan and Ted Heath, and bad news
for John Major.

There were significant differences between Black's *Telegraph* and
Murdoch's *Times*. Where the *Telegraph*'s High Tory instincts made
it monarchist (so long as the royals didn't become politically correct),
Rupert Murdoch was an instinctive republican. But neither paper's
politics suited John Major. Both took Thatcherism as their point of
reference. Both took anti-Europeanism for granted. Nevertheless, the
Telegraph saw a duty to fulfil a Conservative destiny. By contrast, *The
Times*, much altered though it might be since the days when it was
the establishment's house journal, still regarded itself as independent
voice. This was spelled out in a message for the dawn of election year
which promised readers that *The Times* would 'seek to identify the
party leader who best matches the temper of this cautious country in
these changing and often confusing times'. *The Times* added, a mite
pompously some may have thought, that Tony Blair might persuade
the editor that he was the man: 'He or his successors may yet quietly
claim the "conservative" title.' This was indeed worthy of one of
David English's thoughtful silences.

John and John – and Margaret and Emma

By the time the 1992–7 parliament was down to its last couple of years it was hard to see what John Major could realistically do to change either his policies or his style to satisfy Murdoch's *Times* or Black's *Telegraph*. He could have humiliated himself by coming out at the last moment firmly against Europe. But then, he had tried placating the Eurosceptics before, only to find, as placators tend to find, that his tormentors simply came back to demand more concessions.

It was little comfort to him that this sort of thing had happened before: to Stanley Baldwin, supposedly a Major role model.

In the 1920s and 1930s, SB was in trouble with the right wing of the Tory party over a range of things – Indian self-government mainly, but also tariff reform and what was then called Empire trade. He was endlessly baited by the great press lords of the time, Beaverbrook of the *Express* and Rothermere of the *Mail*. Things came to a head when, after the Tories had lost a general election, Rothermere decided he was entitled to influence what Conservative policy should be when the party moved into the next election period. He went further. He laid claim to a say in the composition of the next Conservative Cabinet as the price of a guarantee to the party of the *Mail*'s support. SB had put up with a lot from the press lords, but now he turned on them. He made the speech that has gone down as one of the great pieces of polemic of the twentieth century, accusing the press lords (in a phrase crafted for him by his cousin, Rudyard Kipling) of seeking 'power without responsibility – the prerogative of the harlot down the ages'.

John Major never tried anything so grand as that. He did, however, win an interesting tactical skirmish with the press when he sprang on them – and everyone else – the surprise party leadership election in the summer of 1995. It wrongfooted both the press and his political rivals. It was only a minor triumph, and by the time the general election came, it seemed a long time ago. But the story is worth retelling as a high point of the Major years.

*

Politicians, like farmers and Sloane rangers, know that there is a pattern to the seasons. By the Cheltenham National Hunt Festival the whips are beginning to worry about whether they will get through the parliamentary timetable. By the time of Trooping the Colour and Royal Ascot, if the weather has become hot and sticky, they know the colleagues will be snarling at each other before July. By Wimbledon fortnight and Henley they begin to wonder whether it would help if the PM had a quick summer reshuffle. It was into this natural sporting calendar that John Major inserted the 'put up or shut up' challenge trophy in June 1995.

It was a fine summer's day. In the City, one captain of industry was telephoned by a business acquaintance who thought he could earn a brownie point by being first with the sensation of the year. 'There's a rumour that the Prime Minister is going to resign this afternoon,' he shouted to the secretary at the other end of the line. 'The Chairman ought to be the first to know.'

'Resigning? Really? How interesting,' said the secretary. 'But I couldn't possibly interrupt the Chairman with something like that. He's watching the rugby.'

The Prime Minister had chosen to announce his plan for solving the Eurosceptic problem at the point where England was being defeated by France in the Rugby World Cup. Momentary confusion was caused, and not just in the City, by misunderstanding of the constitutional difference between a prime minister who resigns as prime minister and one who merely resigns as leader of his party.

The announcement was made at a press conference held in the garden behind No. 10 on Thursday 22 June. John was doing something that many people, friends as well as enemies, had always said he couldn't do. He surprised us. When prime ministers decide the time has come to shut up their critics on the back benches, the traditional thing is to table a vote of confidence and to say in effect that if the rebels want to get rid of the premier they have to summon up the guts to go into the No lobby. John had tried that over Maastricht. It had worked, but only just and only for a time. Now he needed to do something completely different. He consulted no more than a handful of his nearest and dearest – and he made a careful judgement about how his most serious rival, Michael Heseltine, would jump. Then he went on to make history. Never before had a Conservative Party leader voluntarily chosen to challenge his critics to put up or shut up *in a secret ballot*.

It was only in 1965 that the modern machinery for electing (or re-electing) Tory leaders by secret ballot was invented. It was the brainchild of two unlikely collaborators, Alec Douglas-Home and Humphry Berkeley, a combination of one of the most respectable Tories and one of the most wayward – as Humphry proved shortly afterwards by walking out of the party. He left as his memorial an electoral formula involving the kind of arithmetical complexities most Conservatives prefer to leave to their tax accountants.

Until 1965 the colleagues had regularly been told whom they wanted as their leader, and then welcomed him with a loyal cheer. Leaders 'emerged', picked by what Iain Macleod called contemptuously the Magic Circle. It was a system that suited the Tory instincts of the time. The reason for changing the system was not that the party particularly wanted to be dragged screaming into the 1960s but that it had been deeply embarrassed by the unseemly scenes on the last occasion the Magic Circle was called on to operate: a process that resulted in Alec Douglas-Home emerging to succeed the ailing Harold Macmillan. Harold's illness and resignation happened to coincide with the Blackpool conference of 1963. The party was guilty of behaving badly. Seriously badly. Campaign buttons appeared on lapels. At least one prospective candidate, Quintin Hailsham, campaigned openly. Up with this the party could not put, and so the Home–Berkeley system was invented to select the leader by secret ballot.

Its mathematical technicalities could almost have been designed deliberately to bring a glazed look to the eyes of a knight of the shires. There was a requirement for a 15 per cent vote 'premium' in the first ballot; the voting could go on to three or even four rounds; and there was even a provision, albeit never used, for that very unTory electoral device, the transferable vote in certain circumstances.

Confronted with the Home–Berkeley formula, many of the colleagues may not have grasped all the detail, but they were streetwise enough to appreciate the essence. It gave mathematical respectability to a principle dear to their hearts. In the selection of leaders, as distinct from the election of MPs, Tories had never believed in anything so simple as 'first past the post'. Everyone recognised the possibility that there might be a popular candidate who was neverthless unthinkable because a significant minority hated his guts. For the best part of a political generation this principle was applied in order to deny the leadership to Rab Butler. In 1990 roughly similar considerations applied to Michael Heseltine. Deep down, Tories still hankered after the idea of an ideal candidate 'emerging' without blood on the carpet.

Nevertheless, they took to the novelty of the secret ballot with alacrity. To Members accustomed to streaming through the division lobbies under the beady eyes, and sometimes subject to the physical persuasion, of the whips, this was heady freedom. They warmed to the possibilities. They could tell their constituency chairman they were voting for candidate A, they could tell candidate B they would vote for him, they could give six different stories in confidence to six different newspapers – and they could never be found out. For the couple of weeks leading up to a leadership election they could behave like children in a normally well-disciplined household who are allowed to run riot at Christmas.

The new freedom brought unexpected results, as in 1975 when the party found itself electing Margaret Thatcher as leader. She benefited from another feature of the system, not built into the rules but assumed to be self-evident: that in a gentlemen's party an incumbent leader should not be challenged by his closest colleagues – at least, not at once. The first round in the election should be regarded as a dummy run. Somebody else had to strike the first blow.

In other words, like most Tory party procedures, the thing was a game, with a few written rules and a lot of conventions. With each new election under the Home–Berkeley formula the party learned how to use the rules of the game to suit its purposes. And it learned fast. A new spin was applied to the ball each time.

Now, in 1995, John Major produced yet another variant by precipitating an election at a time to suit himself. It was also an innovation, almost a presidential touch, to announce it among the rose bushes of Downing Street. (The word 'presidential' was, rather oddly, to be applied to John right up to the election.) He chose good cricketing weather to put his spin on the ball. Sport of one kind or another, indeed, formed the backcloth for much of the drama of the Major re-election campaign. Apart from the Rugby World Cup, being played in South Africa, the press conference took place while many leading members of the Conservatives' natural constituency were at Ladies' Day at Ascot. Others were watching the test match taking place that week against the West Indies at Lord's.

Among the spectators at that test match was the most junior member of the Cabinet. John Redwood had been warned in advance of what the Prime Minister was going to say in the rose garden, but only at second hand (by Michael Howard). He would have chosen to be more closely involved. He was not alone on the Tory right in thinking that he had seen the future and was convinced it would work, but he was considerably more articulate than most right-wingers. He had been in correspondence with the Prime Minister, setting out his own views on how the party could cure its divisions, and felt he deserved a more personal response than an announcement made to all the world at an open-air press conference. His feelings, and his gift of articulacy, were about to complicate the state of the party.

*

Initial reaction to the press conference was muted and puzzled. At least one historically minded Tory was reminded of the story of the ever-suspicious Metternich at the Congress of Vienna who, on being told that one of the delegates had died without warning, asked: 'I wonder what he meant by that?'

The simplest explanation was probably the true one. John said he wanted to clear the air and he meant it. During the previous week or two he had had a bellyful. Things had scarcely been helped by the tacit and sometimes less than tacit support the Eurosceptics had been receiving from his predecessor at No. 10; only the previous week she had publicly rebuked the Prime Minister for disciplining the rebels. Lady Thatcher had had her own ways of dealing with rebels, but she had never had to cope with the parliamentary arithmetic that faced the government in 1995, by which time John's majority was down to single figures.

He said later he had toyed with the notion of resigning the leadership a couple of times before, but had soldiered on. What was new now, in the June heat, was that a lot of people, in the party and in the media, were relishing the prospect of a long, enjoyable summer of doom-mongering, speculation about an autumn leadership election, or, failing that, malcontents putting the frighteners on him to pack his Cabinet with sceptics. Vicarious Cabinet-making always makes backbenchers frisky. And there were transatlantic forces at work. The Tory right wing had been drawing comfort recently from the news out of Washington, where Newt Gingrich's fundamentalist Republicans had been winning battles against the Clinton White House. It gave them ideas about doing the same sort of thing at Westminster.

Back-bench critics were made yet friskier by what they saw as evidence that the Prime Minister was beginning to make sceptical noises about the single currency. They decided it was time for a confrontation. They suggested, and he agreed, that he should meet a deputation from the Fresh Start Group.

The Fresh Start encounter, on Tuesday 13 June, was a turning point in the Major story; it was also a disaster. The two sides had wildly different perceptions of the realities. The critics sincerely believed the government was on the run over Europe: one more push and they could get the pledge they wanted, that Britain would stay out of the single currency. The Prime Minister himself, they suspected, had really come round to that view but simply felt bound to make European noises to pacify the Europeans among his Cabinet colleagues. One member of the Fresh Start deputation explained after the confrontation that he had expected the Prime Minister to 'give us a nod and a wink and say: "You know my difficulties with Clarke and Heseltine."'

Both sides at the Fresh Start confrontation may or may not have been conscious that another meeting was taking place in London simultaneously: a forum sponsored by *The Times* which was providing Margaret Thatcher with yet another opportunity to broadcast her disappointment with her successor. In any event, the Fresh Start delegation miscalculated badly, on two counts. First, they failed to appreciate an important streak in the Major character: guts. This was, after all, the man who had climbed up on his soapbox when all had seemed to be lost at the previous election. The other point, easily forgotten as the war of attrition went on, was that John at that stage did genuinely believe that being 'at the heart of Europe' was wholly consistent with the arguments he had won at Maastricht about maintaining British interests. The rebels, like many ultras, tended to believe they had a monopoly on idealism. They tried to bully the Prime Minister. To their astonishment, he stood up to them. One way and another, there had never been a meeting quite like it between a Conservative prime minister and a group of supposed supporters.

John's boldness paid off, but only in the short term: in retrospect, the delegation were more far-seeing than either they or he realised at the time. A year later, other forces had compelled him to go much of the way down the road the Fresh Start Group wanted him to tread.

*

The right smelled blood in mid-June 1995. That was why the Fresh Start Group took their initiative. Down at Rupert Murdoch's Wapping, *Times* leader-writers were honing the judicious phrases which would both express sadness at the passing of a prime minister who wasn't up to the job and welcome the dawn of a bright neo-Thatcherite future. In the Palace of Westminister, less elegant phrases like 'dead in the water' were heard. A shy, statesmanlike smile was reported to have been seen on the elegantly chiselled features of Michael Portillo.

This was the background to the garden press conference. There was over-excitement on the Portilloite fringes of the party for all of about forty-eight hours; but the party as a whole had a dilemma that failed to disappear, right up to the general election. It was a party unhappy with its leader but not daring to find a substitute. The immediate crisis following the Fresh Start fiasco was resolved when a message filtered down rapidly from the elder statesmen of the right. Roughly, it ran like this: 'Cool it, chaps. We know you think John is impossibly wet on all sorts of things, from Europe to tax-cutting. We know some of you have got excited by all these articles you've been reading in *The Times* and the *Telegraph*. We know some of you think this young Portillo is the greatest thing since Margaret. Maybe he is.

'But' – the message from the elders went on – 'if you hustle John out at this precise moment, don't imagine that you're going to get a chance to flaunt your precious principles. Get real. You're not talking principle here. You're talking panic. Look at the opinion polls. When the chips are down, all the colleagues are interested in is their chances of survival. Have you seen these charts from the opinion poll johnnies showing that about half of them are liable to lose their seats? What the party wants is a vote-winner. John did win the election for us in ninety-two. Maybe he can do it again. Maybe not. But one thing is sure, given the state of back-bench morale today: if you get rid of John the troops will look to Michael as their best hope – and that's not Michael Portillo.'

So the party found itself confronted, yet again, with the Heseltine love–hate factor – which was also, along with the bastard factor and various others, revolving through the Prime Minister's mind in the June sunshine.

The party's electoral prospects were also uppermost in the fertile mind of John Redwood. In mid-June 1995 the Secretary of State for Wales was not looking for a change of Prime Minister – not yet; but he was looking for a change of direction. It was after the Fresh Start meeting that he drafted his suggestions to the Prime Minister about what the Conservative administration ought to be doing if it hoped to be in with a chance of victory at the next election.

He was accustomed to addressing thoughtful words to prime ministers; he had been head of No. 10's Policy Unit in the Thatcher days. He was also a Fellow of All Souls. The Tory party ought to have learned by this time that it is unwise to dismiss thoughts from Fellows of All Souls out of hand. In the 1970s it was Keith Joseph, Fellow of All Souls, whose thoughts put a bomb under the party.

There were other similarities between John Redwood and Keith Joseph. Both were worriers. (When the leadership election was over, and John was a back-bencher once more, his wife Gail revealed that freedom from office had taken years off his life overnight: he could be his own man again.) Both Redwood and Joseph worried about the nitty-gritty of national life as well as about the abstractions. They both worried a lot about one-parent families, for instance. And both had an air of remoteness from the real world.

Twenty years earlier, the newspaper sketch-writers had labelled Keith Joseph 'the mad monk'. Monks were too subtle an allusion for newspaper readers in the nineties; now they took their metaphors from *Star Trek*. Matthew Parris of *The Times*, not realising what he was giving to posterity, had once written of John Redwood as 'a new creature, half human, half Vulcan, brother of the brilliant, cool-blooded Spock'; in 1995, the phrase became the small change of the hacks.

Brilliant, arguably only half-human, and seemingly innocent – it was a combination which made both Keith and John potentially dangerous in any leadership campaign. ('John has never been exposed to germs,' one colleague said.) The shop-soiled, all-too-human bruisers of the front bench – the Ken Clarkes, the Norman Lamonts – carry a lot of baggage with them when they enter a political battle. Norman, with his own ambitions to become a sort of Westminster Gingrich, was the obvious man for the right to put up against the Prime Minister in 1995 if there was going to be an election. Instead he had to grit his teeth and acknowledge that innocence gives a Fellow of All Souls a head start. John Major had less to fear from the toughs on his front bench. If Ken Clarke had chosen to stand, he would have started with with the handicap of a 'disloyalty' label round his neck.

John Redwood had even managed to keep himself germ-free in his Cabinet job at Welsh Affairs. It was the ideal job for a Cabinet minister with a troublesome conscience. In the Thatcher era Peter Walker spent several happy years in the Welsh Office virtually uncontaminated by Thatcherite regional policy. The wheel turned full circle when John Redwood took over. Wales wasn't so much a nation as a laboratory for experiments in neo-Thatcherite economics. He didn't choose to live in his laboratory, preferring to go home at night to leafy Berkshire. 'I'm the only minister ever to get into trouble for sleeping with my wife,' he said, to prove that half-Vulcans have a sense of humour.

Wales apart, he had never seemed particularly troubled by collective Cabinet responsibility on policy. He felt no shame in being, within the privacy of the Cabinet, one of the 'bastards' on Europe. He certainly felt free to call at No. 10 on Wednesday 21 June 1995 to give the Prime Minister his polite warning that the government had to mend its ways if the Tories were going to win the next election.

It was on this very day that the Prime Minister reached his decision to put his critics on the spot by forcing a leadership election. He had consulted nobody but Norma, he said later, but on that Wednesday he confided in the small team of people he was going to ask to run his campaign. There was Brian Mawhinney, the Ulsterman who, it was assumed, would provide Belfast-type no-surrender loyalty; Lord

Cranborne, whose aristocratic background was a particular cause of offence to some of the sceptics; and the canny Scot Ian Lang, who emerged as one of the heroes of the next couple of weeks and got his reward when he succeeded Michael Heseltine at the DTI.

On the following morning the Prime Minister told a selected group of Cabinet members. John Redwood was not one of them. So the Welsh Secretary was in an interesting state of mind when he went to watch England play the West Indies.

He was a guest in the box at Lord's taken by David Evans MP, one-time cricketer, one-time professional footballer and now million-aire chairman of Luton Football Club. David had been John Red-wood's PPS and was still his minder and source of street-wisdom. He had had problems as an ambitious young man about getting into politics (he had failed his eleven-plus and 'didn't have the right accent', as he explained). But he could make money. He had prospered from privatisation. He took in washing on a vast scale when the hospitals contracted out their laundry work. Eventually elected to the House, David was exactly the kind of self-made, salt-of-the-earth businessman approved of by Mrs Thatcher.

He was a man noted for what are called, in the rough trade of politics, robust views. He and his robust views were to reappear – indeed, to explode – on the scene just before the 1997 general election.

The admiration between Evans and Thatcher was mutual. He was believed to have sold her the idea that the problem of football hooli-gans could be solved – assuming that flogging was ruled out – by bringing in identity cards. This was how he had done it at his club at Luton Town. 'I'm not politically ambitious,' he once said. 'Not in the way of a thirty-five-year-old backbencher. I would probably be best persuading the people with the real power.'

He found a willing audience for his persuasion that day in his box at Lord's. All his streetwise instincts told him what John Redwood should do, now that the Prime Minister was submitting himself for re-election. Resign from the Cabinet, he told him, and stand for leader. As they surveyed the cricket field he spelt out an enticing scenario in a mixture of cricketing and other metaphors: 'You'll have a clear run,' he said. Somebody would have to stand in the first round against the PM. It wouldn't be Hezza, he predicted. Hezza would 'bottle out'. So would Portillo. David Evans was no constitutional guru, but he knew how the loyalty factor worked in the Tory Party. Tough old Thatcherite that he was, he had convinced himself that John Redwood had a sporting chance of doing what Margaret herself did as an outsider in the leadership election back in 1975.

It took a little while for John Redwood to make his mind up, and indeed nothing much seemed to happen for the next day or two after the garden news conference. Party, press, pundits – all had been caught off guard. The Prime Minister had achieved a tactical advantage. There was praise for his pluck. When he himself turned up at Lord's, as guest of the MCC president, the crowd burst into applause when he entered his box – upsetting the bowler Curtley Ambrose during his run-up. But it was not the cricket-going public whose votes he had to rely on.

What did happen, though, to affect the equilibrium further was that Douglas Hurd announced he would bring forward his retirement as Foreign Secretary to coincide with the leadership election. This would suit the convenience of whichever leader would be conducting the post-leadership Cabinet reshuffle. But it was also seized on as a new opening for the Eurosceptics. If they couldn't have a Eurosceptic Prime Minister, they wanted a Eurosceptic Foreign Secretary.

It was never clear that John Major, having decided to take the plunge, thought through what might happen in the first round of the ballot. The days were long past when a Tory leader in this situation could have expected to be enthusiastically re-elected by acclaim, *nemine contradicente*. He presumably expected a 'stalking horse' candidate who would get the backing of the obvious basket cases among the dissidents. He knew that six years earlier a previous stalking horse, Sir Anthony Meyer, had won an unexpectedly healthy total of protest votes when he challenged Margaret Thatcher.

It was soon obvious that John had opened the stable door to much more than stalking horses. To its own surprise, the party found itself shaping up for a contest reflecting an ideological divide in the party. This was something new. The first leadership election under the modern rules, when Ted Heath defeated Reggie Maudling in 1965, had been about style, not ideology. There was indeed an ideological third candidate on that occasion, Enoch Powell, but nobody took him very seriously. The next election, when Margaret ousted Ted, was conveniently reinterpreted in retrospect as a great breakthrough in

Conservative thinking, but it hadn't looked like that from the back benches at the time. Electing Margaret had simply been the most effective way of getting rid of Ted.

Now, in 1995, once the surprise had evaporated, ideology was suddenly in fashion. One Nation Conservatism, invented nearly fifty years before, was back as a talking point. Europe was an issue, of course. 'Sovereignty' was another. Nobody was under any illusion, however, that it was ideology which was uppermost in the colleagues' minds when they came to vote: at the end of the day they were looking for the leader most likely to deliver results at the general election. But meanwhile they wanted to talk it through in terms of issues. John Major, an unlikely Aladdin, had conjured up an ideological genie.

It became the accepted wisdom during that strange weekend following the garden press conference that a mere Anthony Meyer would not do as a foil for the Prime Minister in the first round. Over the weekend, MPs met constituents, or got indoors out of the sunshine and, clutching cordless telephones, slumped in their shirtsleeves into armchairs to chat to chums. A limited consensus began to take shape. It might or might not be a good idea for the party to swing one way or another ideologically, and it might or might not have been a good idea for John to have done what he did, but now he had done it, the party deserved a proper choice. Incidentally, the party's metaphors had gone downmarket. The talk now was not of stalking horses but of 'Mickey Mouse' candidates. A Mickey Mouse election was simply not on.

Several Mice were indicating that they were available. Teresa Gorman was one. Another was Barry Field, whom colleagues remembered as a campaigner for capital punishment and a friend of the prison officers (prisons being a growth industry in his constituency, the Isle of Wight). Now they reminded themselves, by checking the reference books, that he was the only MP known to be in the crematorium trade. These qualifications for leadership were never put to the test.

If there was going to be a vote along ideological lines, the natural candidates – in the second or third round – would be the two Michaels, Heseltine and Portillo. Both, it was taken for granted, were bound by the code to express loyalty to the present leader in the first round. Both did so, as did their Cabinet colleagues – with one exception. John Redwood stayed silent. He played cricket that Sunday for the local village team. (The amount of cricketing that went on during the leadership election would have seemed unrealistic if it had been fitted into the plot of a Jeffrey Archer political whodunnit.) Meanwhile Gail Redwood served mugs of tea to the gaggle of reporters camped outside their home. At that stage there was less serious interest in the Redwoods, however, than in the ex-minister who was not bound by the loyalty code: Norman Lamont.

There was an obvious problem for Norman, if he stood. He had been sacked by John Major. Tories don't like a bad loser. Under the conventions, though, bitterness doesn't disqualify candidates in the way that disloyalty does. It seemed, that first weekend of the election campaign, with the telephone lines humming around the constituencies, that Norman was the likeliest candidate to flush out the issues, if issues were what the colleagues wanted. He had the political clout – an ex-Chancellor, for heaven's sake, a flesh-and-blood politician with the killer instinct, rather than a Fellow of All Souls. Yet by the Sunday evening the Fellow of All Souls was emerging as the more credible candidate.

Things happened quickly on Monday morning. John Redwood resigned from the Cabinet; the FT Share Index fell 70.2 points. That was the bad news. The lighter news was that the challenger held a photo-call with some of his more flamboyant admirers posed around him – thereby rapidly establishing a cardinal rule for candidates in future leadership campaigns: you don't allow supporters like Tony Marlow to come anywhere near you wearing their striped old school blazers, even in cricketing weather. The *Daily Telegraph* (where there was a lively Redwood claque) helpfully used a truncated version of the group photo with the blazer out of shot. The version appearing in other papers needed only a ukelele and kiss-me-quick hats to make it look like part of an old *Picture Post* feature on how the British spend their Bank Holidays.

After this knockabout start, the Redwood campaign settled down into a serious operation. The hard-nosed David Evans took a grip on it and kept the striped blazers away from the cameras. 'This bloke is coming on strong,' he was able to say of his candidate a day or two later.

Even without striped blazers, the formal press conference called to present the Redwood programme for the party evidenced its own eccentricities. There was something for everyone. Hostels for the homeless, security for threatened regiments, a future for the royal yacht – a topic which was to re-emerge. It was easy to make fun of the Vulcan, but his basic themes, more tax-cutting and less Europe, were close to the hearts of a lot of the colleagues and their friends in the media.

So the choice facing the party in June 1995 was: John or John. Cynics said it was a contest between the second elevens – no more than a warm-up for the real leadership battle – and the logic of what was happening inside the party demanded a battle between the two Michaels.

It was easy to see why the first of the Michaels, Heseltine, chose to be a dog that declined to bark. To have brought down one Tory leader might be written off as high spirits. To bring down another would be the mark of a poor team player. Moreover, at some stage in the spring of 1995 he apparently reached the conclusion that the realistic thing was to establish himself as a deputy prime minister with real clout – not a Geoffrey Howe but a super Willie Whitelaw.

The case of Michael Portillo was more complicated. Until that weekend, he seemed a far likelier standard-bearer for the right. He was a fully paid-up Bastard. His loyalty to Margaret went back a long way. He liked to recall that he had been with her when she became Prime Minister (as part of her retinue in the 1979 election campaign), and he had been there in her final hours in Downing Street, when he almost literally fought his way into No. 10, over the ample body of Peter Morrison, to plead with her not to resign. Since joining the Major Cabinet he had stretched the rules of collective responsibility more than anyone to get the Thatcherite message across, over the Prime Minister's head. He had wowed the 1994 conference with his 'stop the rot from Brussels' speech: 'Stop telling kids they can't earn pocket money from doing their paper round. Stop telling small businesses they must give three months' paternity leave . . .' That was all on the record. Off the record, he had gone as far he decently could in giving comfort to the Euro-rebels.

To the sceptics, Michael Portillo looked to be the most credible king over the water. To the right, he looked to be the man likeliest to meet the Blair challenge by distancing the Conservative Party from Labour with 'Clear Blue Water' – which was the title of an address he gave to a fringe meeting at the 1994 conference. He had even managed to survive the embarrassing zeal of some of his friends (like the ones who booked Alexandra Palace for a Portillo memorial love-in). Among embarrassing friends might be counted the *Sun*, which decided that the Major–Redwood contest was simply ludicrous: what the nation needed was 'a man who speaks the language of the people . . . That man is Michael Portillo. He must not be kept waiting in the wings.'

Michael himself, however, recognised that waiting in the wings can be the clever thing in politics. Like the other Michael, he knew the perils of backstabbing the leader. He couldn't hope to get away with it as fetchingly as John Redwood seemed to be doing. He was already on everybody's list of usual suspects. Another incidental factor was that he was not a knee-jerk anti-Heseltinist. His inclination had been to prefer Michael over John Major in the 1990 leadership election, but he had given way to Margaret's edict to vote for her man.

On the last weekend of June, when David Evans was still telling John Redwood to 'go for it', Michael Portillo had his own millionaire constantly on the phone – the man who was not the least potentially embarrassing of his friends, David Hart. David Hart had been a loose cannon in the Thatcherite artillery for years. He had given aid and succour to the Federation of Conservative Students when they regarded themselves as the SAS of the Thatcherite right. He had been an irregular in the anti-Scargill campaign during the miners' strike. And he had found his imagination fired at his first meeting with Michael Portillo: 'Like Diaspora Jews,' he was quoted as saying, 'we instantly recognised that element in the other which set us both apart from those around us.' In June 1995 Hart was convinced that the time had come to strike.

Michael himself was more cautious. He believed John Redwood's candidacy could be queering the pitch, and told him so. Nor was he best pleased when some of the Redwood camp dropped hints that he, Michael, simply 'lacked the bottle' to break with the Prime Minister. Leadership campaigns bring out nasty streaks among the colleagues. Michael knew there were mutterings in the lobbies about the disadvantages of a foreign-sounding surname like Portillo, not to mention a swarthy face and thick lips. Niceness is the first thing to go out the window when the modern Tory party elects its leader.

Now, it would have suited Michael Portillo for the first round to be indecisive, but leaving the Prime Minister so seriously wounded that he had to step down. *The Times* declared that a showdown between Heseltine and Portillo was what the party 'needs to have' – a battle between two powerful personalities and between two styles of Conservatism. Clear blue water indeed.

But, as in the old story about the road to Tipperary, the problem was where to start from. Assuming the object was to get a Heseltine–Portillo contest in round two, how on earth should the supporters of either of these two men cast their votes in round one? The Home–Berkeley formula presented the same conundrum in 1995 as it had when the party was replacing Ted and finally picked on Margaret. Tactical voting does not come naturally to Tories – it smacks of third-party flabbiness. But some colleagues in 1995 were certainly prepared to be devious. Not all the people who voted Redwood in the first round were great admirers. It was like a 'phoney two clubs' bid at bridge. You don't want to play in clubs but you are determined to keep the bidding open.

There were rumours of a secret Redwood–Portillo deal: John to stand in the first round, to keep the seat warm for Michael in the second. Yes, they had spoken on the phone, said John. But then, as he said, he was on telephone terms with a lot of people.

Telephones (like cricket) featured largely in the campaign. Ever since Margaret had been defeated in 1990 because, so the story went, she and her team didn't spend enough time on the phone during the leadership campaign, telephone lines were deemed to be of the essence. Suspecting a Portillo plot, or a Hart plot, the press scouted around to find whether a secret bunker was already being kitted out as the Portillo HQ for a second-round coup. Without much difficulty they identified activity by telephone engineers outside 11 Lord North Street, home of Greville Howard, millionaire ex-aide to Enoch Powell. In the House, Labour MPs had fun with the logistics of Lord North Street at Prime Minister's questions. The PM was nothing if not chipper. If it was indeed true that forty telephone lines had been rushed in, he said, it was yet further evidence of the efficiency resulting from the privatisation of British Telecom.

*

When voting day came, it was an anti-climax. The colleagues, after all the predictions of blood on the carpet and the coming of the second Thatcherite revolution, decided to play safe. They opted for a formula which annoyed the ideologues. The solid middle of the party was still less interested in ideology than in the best formula to give them a sporting chance of winning the next general election.

Ultimately, 'it's the economy, stupid.' But the old Hezza magic might just help electoral prospects. Polling day for the first ballot was Tuesday 4 July; it was also the day of the famous Major–Heseltine summit. Officially they were discussing the economy. After the summit, Michael spent a long time that Tuesday prowling the corridors behind Downing Street to select his physical power base and to work out how to get some functioning reins of power into his hands. He had declined to be no more than party chairman in the run-up to the election. The summit deal was to defeat the John Redwood–Michael Portillo challenge by harnessing the other John and Michael in tandem. An unikely mix, maybe, of two very different men thrown together by the strange mixture of brutal democracy and schoolboy honour which added up to the ritual for electing the party leader. The deal done, Michael went to the committee room to cast his vote. He ostentatiously put his mark against the the Prime Minister's name.

The vote was 218 for Major, 89 for Redwood. The rose-garden *putsch* had worked – for the time being.

*

'The election has been decided,' John Major said afterwards, 'by MPs in Westminster, not by commentators outside Westminster with their particular views.' Put more bluntly, he had seen off not only John Redwood but the supposedly Conservative press. For how long, remained to be seen.

The press campaign against John during the leadership campaign demonstrated the contempt in which he was held by many of those 'commentators with their particular views'. On the day of the ballot the *Mail*'s headline was 'Time to ditch the captain'. The *Telegraph*, which had made the same point, was gracious enough after the event to admit that the Prime Minister had licked the pack: 'It is healthy for democracy when MPs, or the electorate at large, force a brief spell of humility upon the scribblers.' The *Sun*, which had displayed headlines like: 'Redwood v. Deadwood . . . Goodbye Johnboy', was less contrite on the day after: 'It's worse than that, he's won!' *The Times*' morning-after comment made the same point in *Times* language: 'Yesterday Conservative MPs threw away their last best opportunity to win the next election.'

In due course they could say, 'We told you so.'

Meanwhile it was a famous victory, and John, for once, chose to follow it up by carrying the battle into the enemy's camp. He hadn't forgotten or forgiven the experience of being roughed up by the Fresh Start Group. Having secured his left flank with Michael, he showed few concessions to the right when he reshuffled his Cabinet. To replace Douglas Hurd he promoted Malcolm Rifkind (who was not among the sceptics at this stage, though he was to join them later). Michael Portillo, preferred candidate of the right for the Foreign Secretary's job, was given defence – the old trick of putting a tax-cutter in charge of a spending department. Tristan Garel-Jones, shrewdest of ex-whips (and of Europhiles) remarked, when news of the reshuffle came through: 'I couldn't have done it better myself.'

In the event, defence proved a good education for Michael. He grew up over the next eighteen months. Nor was the other Michael, newly appointed Deputy Prime Minister and already the elder statesman, past learning, as he now proceeded to show. During the last couple of years of the Major government nobody was better at projecting the sweet reasonableness that was to be supposed to be the hallmark of the Major policy. One Nation . . . Common sense on Europe . . . Like the old pro he was, Michael became a regular performer on the BBC *Today* programme, slipping naturally into the company of the morning papers, folksy rabbis and constitutional experts on royal marriage and divorce. 'Now, we have with us in the studio the Deputy Prime Minister. Good morning, Deputy Prime Minister. You've heard what the Labour Party is saying about the European Commission's proposals for the privatisation of the Brigade of Guards. Tell us, please, Deputy Prime Minister . . .' Europe, lower taxes, global warming, naughty schoolchildren – whatever it was, Michael could come up with an easy, authoritative answer that breathed the message that we, the Tories, are the natural party of government and nobody in their right mind could think of voting for the other lot.

But the fate of the Tory party was not being decided wholly in Downing Street or in the new tennis-court-sized office of the Deputy Prime Minister. Lady Eden once remarked that the Suez Canal seemed to be flowing across the carpet in her drawing room. Norma Major, during her husband's last two years in office, had to get accustomed to all sorts of murky waters washing over the floorboards of No. 10. Some of the seepage was still coming from the direction of Grantham. A number of left-wing Tory MPs found their consciences worrying them, and the electorate showed no signs of reversing the impulse which had been eating away at the Conservative parliamentary majority at by-elections. There was also a small tidal wave, terrifying for timid Conservatives, about to sweep in from the Gulf of Mexico: 1996 was the year when the Conservative Party, unforgivably, allowed itself to be manipulated by the maverick expatriate billionaire James Goldsmith. In and around Downing Street, life's rich tapestry was becoming, to borrow the words used by the Princess of Wales in another connection, a bit crowded.

In January 1996 the Church of England, once the Tory party at prayer, marked the new year by issuing a judiciously worded new statement on hell: some Christians, it seemed, had been alarmed by taking hellfire too literally. Within days doubters were put to rights by Margaret Thatcher, never slow to challenge sloppy Anglican modernism. She launched brimstone on the party leadership. The occasion was the memorial lecture for Keith Joseph, who had died a year before. Her address developed into a set piece out of the *Inferno*, a grim warning to backsliders.

The lecture was important because it telescoped two of her favourite themes into a slogan for the Tory right. One theme was, of course, her successor's backsliding on Europe; the other was an attack on an image of Conservatism that had been central to John Major's speeches ever since the leadership election: One Nationism. It was also important because there was a sub-theme in which she put her own slant on the feelgood factor. A major weakness of the current Conservative government, Margaret told her audience, was its failure to keep faith with the middle class – 'and those who aspire to middle class values'. This was her explanation for the party's by-election defeats and poor showing in the opinion polls. Through every sentence of her lecture there breathed her sense of outrage that after all her success in bringing the new middle classes – the upwardly mobile, the Essex men and Essex women, the owner-occupiers of the old council estates – into the fold, her successor in Downing Street had managed to frighten them away.

Middle-class values had been basic to Margaret Thatcher's philosophy since girlhood. But a sharp edge was added to that philosophy in her early days in the Conservative Party when she came face to face with important party members whom she suspected, rightly, of patronising her, and patronising the homespun virtues she valued. It is hard to quantify the impact of her resentment, which could surface unpredictably. She devoted a substantial amount of space in her memoirs, for instance, to a trivial episode back in 1974 when she was standing against Ted Heath as a contender for the party leadership. She was interviewed by a magazine for the elderly, to which she offered some common-sense housewifely tips for saving money during times of rising prices: for example, you stock up your store cupboard with tins of food when you see a bargain in the shops. The media seized on it. Overnight she became Maggie the Hoarder (as she had once, as Education Secretary, been Maggie the Milk Snatcher). The point was that this was happening in the bad old inflationary days when the price tags in supermarkets were being marked up almost daily. Rising prices were one of the reasons the Heath government had got into trouble and had tried to get out of it with a 'prices and wages policy'. The accepted wisdom was that the key to dealing with inflation was 'restraint'; and 'restraint' was supposed to be the civic duty of shoppers no less than of trade unions.

Margaret never forgave the media for turning her into a hoarder. More than that, she was convinced they had been put up to it. The real villains were the Tory 'establishment'. 'In its way it was cleverly done,' she recalled in *The Downing Street Years*. 'It played to the snobbery of the Conservative Party, because the unspoken implication was that this was all that could be expected of a grocer's daughter.' Her suspicions had been strengthened when that pillar of the establishment, Lord Redmayne, once Harold Macmillan's Chief Whip, was persuaded on television to condemn the shopping techniques of the Thatcher household. 'Any sort of inducement to panic buying,' he solemnly warned the viewers, 'is against the public interest.' Lord Redmayne was deputy chairman of Harrods and, Margaret noted acidly, his larder 'probably contained something more enticing than a few tins of salmon and corned beef'.

Her account of the episode in her memoirs didn't stop there. 'Sometimes I was near to tears,' she recalled (this was twenty years after the event); 'sometimes I was shaking with anger.' A particular cause of that anger was her consciousness of what the media had done to her friend Keith Joseph. Just weeks before the 'hoarding' episode, he had seemed well placed to win the leadership from Ted, but then he made a single slip and the media were on to him – and not only the media, as Margaret saw it, but the establishment too. 'I saw how they destroyed Keith,' she had told a colleague when she effectively took over Keith's candidature. 'Well, they're not going to destroy me.'

All this anger welled up again, in the context of the 1990s, in the Keith Joseph memorial lecture. She took it out on the Major government. She took it out on the One Nation Group. Her assault on this group, which had drawn support from all parts of the Conservative Party, involved a curious rewriting of history: now, it seemed, it was a hotbed of near-traitors. She built up to the most important of the soundbites written into the lecture: some One Nation Tories, she said, judging by their views on European unity, would be better called 'No Nation' Tories.

At Central Office the lecture was seen as the end of a chapter. It was a double attack on the Prime Minister: a deliberate insult to the Major version of One Nation on which he was planning to win the election, and a deliberate flouting of the party strategy for knives to be sheathed on the issue of Europe. The leadership election was, after all, supposed to have drawn a line under that question. But things were shortly to made worse: Margaret wrote out a cheque for Bill Cash's European Foundation. A year or two earlier, it might have been possible to ignore this; but the European Foundation was now known to have had financial support from Sir James Goldsmith, founder of a separate party, the Referendum Party, which was determined on taking votes away from Conservative candidates.

In Smith Square, those in charge of preparations for the general election felt like kindly magistrates who have shown every leniency over the years to the local bag lady who makes trouble in the streets at closing time every Saturday night and now feel the time has come to lock her up for her own good. They sighed and started planning

for the 1997 election on the working assumption that Margaret was
. . . well, not a team player.

It happened to be about the same time that similar working assumptions were reached in Buckingham Place regarding the Princess of Wales. Indeed, the winter of 1995–6 confirmed the prejudices of male chauvinists everywhere that women in public life and team playing do not go together. For there was another little difficulty facing Central Office.

On the face of it, Emma Nicholson looked a dream of a team player. An Angela Brazil headmistress couldn't have wished for a spunkier head girl. Public service was in the Nicholson blood. One of Emma's great-grandfathers was predecessor of John Major as Tory MP for Huntingdon. When you scratched the surface, though, there was much that might have made the whips uneasy. Emma's father, a knight of the shires – a baronet actually – who sat on the back benches in the days when the party was run by the nobs, was a loyal, charming Tory, but quirky, and capable of putting the boot in: on the eve of Britain's finest hour he had been one of the minority who backed Churchill against Chamberlain. Her great-grandfather had been a floor-crosser – a Liberal MP who joined Disraeli's Conservatives. A more distant ancestor was one of the knights who took King Henry II at his word about what needed to be done with Becket, the turbulent priest. And on the maternal side Emma was descended from the Earls of Crawford and Balcarres, whose lineage goes far back into Scottish history and who were latterly distinguished for enlightened interest in the arts – in itself enough to set warning bells clanging in the whips' office.

Emma entered Parliament in the last years of the Thatcher era. She was to be vilified later as a hopelessly out-of-date Wet, but she was a child of her times. The smart watering-holes of the Thatcher years were full of Emma Nicholsons, robust professional women, talented, ambitious, independent-minded, pragmatic on women's lib issues and determined not to slip into conventional marriage. Such women throve under the conditions created by many of the Thatcher government's radical reforms, but they were a type of female with which Britain's first woman Prime Minister was never wholly at ease.

Emma's chosen profession was very much of the Thatcher years – computers. She divided her professional life between computer consultancy and charity organisation (fund-raising for Save The Children). She was sharp – she had played chess against Kasparov. And she was manifestly an achiever. Born with a hearing defect, she won a scholarship to the Royal College of Music. All this added up to a character bound to spell trouble for the Conservative Party in the 1980s, or perhaps in any decade. But her first involvement with Central Office was non-doctrinal: she was brought in to do something about the party's computers. The congenial Lord McAlpine, party treasurer and then deputy chairman (and later, incidentally, a leading light in the Goldsmith Referendum Party), and himself looking like a player of a bit part in an Angela Brazil story, thought it would be a jolly wheeze to make her a vice-chairman of the party. Her brief would be to find more women candidates, something the party felt it ought to be doing although its heart may never have been in it. But there was little meeting of minds between Emma and the party chairman Norman Tebbit, and her time at Smith Square was not an unqualified success from either point of view.

Elected as MP for a Devon seat in 1987, Emma showed early stirrings of mutiny. From the start she had Doubts, as they used to say of curates, about the poll tax. When Margaret attacked Conservative-led Devon County Council over their budget, Emma stood up for the councillors. On EC matters, she was pro-European. She got into trouble for expressing an ambition to serve in the Westminster and European parliaments simultaneously. At the time of Margaret's downfall in 1990, she planted herself publicly in the Heseltine camp. Chauvinists, of one kind or another, did not forget.

She fretted under the Major regime. The Conservative Party, she was to write afterwards, 'is increasingly unattractive to someone like myself. There is an endless search for scapegoats: single mothers, asylum-seekers, young people, ethnic minorities and many others are used as political targets by ministers seeking to deflect blame.' She fretted over Europe and 'cheap flag-waving populism'. For her, and not only for her, the 1995 Blackpool conference (with Portillo's silly anti-European speech) marked some kind of turning point. She had discussions with colleagues (including Alan Howarth, who had similar difficulties and eventually resolved them by crossing the floor to join the Labour Party). Later, Alan rationalised for both of them: 'Her frustration was above all at John Major's failure, after Thatcherism had run its necessary course, to bring the Conservative Party back on to its traditional ground.'

Come summer 1996, Emma imagined that the Heseltine–Major alliance would mean a fight-back to that traditional ground. She took her Doubts to Michael. If she hoped for reassurance, or for a hint that there might be a place for her in government to help with the fight-back, neither was forthcoming.

The next development took place, as is often the way with parliamentary developments, during a late-night sitting. Whiling away the long hours waiting for the division bell to call her back to the Chamber, Emma got into conversation with a fellow west country MP, the Liberal Democrat Nick Harvey. The extent of her Doubts was no secret, and Nick Harvey decided to pull her leg. You're in a sinking ship, Emma, he said; why aren't you jumping overboard and swimming to something safer? Perhaps she might, she told him. If she were asked. It was all playful, late-night stuff. But maybe there was a glint in her eye. The exchange sparked off a Lib-Dem cloak-and-dagger operation which did credit to the only party leader ever to have trained in the SBS Commandos. Paddy Ashdown himself kept behind the scenes until the last moment, after his lieutenants had done the preliminaries – guarded phone calls, a secret rendezvous in the Meridien Hotel (with a harpist providing mood music), then the definitive meeting in a safe house in Devon.

The object of the operation was not simply to spirit Emma away to the safety of the Lib-Dem benches but to bring the maximum firepower to bear on the Tory leadership. Tactical surprise was to be achieved. H-hour was to be 2100 hours on the Friday evening at the end of the Christmas holiday, as the opening titles of the BBC *Nine O'Clock News* rolled. Emma's courtesy letter of regretful resignation was faxed to Downing Street only minutes earlier, and by the time it was faxed on to Chequers the Prime Minister had learned the news from his television screen. The shock did not stop him doing a quick sum in his head: his Commons majority was now down to just one.

Arithmetic, team spirit, personal ambition, hurt pride – they were all there in *l'affaire* Nicholson. It wasn't just the Eurosceptics who were fed up with the reasonableness of John Major. In fact, there were a lot of bright people of the Nicholson generation, in both parties, much troubled, that winter, that their parties weren't getting things right. Which brings us to the Dromey family of south London.

Jack Dromey, a trade union official, and his wife, better known as the Labour front-bencher Harriet Harman, were faced in January 1996, like hundreds of other south London parents of eleven-year-old children, with the problem of where their son should to go to school the following autumn. After thinking long and hard, they fixed, not on the local comprehensive, but on a highly regarded grammar school out on the fringes of Kent.

The comrades were duly outraged, the Tories duly delighted. Education was something Conservative polemicists had been hoping to get a grip on for years, but the comprehensive schools issue never quite gelled for them. Now they had an issue. Within hours they had a slogan too: 'Labour says one thing, but does another.' The real joy was that it applied not just to Harriet Harman's family but to Tony Blair's. Both families had turned down comprehensive schools *run by Labour local authorities*. This was not just an issue, but an issue where you could shout 'Hypocrite!' It lasted the parliamentary Conservative Party through several happy weeks' question times, weeks during which Prime Minister's questions showed John at his most relaxed and most confident.

He knew his party needed something like this. It was obvious, at that stage of the 1992–7 parliament, that the economy – the one thing the party had traditionally been able to sell to the voters in the country once the chips were down and an election was called – hadn't been playing so well on the doorsteps since Black Wednesday. Then there was law and order. The traditional refrain had been: Labour is soft on crime. But by 1996, the Tories faced difficulties over the crime statistics during seventeen years of Conservative rule. The numbers had risen. Moreover, Michael Howard, having locked more and more people up, didn't seem able to stop them running away again. The third old faithful had always been standing up to the Reds, but that hadn't sounded the same since the Iron Curtain came down. For the Tories of 1996, Harriet Harman was a godsend.

The Labour Party had a real problem. Indeed, it had a long history of problems with the likes of Harriet Harman. As with Emma Nicholson, pedigree came into it. Harriet (educated, through no fault of hers, at St Paul's Girls' School) had a family background linked to the Longfords and the Pakenhams. The People's Party had been uneasy about such people since the days of Beatrice Webb. Back in the 1960s, when Hugh Gaitskell was trying to get rid of Clause Four, if you wanted to irritate the comrades you only had to mention that Hugh had been getting ideas from his friends over sherry in Hampstead. Now it wasn't Hampstead and sherry; it was Islington and cheeky little wines from Bulgaria. Labour had a leader educated at Fettes. One of the jokes was that in Islington the dinner-party chat was about how one got round the defects of the comprehensives by sending one's kids to a really good tutor on Saturdays and to an exciting summer school in the Cévennes. Tories laughed their heads off.

In the event, Harriet Harman (and Tony Blair) got off more lightly than they had at first feared. The fact was that the whole Blair generation was having doubts about the comprehensive ideal as it applied to the inner cities. Harriet found an interesting ally in the shape of Bernie Grant, archetypal spokesperson for the deprived urban areas, who observed bluntly that his kids had gone to the local comprehensive and he wished they hadn't. Harriet Harman's crime, like Emma Nicholson's, was that of the child in the story of the emperor's new clothes. But while Harriet probably helped the Blair leadership in developing its own kind of *realpolitik*, Emma, on the other hand, posed awkward questions about Major's. The emperor may have been confirmed in office, but his apparel was looking a bit threadbare.

Money Matters

Back in the 1960s and 1970s Jimmy Goldsmith was one of the early
enthusiasts for Britain going into Europe. Maybe he had been listening
to the fashionable left-wing line of the time about the European
Community being a rich man's club. Probably he was also among
those – like Ted Heath – who believed that going into Europe could
be a remedy for the 'English disease' that had been debilitating industry. In fact, the future founder of the Referendum Party even offered
a deal to Ted in the Conservative leadership contest that followed
the demise of the Heath government at the hands of the miners in
1974. Goldsmith (not yet Sir James) was convinced that Britain, with
Harold Wilson back as Prime Minister, was well on the way down
the slippery slope to Marxism. He was not alone in thinking this:
1974 was the year when various distinguished military men were writing letters to the papers calling for public-spirited citizens to volunteer
to man the road blocks when the Reds tried to take over. The Goldsmith proposal was not military. Broadly, it was that the European
dream, backed by Goldsmith money, could rid Britain for ever of
Harold Wilson and all he stood for. Ted declined the offer. An interesting footnote to the episode is that it was Harold Wilson (in his
controversial resignation honours list a couple of years later) who gave
Goldsmith his knighthood.

Sir James continued to push for his own brand of Europeanism and
entered the European Parliament. He wanted a 'strong Europe' and
set out his dream in detail in his published works. In the 1970s, as a
Euro-enthusiast, Sir James believed in unity of policy-making and
unity of financial strategy; read today, his ideas convey an image of a
Europe remarkably like the one that was to be denounced by the
Eurosceptics in the 1990s.

Logic, however, was never the strong point of the Eurosceptic case.

By the mid-1990s Goldsmith, now operating from power bases in Mexico and France, was the ally of the Eurosceptics with their spiritual power base in Essex. Where Sir James was wholly consistent was in his underlying philosophy: that of a rich man contemptuous of wishy-washy politicians. It had evolved into a mind-set which looked extraordinarily attractive to a lot of John Major's critics, those same critics who had been so patronising towards him during the leadership election campaign.

After the 1997 election, the Goldsmith Referendum Party seems a tattered irrelevance. For those who remember reading about them in the political theory textbooks, Major Douglas's Social Credit Party or Sir Richard Acland's Commonwealth Party look statesmanlike by comparison. But before the election, it seemed to have the potential to wreak havoc in the Conservative Party.

Sir James wanted a broadly worded referendum on the UK's relationship with Europe. Traditionally, government by referendum was anathema to mainstream British politicians, not least to Margaret Thatcher at the height of her powers. The fact that she had since changed her mind, and that the Referendum Party won the loyalty of well-loved members of her entourage – Alan Walters, Alistair McAlpine, Carla Powell (spouse of Sir Charles) – merely added to the oddness of the Goldsmith phenomenon. Even odder was the spectacle of politicians who were ready to go to the wall to preserve the integrity of the Westminster Parliament arguing that of course that Parliament couldn't be trusted to vote on the EU.

Why, in the spring of 1996, did a lot of normally level-headed people suddenly take Sir James and his party seriously? The Goldsmith party added remarkably little to the European debate. Tory MPs were divided over Europe; but then, they had been divided on this topic for twenty years. Many of their constituents dislike foreigners; but then, this has been true for a couple of hundred years at least. With a small majority, the Tory leadership had had to give in to the sceptic minority more often than they ought to have done; but then, the Prime Minister had been remarkably successful in seeing them off in the leadership election. So what was new?

The Commons arithmetic, the majority down to one, concentrated minds – or at least, it concentrated fears. Sir James – Britain's eleventh richest man, according to the annual *Sunday Times* survey of personal

wealth – was threatening to put up candidates, not in every constituency, although he could have afforded even that, but in those constituencies where the Tory candidate declined to give an assurance of
support for a referendum on Europe. There is an old joke about how
the great strength of the Conservatives is that they never panic –
except in a crisis. By that definition, the Goldsmith *démarche* counted
as a crisis.

But it was not just the arithmetic within the existing House of
Commons that frightened the colleagues. Jeffrey Archer, who always
had a distressingly accurate sense of what the country's Conservatives
are thinking out there in the grass roots, used to invite political
acquaintances to his penthouse, overlooking the river and the Palace
of Westminster, and invite them to play a jolly little game on his
computer. Suppose, just suppose, he would say, that this strange new
party attracted a respectable smattering of votes. Nothing like as many
as the Lib Dems, of course, but enough to justify feeding the figures
into the computer. Think of a number to represent the Referendum
share of the vote and enter it into the computer. Then put in your
guess of the Tory share of the vote and the Labour share. Jeffrey had
programmed the computer to calculate the outcome for each individual Tory MP, given any particular figures for overall shares of the
vote. As each guest entered his estimates of the parties' vote, out
spewed a printout of the Conservative MPs who could lose their seats
if Goldsmith put up a candidate against them. Nothing focuses an
MP's attention like a list with his name on it. Jeffrey's little game
gave colleagues nightmares in which they saw their names in brass
letters on coffins.

The single currency was not the only matter at issue. Spring 1996
was the time when the Great Beef War with Brussels got very bloody
indeed and Great Britain's representatives in Europe were instructed
to enhance their country's standing by refusing to talk to anyone. It
was also the time when, back home, the Conservatives were virtually
wiped out in the local council elections. The party had over a thousand
councillors up for re-election in 150 English local authorities. More
than half of them were defeated. Manchester, for instance, no longer
had a single Tory councillor. Even before these elections, the Tories
had been edged down to third place in local politics, and now the Lib
Dems had increased their margin over the Conservatives to several

hundred seats. These were real people voting with their feet out there, not blips on Jeffrey Archer's computer or notional voters in an opinion poll. It added up to scary stuff for salt-of-the-earth party activists around the country, many of whom had already seen their morale undermined through the Thatcher–Major years as central government, in the name of democracy, had taken more power from the town hall into Whitehall.

Central Office during this period resembled the BBC in one of those situations where 'viewers swamp the switchboards' after somebody uses a naughty word on *Newsnight*. The party grass roots were, in a manner of speaking, revolting. Europe was a major ideological battleground, but it wasn't the only one. Lord Mackay's Divorce Bill was running into trouble in the Lords (and in the *Daily Mail*) at the hands of miscellaneous Tory pundits. Like a banana republic dictator who decides he needs a good war to distract attention from unrest among the masses, the Conservative Party collectively decided that the secret weapon which would simultaneously see off Sir James, the beef lobbies, the House of Lords and disgruntled local electors would be capitulation on the referendum issue.

When Sir James arrived in London for a spring reconnaissance of the battlefield, John Redwood sought to play honest broker by calling on him in his suite at the Dorchester, but Sir James saw no reason to go out of his way to pull the Conservative Party's chestnuts out of the fire. It was against this background that the Cabinet agreed on a change of policy: not, indeed, to go for the broad referendum the Goldsmithites demanded, but to make a pledge that if the decision were taken by government to enter the single currency it would have to be ratified by a referendum.

Even back-benchers and front-benchers with sensible views on Europe had been swept along. The man best suited to stop the rot, Ken Clarke, allowed himself to be wrongfooted in Cabinet. The U-turn happened, but it stiffened Ken's resolve not to be caught out again, and to make sure the Tories didn't go into the general election as a hopelessly anti-European party. The fact remained that James Goldsmith, plus the failings of the UK agriculture industry, had changed the terms of trade on the Europe issue.

*

By the time the country entered election year, Sir James was already looking like an irrelevance. The same could not be said of the range of difficulties summed up in the word 'sleaze'.

No photo-montage of the Major years is complete without the press photograph of Neil Hamilton flourishing his biscuit. This biscuit had been presented to him when he visited a school, as MPs have to do, and Neil, forced to resign as a minister pending investigations into earlier activities while a back-bencher, took the opportunity to demonstrate that he was always meticulous in declaring any gifts received in the course of his duties.

The Hamilton case was the best known but not, regrettably, the only case during the 1990s of a Member alleged to have to been offered gifts in cash or kind in return for his advisory skills in and around Westminster. The Hamilton case was high-profile stuff, linked to the battle between Lonrho and the Al Fayeds for the control of Harrods. (If the Conservative Party was going to be embarrassed over coarse matters like shopkeeping, it liked a good class of shop.) The *Guardian* accused Neil of accepting money from the lobbying firm Ian Greer Associates for asking questions in the House. He sued. So did Ian Greer. After a while, the lawyers found they were hampered in preparing their case by an ancient statute. The 1689 Bill of Rights had not been a subject of much discussion at Westminster for some time, but mostly it was regarded as what *1066 and All That* calls a Good Thing, or at least a thing which wasn't doing any harm. Now, when the libel lawyers decided that they needed to present the court with certain government documents potentially useful to their case, it emerged that the Bill of Rights, designed to protect the privileges of Parliament, made it difficult for an MP to publish such material.

The government, perhaps rashly, accepted that the issue in the Hamilton case was important enough for the Bill of Rights to be amended, and a Law Lord was persuaded to introduce the necessary provision in the Upper House. He had second thoughts when he turned up and found the Lords benches packed with Conservative worthies evidently more interested in the politics of the thing than in its constitutional niceties, and abstained on his own motion. However, the Bill of Rights was amended, and Whitehall proceeded to make a search – a fairly costly search – for the files required.

When the information arrived on their desks, the lawyers who had been acting jointly for Ian Greer and Neil Hamilton found that it contained evidence which could create a 'conflict of interest' between the two clients. It was decided that the only realistic course was to drop the case.

There is less corruption in British public life than anywhere else, we are told. Maybe it was because of our good record that the 'cash for questions' affair upset so many people.

There have always been convenient fictions about the financial realities of an MP's life. The Mother of Parliaments has never really come to terms with the idea that its Members should be paid at all. Built into the constitutional infrastructure, along with Black Rod's breeches and the cloakroom facilities for Members to hang up their swords, are folk memories of the world of Trollope, when gentlemen reckoned that there was a price to be paid for, not an income to be earned from, the privilege of sitting on the green benches. The archetypal Victorian legislator got his income from his broad acres or the fruits of the industrial revolution. When his colleagues got fed up with him, or when he couldn't stomach government policy any longer, he could retire gracefully to his country seat and fill his days happily killing the fauna of the estate or, according to taste, fondling the incunabula in the library.

There was a lot to be said for Trollope's world. Legislators needn't hang on because they couldn't afford the alternative. But even the stiffer elements in the Tory party recognised years ago that its time had passed. Not only, in the celebrated words used by Michael Jopling, Margaret's Chief Whip, of Michael Heseltine, are there chaps in the House who had to buy their own furniture; there are some who are unsure where the money is to come from to do so – not to mention building up a decent cellar, raising the school fees to give their two-point-something children a proper start in life, and maintaining a modest base in Tuscany or the Midi from which to take a grassroots view on the EU.

The plain fact is that while an MP's income is higher than that of his average constituent, it is less impressive than that of the decision-makers in almost any organisation, private sector or public sector, with whom he expects to mingle. No doubt MPs should be able to rise above base temptation, but some of them had been sorely tempted to envy in the heyday of Thatcherism. During the enterprise years of the 1980s they increasingly found themselves hearing about people, no cleverer than they, earning telephone-number salaries in the City; and while MPs' expense accounts are not to be despised, they compare modestly with the bonuses, share options and all the rest of the perks of the Square Mile.

This was a mounting source of frustration – on top of the well-known occupational frustrations of back-benchers who have not yet made it to the front bench. British ministerial salaries may not be enormous but ministers enjoy what recruitment agencies call a highly attractive package. When ministers leave office, voluntarily or unwillingly, what really hits them where it hurts is no longer having the use of the chauffeur-driven departmental car. Even if the ex-minister has found himself a private sector niche where the perks include a car and driver, there was something about the Whitehall car pool that bestowed an enormous sense of comfort. If the British ever wanted to go in for radical democracy, the first step would not be to put the royal family on bicycles but to make ministers fight their own way through the London traffic. The conferral of a ministerial car, plus the pampering by private secretaries and the other luxuries of the machinery of Whitehall, is a powerful way to flatter a man.

When illness forced Harold Macmillan to resign the premiership, the change first hit him with the arrival of an engineer at his hospital bedside to disconnect his telephone. Now, he complained to friends, he had to pay a penny-halfpenny per call. Keith Joseph, while a Cabinet minister, was known to leave his desk to queue up at the Post Office for stamps to put on letters which weren't strictly concerned with departmental business. But Keith was an exceptional man. On the whole, Conservative politicians like their little comforts, and this is no less true after their party has been in office continuously for years, as the Tories had in the 1990s.

A new piece of Tory orthodoxy had evolved on the question of how Conservative MPs should finance the life to which they thought they should be accustomed. The ideal Tory was now assumed to be a man of substance not because he was a knight of the shires but because he had proved his market value in the business world – how much better, after all, it was for the country to be governed by people good at running a business.

So the argument ran. In fact, it is not a practical proposition to be an

MP while running a business. Typically the able modern businessman works an eighteen-hour day keeping up with the competition, which doesn't leave much time or energy for politics. The one-time gentlemanly ways of earning a living – the old-style family merchant bank or the estate agency serving the upper end of the market, which left time for extra-mural interests – have sunk under the pressure of market forces. Successful businessmen have indeed graduated to the House: take Michael Heseltine. But then, take Robert Maxwell. And there have been plenty of businessmen who didn't transplant well, shrewd men whose friends persuaded them, in their middle years, that they would be the greatest thing since sliced bread if they would stand for the Commons, and who within a month or two of arriving in Westminster decided it had all been a terrible mistake. The place was unbelievably more boring and unbelievably less efficient than the real world they knew.

While getting genuinely successful businessmen into the Commons has been a problem, there has never been any difficulty about getting lawyers in. The back benches have always swarmed with them: the Bar is notoriously a convenient profession to practise alongside politics. This was still the position in the 1980s, when professional politicians watched what was happening to the real disposable incomes of their opposite numbers outside politics and, unsurprisingly, began to cast their eyes around for some new profession, comparable to the Bar, which might provide an agreeable standard of living.

Enter Mr Ian Greer. But it is unfair to lay too much blame on him. He didn't invent the profession of parliamentary lobbying, nor indeed that of business consultancy. The systematic lobbying developed by him and some other skilled individuals formed part of a wider pattern that became established in the 1980s. The enterprise culture, the market economy and the new spirit of the Thatcher years were all bound up with the processes of communication – public relations, marketing, 'networking', image-making. Capitalism had thrived through the early part of the twentieth century using the skills of the advertising industry. By the 1980s, the business world was still devoting millions to its advertising budgets, but now realised that in some circumstances there are more cost-effective ways of communicating with the people you want to impress. 'Targeting' became the buzzword: you 'target' your message rather than sowing it broadcast. A host of agencies and consultancies sprang up during the Thatcher years, showing sales directors how to home in on the customers most likely to buy their products, advising finance directors how to persuade the City that their company's shares are worth buying, or more generally offering counsel on how to make friends and influence people.

The targets aimed at obviously include Westminster and Whitehall. Even in a privatised world – sometimes especially in a privatised world – the government machine still calls the shots and can move the goalposts. Ministers and officials make rules about everything from green belts through health and safety regulations to selling arms to dictators. 'Market testing' simply made it more, not less, important for businesses to know what officialdom was up to and to have the ear of ministers.

To the business world, the lobbying firms offered contacts and channels of communication. To professional politicians they offered a supplementary career as consultants. The lobbying firms themselves, if they built up a reputation, could earn substantial fees. Many of their clients were organisations accustomed to forking out big money to merchant bankers, City solicitors and various other experts who prospered during the 1980s. Thus parliamentary consultancy became yet another of the highly rewarded specialisms of the Thatcher–Major years. Many of the new consultants are clever people, many are even charming, few of them beat their wives and no doubt they are kind to animals. But by the 1990s the well-paid experts on the fringes of the enterprise culture, oiling the wheels of the market economy, tended to be unpopular with the politically correct. To the man in the street they were people being paid far too much for jobs which arguably weren't worth doing anyhow. The fact that they provided second (or third) incomes for politicians made things worse.

Those second and third incomes niggled when the electorate came to pass its verdict on eighteen years of Conservative government. The enterprise culture had generated another subliminal election issue. But the cookie had visibly started to crumble long before polling day was announced.

The process was set in motion in July 1994 with the exposure by the *Sunday Times* of two back-benchers who fell for the bait, offered by a reporter posing as a businessman, of a fee for asking a parliamentary question. The press, far from being ashamed of using this stratagem, dug deeper, and it was now that Neil Hamilton's name began to generate interest.

The Prime Minister acted characteristically. His gut instinct, as the decent chap from Brixton, was to throw back curtains when faced with shadows and let daylight flood in. This was the instinct that led him to appoint the Scott inquiry into arms for Iraq, and to encourage Scott – or at least to allow Scott to think he was being encouraged – to take the widest view of his remit. His reaction to cash for questions allegations was to set up the Nolan Committee, which also ranged far wider than some colleagues thought wise. Throwing back curtains is never popular with Whitehall professionals. Sadly, it didn't seem to win the Major government many brownie points with the ordinary voter.

Conservative governments in the past have often been often accused of doing too little too late. John Major, more than once, sometimes seemed to do too much too guilelessly. And there was another thing about John. By the time he became Prime Minister the gut instincts of the decent chap from Brixton had to compete with the instincts of a party politician who had worked in the whips' office. By the time Nolan and Scott were ready to report, it was John the ex-whip whose instincts predominated when it came to dealing with their conclusions.

The cash for questions business was only one way in which the currency of political integrity was seen to have been debased through the 1990s. Perhaps, as was often said, it was just that the blighters had been there too long.

The more literate kind of Tory has never been slow to quote Macaulay's dictum on the propensity of his countrymen from time to time to make a concerted dash for the moral high ground. 'We know no spectacle so ridiculous,' he said, 'as the British public in one of its periodical fits of morality.' The Conservative Party has never believed that the electorate, overall, wants its rulers to be straitlaced; but politicians can never afford to ignore sexual morality. Scandal may not actually have brought down Harold Macmillan but it heralded his fall. Christine Keeler still haunts No. 10. 'It *is* a moral issue,' *The Times* had thundered. However, the reaction of voters to such episodes is unpredictable. In America, the Republicans believed they had President Clinton on the run as unsavoury shadows emerged about his past. Then he trounced Bob Dole in the 1996 presidential election.

John Major had at least his fair share of sexually indiscreet colleagues to cope with. His heritage minister and friend David Mellor attracted the notice of the tabloids with the details (some of them true) of his friendship with the actress Antonia de Sancha. The jolly accounts of their relationship seemed not to shock the public overmuch. But the press, like the electorate, is unpredictable. Having got a taste for probing into the heritage minister's private life, the newspapers dug up the fact that he had accepted a free holiday for himself and his family. Sex and money can be a dangerous mixture. It was the gift of a holiday – although legitimately offered and legitmately accepted – that put paid to his ministerial career.

The departure of David Mellor was a real loss to John Major. David, like Norman Lamont, had been part of his circle, and when prime ministers feel they are losing the people who talk the same political language as themselves there are problems ahead (as Margaret found). More damaging still was that the Mellor episode showed John as a prime minister who stood four-square behind a colleague in trouble – until the Chief Whip told him enough was enough. Perhaps sexual peccadilloes damage political credibility less than U-turns.

*

There were more ministerial departures to come. There was the unhappy case of Tim Yeo, a junior environment minister who was revealed in the *News of the World* as the father of a child born to a fellow Conservative whom he had met at the 1992 Party Con- ference. When journalists went to their cuttings libraries to fill out their stories they were delighted to find that Tim was among those Conservatives who had gone on rather a lot about how single parent families threaten the fabric of society. Again, as with David Mellor, the Prime Minister was sympathetic – then decided that Tim had to go. Another cliché was added to those which, for cynics, summed up the Major years: when a minister asserted confidently that he 'enjoyed the full support of the Prime Minister' it was time for him to clear his desk. As when John made brave pronouncements about standing up to the Eurosceptics, the sensible approach had a way of coming to grief.

In some respects the most embarrassing case was that of the trans- port minister Steven Norris, who was revealed as having been involved with a range of mistresses following the breakdown of his marriage. The particular problem with Steven was one of timing. It happened that his private life became public knowledge in the same month, October 1993, which No. 10 had chosen to launch its new initiative called Back to Basics.

At the time, Back to Basics had seemed such a good thing. In the first place, it picked up fashionable concerns about the state of British education: why can't children read and write and do arithmetic? Then again, the words had a reassuring ring of muscular Christianity: play the game without getting too pious. They also had the merit of being alliterative. With any luck, it was a campaign which would wrongfoot the opposition. And, not the least important aspect, it wouldn't frighten the Treasury by costing a lot of money. Back to Basics was intended to roll on into the general election; in the event it failed to survive the Norris affair, or affairs. And Steven was to emerge nearer the election to haunt the party yet again, this time on a purely political issue.

Yet there was a receptive audience, out there among the electorate, for the politics of morality. This grassroots feeling surfaced as the 1996–7 academic year was getting under way and news began to flow in of schools where behaviour was not just bad but frighteningly criminal. A headmaster was stabbed to death when he tried to defend a pupil. His widow made a moving appeal for a moral crusade. In a vague way, the public mind associated all this with the horror of the mass murder at the infants' school in Dunblane.

If the public wanted a moral lead, it was far from clear that politicians were the right people to deliver it, especially with a general election on the horizon. Of politicians who ventured into this dangerous ground, few emerged with glory and some behaved with sheer crassness. The parties bickered. They bickered about the size and design of knives that hooligans should be allowed to buy over the counter; they bickered about which types of guns were safe to sell and which unsafe. What started as highminded debate foundered in squabbles about weapon calibre. The education secretary, Gillian Shephard, took the opportunity to suggest more caning of children and seemed genuinely surprised that she wasn't hailed as a stateswoman. The Conservative Party is not always at its best on crime and punishment, and rarely so on punishment in schools.

It wasn't John Major's fault that the closing months of his government witnessed spectacular horrors, including mass murder. But what irritated many – whether the subject was crime, or disastrous schools, or feckless pregnant teenagers, or unpleasant vagrants camped out in shop doorways – was the rhetoric of ministers who acted and talked as if they had suddenly arrived like trusty, disciplined firemen on the scene of a tragedy, skilled and trained to bring order out of chaos. These same ministers had been around for eighteen years. It might have been more seemly, in the minds of at least some voters, for them to have paid at least lip service to the responsibilities that have accrued to a party that has been in office for the best part of a couple of decades. Eighteen-year-olds, well or badly behaved, had been in nappies when the Labour Party was last in power; they had completed their education, from kindergarten to sixth form (or youth detention centre) under a Conservative government. Yet some of the ministerial rhetoric resembled that uttered by Harold Wilson when he arrived brandishing the white heat of reform after thirteen years of government by the other party. The Tories had been there for an awfully long time. Any government in that position has a problem, maybe an insoluble problem.

*

John himself was more aware than some of his colleagues of the danger that the years can bring complacency and arrogance. That was why he sensed the threat posed by the most complex of the scandal allegations of his time, which the Scott inquiry was set up to investigate. Apart from anything else, he remembered Westland. Whitehall, too, was still sensitive to the memories of one of the great crises of the Thatcher years. Even in the mid-1990s you could make the flesh of higher-grade civil servants creep by mentioning the word Westland.

The Westland crisis of 1985–6 not only came within a whisker of bringing down Margaret Thatcher, it seriously embarrassed the Civil Service. Civil servants don't like being accused of breaking the rules to suit the convenience of their political masters. Nor, it must said, do mandarins enjoy having the processes of decision-making thrown open to public gaze. After Westland, two select committees spent long and often fascinating hours trawling the corridors of power for evidence about the source of the celebrated leak of the law officer's letter which had been designed to embarrass Michael Heseltine over his negotiations on the Westland company. Committee members trying to trace just what had happened to that letter as it passed from hand to hand around Whitehall were confronted with a classic performance of departmental stonewalling by no less a figure than the Cabinet Secretary himself, Sir Robert Armstrong, who was subjected to public examination. Nothing like this had ever happened to Sir Robert before. The repercussions among Whitehall professionals lasted for years. Happily, Sir Robert Armstrong did not allow it to undermine his confidence. Before long he was stonewalling for England once more, in Australia when the *Spycatcher* case came before the courts there. It was in Australia that he earned his place in the dictionaries of quotations with the phrase 'economical with the truth'.

Westland and *Spycatcher* all happened long ago. (You can always identify a pouring-of-cold-water operation when politicians say: 'It was all a long time ago.') Politicians know, too, that few ordinary voters bother much about the workings of the policy-making machine. Departmental memos, red boxes, briefings, leaks, Cabinet papers – such things are caviare to the general, not the bread and butter of winning elections. Westland certainly wasn't an issue at the general election which followed in 1992, by which time the principal player had moved on from Downing Street. Nevertheless, the earth did move at Westminster during the Westland drama. And, as John Major was to find out within a very short space of time after taking over at No. 10, there was another earth-moving drama waiting to happen in the murky waters in which the defence industry, intelligence and Middle East policy swim warily round one another.

*

The Scott inquiry into the sale of arms to Iraq was the classic case of John Major's instinct of outrage at political chicanery – or, more accurately, his instinct to react to a public sense of outrage when the chicanery came into the public domain.

The alleged chicanery was that ministers had signed certificates, on grounds of national security, which denied a handful of businessmen the right to put forward the defence that would have prevented them from going to prison. This had emerged when the Matrix Churchill trial was aborted in the autumn of 1992. Autumn 1992 happened to be a bad time for the government. Taxes had had to go up, just months after an election fought largely on the Conservatives' credentials as tax-cutters. The Eurosceptics had been causing grief again. And the badly handled episode of the latest pit closures had been a further embarrassment.

John wanted to prove that his government would act fearlessly to get to the root of the Matrix Churchill fiasco. No stones were to be left unturned. No fear or favour was to be shown. He looked for a fearless judge, and turned to Lord Justice Scott. There have been few cases of a Conservative prime minister, or a Labour prime minister for that matter, doing so much, with the best of intentions, to upset the British establishment. Scott fazed even some of the least fazable of Conservatives (Geoffrey Howe, for example, who was involved as an ex-Foreign Secretary). And he fazed officialdom even more than the Westland inquiry had done. The shock to the political and administrative establishment was all the greater because those of its members who were involved embarked on the inquiry process confident that there was nothing to worry about, provided everybody behaved sensibly. What happened then resembled the social drama captured in Priestley's *An Inspector Calls* when the family in a respectable Edwardian house are invited to answer a question or two about how a serving girl was got into trouble, then to their horror find themselves treated like common criminals.

The chattering classes were pleasurably enthralled by the Scott inquiry, although eventually even they became bored as the proceedings dragged on for month after month. The Whitehall establishment was traumatised. Scott presented Whitehall with the greatest upset to its equilibrium since – well, since Margaret Thatcher arrived in 1979 and civil servants suddenly realised she wasn't going to play the Whitehall game by the Queensberry Rules; and *that* had been the biggest upset since 1940, when Winston arrived in Whitehall and permanent secretaries, it is said, were to be seen *running* down the corridors carrying files demanded by the Prime Minister.

Many hundreds of hours of departmental time were spent digging out files that Lord Justice Scott demanded, and huge amounts of Wykehamist brainpower devoted to containing what was seen as Scott's assault on the decencies of proper administration. All the tried techniques for neutralising the inquiry were used, including a whispering campaign against Scott himself ('the wettest, most liberal judge they could find', according to Bernard Ingham, himself no whisperer). But Scott would not be deflected. He would simply ask 'Why?', when officialdom thought the proper question would have been 'What are the precedents?' It was a confrontation between common sense and accepted wisdom.

Day after day, having cycled (yes, cycled, as was frequently pointed out by the whisperers) to his makeshift court-room in Westminster, Sir Richard Scott produced revelations of interdepartmental infighting and evidence of how ministers seemed less concerned with realities than with appearances. It all added up to top-quality caviare, but did the general care? It had all been a long time ago.

The Scott Report resulted in no resignations (unlike the Westland affair, after which the political casualties lent the stage an air of the final scene in *Hamlet*). At the end, partly because the inquiry had dragged on so long, the report could be seen as no more than a small earthquake in Chile, or some other faraway country of which we knew little. Even the indignation of the chattering classes had its limits.

And yet, and yet . . . Maybe the chattering classes don't have as much influence as they like to think, but they are a barometer. In the declining years of the Macmillan premiership, the satirists of the BBC's *That Was the Week That Was* may have been self-indulgent pranksters, but they can now be seen as more than that, as minstrels chronicling the decline of a political era. The Scott Report chronicled the culture of a governmental system which many saw as arrogant and careless of the distinction between the public interest and political convenience.

Again and again the Whitehall files, ruthlessly exposed by Scott to the public gaze, produced fascinating weasel phrases. One gem of Civil Service verbiage was the comment that 'we could find ourselves in a presentational difficulty' if a certain event became public knowledge. 'Presentational difficulties' was the euphemism for the danger of being found out. In the past, people had shrugged their shoulders at the Whitehall mind-set. Now it was being spelled out. A key aspect of that mind-set was a marked reluctance to accept that anything could possibly be wrong provided accepted practices had been followed. 'You have a misunderstanding about how the system works,' Scott was told magisterially by one mandarin. Laymen, by contrast, might think the truth was rather that the Scott Report demonstrated a very shrewd understanding of how the system worked during the Thatcher–Major years, and of course for long before that. Arrogance was not a new phenomenon in Westminster or Whitehall. Nor was Whitehall's penchant for playing the 'security' card – 'the need to protect intelligence sources' – as a reason for keeping documents secret. But the Scott Report dotted i's and crossed t's about how the cards were played.

Why did the Prime Minister choose Scott for the job? What impressed him was not what Bernard Ingham called wetness but simply Scott's reputation as a strong, intelligent judge. He had handled politically sensitive cases, in some of which he had offended liberal susceptibilities. He had ordered the *Guardian* to surrender an improperly obtained copy of a Foreign Office document – a decision which led to the imprisonment of Sarah Tisdall for leaking it. During the miners' strike he granted an injunction to a group of miners to stop NUM officials from organising picketing. He was one of the judges to play a part in the *Spycatcher* case, rejecting the government's plea for a permanent ban on the reporting of Peter Wright's story. It was more difficult than Bernard Ingham seemed to think to fit him into a slot. Bicycle rider he might be, but he also had the impeccably Tory virtue of riding to hounds (with the Grafton). He came of imperial stock, born in India and brought up in Natal. In South Africa, it is said, he developed at least one clear view about governments: that dangers arise when they become too powerful.

It is not hard to see why someone like John Major should have approved of Scott as a man who would demonstrate that his government believed in square dealing. John's intentions were good. Unfortunately for him, the Scott Report could also be seen as demonstrating with disastrous clarity how a government works when it has been in place too long for its own good.

The whole arms for Iraq saga was, in a sense, a tale of good intentions gone wrong. For years, successive governments had seen arms exports as 'good for UK plc'. Labour politicians knew it was tricky to criticise arms contracts: they create jobs for good trade unionists. But everybody agreed that there had to be rules – guidelines – about whom you sell arms to.

In his day the Shah of Iran was seen as a good customer. Things changed when he was deposed, and it then made sense to arm the Iranians' enemies, the Iraqis, who stood the best chance of anyone in the Middle East of standing up to the regime which took over from the Shah. The pattern became more complicated when full-scale war broke out between Iran and Iraq, and yet another factor was built into the equation when the Ayatollah pronounced his *fatwa* against Salman Rushdie. Liberal opinion and conservative imperial instincts found themselves on the same side.

The Iraqi regime might be a cruel one – the files released to Scott proved, if nothing else, that Whitehall had few illusions about Saddam Hussein. But, then, who is perfect in that part of the world? British intelligence had been reasonably effective in establishing what Saddam was up to. That was the problem at the Matrix Churchill trial. The documents which would have been useful to the defence in that trial would have revealed intelligence methods; hence the decision to keep them under wraps. The Matrix Churchill boss had himself been working for British intelligence. The plot was thickening and the road to political hell was being paved with good intentions as well as blood-stained rubble.

The government became aware of the makings of a 'presentational difficulty' within days of John Major's appointment as Prime Minister in November 1990. The previous month, Customs and Excise had arrested Paul Henderson and two fellow directors of Matrix Churchill for allegedly breaching the official guidelines for arms sales. At that time the whole question of exporting militarily sensitive engineering materials to Iraq had acquired a high political profile because the Middle East was shaping up for the Gulf War following the Iraqi invasion of Kuwait. Saddam, so far from being a quasi-ally of the West against an evil Iran, had now emerged not just as a cruel dictator who terrorised his own people but as an international aggressor. Britain, under its new Prime Minister, was standing by to send troops to help repel invaders – invaders who, it now seemed, had been armed by British industry.

Into this delicate situation the *Sunday Times* – this was on the Sunday following Margaret's tearful departure from Downing Street – made an unhelpful intervention with a front-page story alleging that a few years earlier Margaret's trade minister had given nods and winks to British machine tool manufacturers about how they could get round the arms export guidelines in order to sell militarily useful machine tools to Iraq.

The minister concerned (who had retired along with Margaret) was Westminster's incomparable loose cannon, Alan Clark.

On the Monday morning following publication of the *Sunday Times* story the new Prime Minister called Alan into Downing Street, where he apparently offered an explanation that satisfied both the Prime Minister and the Cabinet Secretary, who was present; but Whitehall remained understandably apprehensive about what would come out in open court at the trial of the Matrix Churchill directors. The hope was that the prosecution might be stopped, though it was accepted that HM Customs and Excise were well known to be jealous of their right to initiate prosecutions without interference from other parts of the government machine. If the trial did go on, Whitehall strategy was to ensure that civil servants called as witnesses gave away as little as they decently could. This might make it harder for the defence to prove that Matrix Churchill had acted with tacit government approval; but – so the argument ran – people who work for intelligence ought to know that they will be disowned when or if the debris hits the fan. Security interests must prevail.

The legal preliminaries to the trial ground slowly on – for a year and a half. The stress factor in Whitehall cannot have been very healthy for the interests of good government, even at that stage, let alone when the pressure really stepped up during the Scott inquiry. Eventually, a date for the trial was set: it would begin in the autumn of 1992. Alan Clark was to give evidence. A few weeks before the scheduled hearing he gave an interview to the *Sunday Telegraph*. The paper put to him the allegation made by the *Sunday Times*: was it true that as trade minister he made suggestions to machine tool manufacturers about how they should word their export applications so as to get around the guidelines? Yes, it was, Alan was reported to have replied. 'And I did it for two reasons. First, I was minister for trade, so it was my job to maximise exports despite guidelines which I regarded as tiresome and intrusive. Second, Iran was the enemy – it still is – and it was clear to me that the interests of the West were well served by Iran and Iraq fighting each other, the longer the better.'

Alan had done it again. It was like a Bateman cartoon – 'The Politician Who Told It Like It Was'.

The lawyers prosecuting the Matrix Churchill directors saw their case collapsing before their eyes. Then they pulled themselves together and seem to have assumed that Alan couldn't possibly have said what he was reported to have said. They tried privately to get him to spell out what his policy had really been, but didn't get very far. The trial went ahead.

When the day came for Alan to stand in the witness box at the Old Bailey, he literally stopped the show. Defence counsel put it to him straight. The official position was that the machine tools in question would be used by the Iraqis only for 'general engineering' purposes. But in fact he, the minister, knew, did he not, that the Iraqis would be using the order for making munitions? The following exchange then took place:

Clark: Well, it's our old friend being economical, isn't it?
Counsel: With the truth?
Clark: With the *actualité*.

Do official reports ever get hold of the whole of the *actualité*? Scott tried hard enough. His report passed over most heads. But it must have left an impression in the electorate's subconscious – an impression deep enough to serve as another reason for abandoning the Tories come election time a year and more later.

*

The last couple of years of the Major government often seemed like an exercise in cliff-hanging at a congress of unsuccessful suicides on Beachy Head. Again and again, the ritual was played out as the whips marched up to the clerks and announced, 'The ayes to the right . . .', and the colleagues made their triumph noises as the figures showed a government majority of three, or two, or one. 'A majority of one is enough' became one of the catchphrases of a government on the way out.

In February 1996, the Major government survived the Scott Report crisis by one vote. Within minutes of the whips' lining up to announce the result, the official version was sweeping around the corridors: 'We have drawn a line under Scott. A majority is a majority.' Constitutionally, there can be no quarrel with this. British politicians have a touching faith in the 'first past the post' principle. The party with a majority, however small, in the House of Commons calls the tune. Other countries have sophisticated checks and balances – supreme courts which can overrule the legislature, powerful second chambers, regional legislatures sharing power with the national parliament. The British have always looked down on such alien fripperies as something for lesser nations – like proportional representation. It is a great comfort for a prime minister, with a strong chief whip at his elbow, to know that once he has taken a decision he can assume that it will be carried through the Commons; for the Chancellor, having done his sums, to know he can get the budget through; for party managers to know that vital bills aren't going to have the guts ripped out of them in the way that Congress can disable an American administration's legislative programme in Washington.

That comfort was increasingly denied to John Major. His glory day had come when he unexpectedly triumphed in the 1992 general election, but it had been a small-scale triumph. His party had lost forty seats. The overall majority was down to twenty-one, a figure which was to be slashed cruelly by defections and by-election defeats. But the real headache for the Chief Whip was not the simple arithmetic so much as the fact that the Commons was now in the unhappy state of one of those despised foreign legislative assemblies where minority parties call the tune. The Eurosceptics were behaving like one of those small parties in the National Assembly of the French Fourth Republic, redolent of comic opera but able to force the country into yet another general election. Then there was a real minority party to worry about. We heard a lot during the 1990s about 'single issue' politics. One single issue forever causing grief for British politicians is the constitution of Northern Ireland. The Ulster Unionists, with their dozen votes, may have been less theatrical than the Eurosceptics but by the mid-1990s they were potentially more dangerous.

Never forget the Irish. Churchill, in an affectionate tribute to Lloyd George, once noted that if it was the Irish question which caused that powerful politician to fall, he was in good company – 'with Essex and with Strafford, with Pitt and with Gladstone'. The Irish question ripped the great Victorian Liberal Party asunder; a century and more later, it loomed over the Conservatives. One of the great might-have-beens of the Major years was peace in Northern Ireland. Anyone who doubted that courage and perseverance were among John's virtues had only to look at his part in the 'peace process'. At times it seemed as if that was the only thing which was going right for his government. In the Province there was literally dancing in the streets. An American President came and, with tears in his eyes, set his seal on the peace process. It could have been an election-winner. The ceasefire seemed too good to be true. It was. The hopes slipped away and were finally exploded by a massive bomb that ripped out the heart of one of the monuments to Thatcher's England in Dockland.

Ulster Unionists apart, Northern Ireland lent itself to consensus at Westminster much more than Europe did. Even as the Conservative majority crumbled, the Labour Party was not going to play the orange card or the green card just to bring down the government. But there wasn't all that much comfort to be had from this; the Unionists had views on lots of other things, from the Scott Report to mad cows, where they might find themselves voting along with Labour. Their dozen votes gave them power out of proportion to their strength. They were like a religious minority party in Israel, able to shape events across the Middle East.

The Europe debate went back to the days of confused patriotism after Suez when Britain, to borrow Acheson's much-quoted phrase, had lost an empire and was searching for something else. There are still people around who can remember being inspired by the message that Harold Macmillan brought to the Tory party, when he replaced Anthony Eden, of a new world role for Britain. He didn't impress all his colleagues: Enoch Powell saw the performance of 'the old actor-manager' as 'one of the most horrible things I can remember in politics'. Neverthless it was the old actor-manager of the late 1950s who patched together a grievously demoralised party, mended fences with the Americans and earned the respect of the third world. In the 1990s, John Major lacked the skills of an actor-manager. And of course he didn't have the luxury, which Harold had, of a huge Commons majority which allowed him to laugh off his little local difficulties.

The year of Suez, 1956, was also the year that John Osborne invented Jimmy Porter, the young man who was angry about everything England stood for. Now, in the Major years, an ageing Osborne wrote a more relaxed play, *Déjà Vu*, in which he reinvented Jimmy Porter as a gruff old man who had decided that England wasn't so bad after all. What infuriated the new Jimmy Porter was 'a country called the Yookay'. By the mid-1990s, the Yookay had attracted some unappealing camp followers. In the name of the Yookay, grim-faced men in fancy dress marched with bowler hats and umbrellas across dismal townscapes in Northern Ireland. In 1996 there was a serious wrangle in Cabinet over whether to incorporate a Union flag in the design of the new driving licence. We had a defence secretary who sneered at his European allies because he knew it would get a quick cheer from a Conservative conference. This was the same Michael Portillo who told an undergraduate audience, when he imagined he wouldn't be reported, that students in Europe were accustomed to buying their examination passes. And even hardened observers of the UK's newspapers were shocked by journalistic chauvinism during Euro '96. We had got used to the *Sun* telling the Frogs to hop off, but eyebrows were raised when the *Daily Mirror* thought it was funny to address visiting German football fans as invading stormtroopers: 'A state of war exists between us,' its front page warned them. Only joking, of course. Nor was this kind of crudely nationalist under-current exclusive to the tabloids: a surprisingly large segment of the broadsheet press seemed to think that the BSE crisis, a problem that in saner times might have been sorted out by civil servants and veterinary experts round a table, was a war between the Yookay and the rest of Europe. By midsummer 1996, Britain's relations with the rest of Europe were embarrassing for those of us brought up to believe that flag-waving was something that should only happen at the last night of the Proms.

'The United Kingdom' became a Conservative election issue because it was a convenient way to rally the anti-European vote and simultaneously to exploit the absurdities of Labour's plans for devol-ution in Scotland and Wales. Scotland, like Ireland, does funny things to Westminster politicians. John was but a lad in short trousers when the Stone of Scone was stolen from Westminster and there is no evidence that he got emotionally caught up in the drama. But in July 1996 the adult John Major announced that the Stone was to be taken legally back to Edinburgh. John believed he had a special appeal for the people of Scotland. When he led the party into the 1992 election, he had played the Union card in his Scottish campaign. In the event, Scotland swung, slightly, towards the Tories while England swung the other way. Nobody within the party organisation liked to mention what was obvious to everyone in Scotland, that John's merit north of the border was simply that he was not Margaret Thatcher. During her electoral triumphs of the 1980s in England she had brought the Conservative cause in Scotland to an all-time low. John had merely gone some way towards redressing the balance.

Devolution aside, the mechanics of governing the United Kingdom had become a matter of serious concern, and not only to constitutional theorists.

Power-sharing, and checks and balances, had not been in the nature of Prime Minister Thatcher. 'I couldn't waste time having any internal arguments,' she had said when she was asked, before she became Prime Minister, how she would run her government. For her, certainly, a majority of one was enough. She broke tradition by refusing to appoint royal commissions to advise her: there was to be no broadening of the decision-making process by bringing in the great and the good, who might have been Conservatives but not 'of us'. Her successor in Downing Street took a less hard-line view, but ironically found himself, too, at loggerheads with the great and the good: his ministers seemed forever to be having their decisions declared illegal by the courts. At local level, meanwhile, it became apparent that the Conservatives believed in privatisation but not in sharing authority. Local government had become a joke. The Thatcher government's way of dealing with the 'loony lefties' in 1980s town halls had been to strip them of their powers and take control back to Whitehall. Ken Livingstone's London had been left with no recognisable local government at all. This high-handedness led to irritation not only among Labour Party members but among local Tories as well. Conservatives around the country don't ask for a lot. They dip uncomplainingly into their pockets at wine and cheese parties and rubber chicken lunches, and when elections come round they happily stuff envelopes and push leaflets through letter-boxes. But they do like to have some input into policy, and the keener ones like being on local councils.

There was a paradox about a government which talked so much about rolling back the boundaries of the state while it took power away from local councils and created Whitehall-appointed quangos. Years earlier the politician-philosopher Quintin Hailsham had warned about 'elective dictatorship'. Now Simon Jenkins, a former editor of *The Times*, summed up the developments of the Thatcher years, perpetuated under Major, in a book entitled *Accountable to None: The Tory Nationalisation of Britain*.

Across the Channel they have less difficulty in accepting the idea of sharing power. The Germans feel their system is strengthened, not weakened, by a federal system, with some powers concentrated in the capital, others devolved to the *Länder*. And they find it hard to see why a national government can't live happily with a powerful European Union. The Eurosceptics had a point. Over there, they think differently from us. At the end of the Major years, though, a visitor arriving from Mars, and looking at the state of the British party system, might not have been immediately won over to the proposition that British is best.

*

As much as a year before the general election, even Conservatives not noted for historical analysis were heard muttering about what happened to the Tories under Peel in the 1840s or to Gladstone's Liberals, split over Irish home rule. After long years in government, any political party, according to the conventional wisdom, inevitably looks arrogant, sad and devoid of ideas. By 1996 the Conservative administration looked all these things – and often it looked more like an opposition than a government.

They say you can tell which is the 'natural party of government' by looking for an air of effortless superiority in the House; you can tell the other lot because they have nothing better to do than play games at trying to catch ministers out at question time. For the last couple of sessions of the 1992–7 parliament it often seemed to be the government party that was playing the question-time games. What will Labour do about income tax? they would shout from the government front bench. And what schools do Labour front-benchers send their children to? And why – this, incredibly, became one of the commonest interjections from the Treasury bench – why will the leader of the opposition not give us a straight answer? In this topsy-turvy world, it was the Labour opposition who suffered from all the occupational failings of ministers – reading boring briefs from their experts, dissembling, patronising or, at best, trying to demonstrate that they had that surest qualification for a natural party of government, a safe pair of hands. Rab Butler could have been proud of the Blair team.

Meanwhile a great moment of triumph for Margaret Thatcher came at the pre-election party conference in the autumn of 1996. The Labour party conference, that is. Thanks to the Thatcher revolution, Labour had not only ditched Clause Four but had persuaded the comrades to sound excited about the opportunities that lay ahead under capitalism. For the first time since the First World War, British voters had a choice between two parties both claiming to believe in the profit motive and market forces. When Tony Blair addressed his party at Blackpool in 1996, the words flashed up on the autocue screens could have been coming from a Conservative computer. 'Strong families are the foundation for strong communities,' he told New Labour, and it went down a treat. It might have been a Conservative ladies' luncheon club. Never had the Dennis Skinners of the party been so well behaved – at least until they were out of reach of the cameras. One young Labour MP warned her colleagues not to shy away from 'advocating material self-improvement' – 'don't neglect the man with the huge BMW in the driveway when you go out canvassing,' she counselled. A potentially embarrassing exercise in old-fashioned socialism in support of old-age pensioners by a frail but determined Barbara Castle was gracefully contained by conference. The comrades gave the impression that they actually liked each other. Not even the spin doctors were sticking knives in each other's backs.

The Tories' pre-election conference was more complicated, partly because of Neil Hamilton and his biscuit. The representatives had psyched themselves up for trauma because the conference had been scheduled to coincide with the rival attraction of the High Court action of Hamilton v. the *Guardian*. The action was withdrawn only seventy-two hours before they assembled, nervously, at Bournemouth and the media found themselves wrongfooted for having believed their own stories about the blood that was going to cover the conference carpet.

The Hamilton fox having been shot, the Conservative representatives settled down at Bournemouth to the best-behaved conference since Maastricht. The party establishment, after long months of peddling the story-line of a united party, found that it actually seemed to be true: with an election coming, the party remembered its manners and stopped bickering while the servants were in the room. 'Unity, unity, unity,' the conference was exhorted by Michael Portillo. At the fringe meetings there was flag-waving and shouting, but at the conference proper it was the solid middle-of-the-roaders who were hailed with the faithful stamping of loyal feet. Some of the Eurosceptics had been hoping that they had won over the Foreign Secretary, Malcolm Rifkind, and that he would deliver a Europe-baiting rant; in the event Rifkind's conference speech skated elegantly over the logic of the wait-and-see policy on the single currency. The Prime Minister, stripped to his shirtsleeves on the conference platform, played the confident man of action, and a bit of a wag with it; Chairman Mawhinney played his straight man. In pre-election mode the conference was happy to take John to its heart. He was the man who had won the previous election against the odds and was their best hope of doing it again.

Most surprising of all, Ken Clarke had a good conference. The right wing didn't trust him, of course. He was on record as making revolutionary statements such as that if it were proved, beyond all reasonable doubt, that a single currency would demonstrably be of substantial value to the United Kingdom and the British people, he might consider joining it. What is more, he was the man who had put taxes up to balance the books. On the other hand, the right wing had to concede that at least the books *were* balanced in time for the election campaign. Traitor he might be on Europe, but there was a gut feeling in the hall at Bournemouth that the party needed Ken, as well as John, if they were to have a chance at the general election. So the representatives reacted like an old-time music hall audience who don't like all the songs or all the jokes they are hearing but recognise a real trouper when they see one. The Tory rank and file, their minds concentrated wonderfully, seemed to be turning back to the tried and tested, as they might gratefully pull on a comfortable old pair of boots when they know there is a rough path ahead of them. Ken had put the economy to rights. The economy was more important than Euroscepticism. Unfortunately, within weeks of the rank and file showing that they could meet at Bournemouth without tearing each other's eyes out, those supposed to be providing them with leadership at Westminster found the death wish too strong for them.

The strange story of Ken Clarke in the months leading up to the election summed up the plight of the party. He had been a better Chancellor than most. He had given the party the winning trump card they always want to have: they could go before the electorate brandishing a set of national accounts that looked reasonably respectable. Moreover, if the party had been in a state of emotional stability, it might have appreciated that Ken was a man with qualities that have always gone down rather well with Conservatives both in the House and in the country. Nothing to do with being left-wing or right-wing. He was a clever lad of parts but with the gumption not to look too clever. A bit of a bruiser. A bit of a lad – not in the sense of serious mischief, but a man who liked his pint, liked a smoke and liked spending Saturday afternoon at a football match. If he had a bit of a beer belly, and preferred wearing the kind of shoes you can't polish, well, this was true of a lot of people whose votes had to be won. And since becoming Chancellor, Ken Clarke had arguably been the best political friend John Major had in a hostile world. His promotion was part – and not the least important part – of the spin-off from Black Wednesday in September 1992, when his predecessor, Norman Lamont, had had to take sterling out of the European exchange rate mechanism. He was Chancellor through the worst of the soul-searching and backstabbing of the Eurosceptic years, and was in a position to put it all into perspective: he knew that at the end of the day, come the election, 'it's the economy, stupid'.

By any reasonable reckoning, the Tory party had got a good deal out of Chancellor Clarke. He had inherited an economy with problems. The public sector borrowing requirement had reached £50 billion. He behaved with Tory rectitude, which meant raising taxes. The back benches cheered his first budget. He seemed to be presiding over the dream economy, a tangible boom with no prospect of bust to come. But the party knew, like a wife who knows her husband has a secret drink problem but doesn't like to say too much about it so long as he is bringing home a good wage packet, the party knew all about Ken's little problem over Europe. Truth to tell, the sceptics were slightly afraid of him. He was bigger than they were.

The colleagues cheered Ken at the pre-election conference, and a few weeks later they cheered his pre-election budget too. But within weeks they decided to disown him.

It had been a ghastly year, 1996. As month succeeded month, with the opinion polls refusing to offer any grounds for hope, the party forgot everything but its election prospects. By December its refrain was like one of those stories heard every week at meetings of Gamblers Anonymous: I thought if I pawned grandma's silver candlesticks and put it all on the sure thing in the three-thirty I could win back all my losses and look the world in the face again. Even back-benchers who ought to have known better had persuaded themselves that if only the leadership would renounce Europe once and for all, they were in with a chance.

Gamblers don't ruin themselves with a single flutter, and the tragedy of the last year of the Major government was that we could see the step-by-step descent down the slippery slope. Since Maastricht the sceptics had been gathering at the bottom of that slope beckoning the others on down. They had now decided that, with a mixture of patience, *chutzpah* and sheer naked force, they could tempt John Major to take the next step. The party had persuaded itself that the policy of 'wait and see' was the one that could hold them together over Europe. Then came the referendum. Rejected for years as a constitutional monstrosity, it suddenly appeared as that month's sure thing, even if it came from a dubious stable.

There was once a *New Yorker* cartoon showing a politician apparently coming to the end of a long speech. 'Ladies and gentlemen,' he was saying. 'These are my views. And if you don't like them . . . I'll change them.' Ken Clarke, almost uniquely, it sometimes seemed, among his colleagues, wasn't tempted down that road.

This was the background to one of the few pieces of light relief during a depressing winter that preceded the election: the showdown at 90 Park Lane shortly before Christmas 1996. Nobody came out of the Park Lane episode with great credit, except perhaps Nico, proprietor of Nico at Ninety, and his wife, who declined to give away any secrets about conversations between guests in their restaurant, which was routinely patronised, as she explained, by 'politicians, royalty and heads of industry'. Complete confidentiality was in this case unrealistic since, on the day in question, the luncheon guests included a vociferous Ken Clarke, being entertained, 'off the record', by one department of the BBC while, on the other side of the room, a member of the shadow Cabinet, Frank Dobson, was being entertained by the Corporation's political editor.

The licence-payers got their money's worth. Over the claret the Chancellor indicated his displeasure at the way he was being bad-mouthed by his Cabinet colleagues, and their camp followers, as the evil genius who was going to lose the Tories the election. He had heard the Chairman's office was toying with the slogan 'New Chancellor, new chance'. So, he explained, he had warned Chairman Mawhinney to 'tell your kids to get their scooters off my lawn'.

The restaurant watched, fascinated. By the end of the week, so did the nation.

It had been a bad week for party credibility. The Prime Minister had decided, not for the first time, that he had identified a reasonably painless way to widen the channel of 'clear blue water' between the Tories and Labour on Europe. They would continue to pay lip service to the official line – 'options open', 'best interests of the British people' and so forth – while making it clear that the Conservatives were in practical terms putting the boot into the single currency. As a communication strategy this was more familiar in Irish than in English politics. Sinn Fein goes through the motions of assuring the public. The IRA goes on planting bombs and earning the cheers of wild men in the pubs of Kilburn.

The details of the strategy were never clear. It was widely believed the Prime Minister was involved in leaks in both the *Sunday Telegraph* and *Daily Telegraph*, signalling a change in government policy. These papers, which had been increasingly strident in tone, published relevant stories on the Sunday and Monday respectively before the lunch at Nico at Ninety. If the Prime Minister was personally involved, he had not talked things through with either his Chancellor or his Deputy Prime Minister. Both these men were about to show their muscle.

If this was supposed to have been a managed leak, the party's management needed refurbishment. On the Monday morning, Ken was in Brussels for a finance ministers' meeting and saw the dangers implicit in the *Telegraph* story as soon as it was faxed to him from the Treasury. He had already agreed to appear that morning on the BBC *Today* programme, and used the interview to deny the story. A switch of European policy? 'Quite preposterous.' Later that morning Michael Heseltine was chairing the Cabinet committee on presentation of policy – a body which, understandably, he felt should take a view on the *Telegraphs'* stories. He added his own rebuttal to Ken's.

When a delighted Tony Blair confronted the Prime Minister with all this confusion, what could he do but deny what he had laboured to suggest? The policy hadn't changed. All that was left behind the leaking operation was a lot of seething sceptics and a lot of continuing vehicular activity on the Chancellor's lawn.

The irony was that by the spring of 1997 it was even more clear that Ken Clarke was a rare asset to a party which had all too many electoral liabilities. He had delivered a set of national books of which Samuel Smiles might have approved. He had gone a long way towards restoring the party's reputation for soundness of economic management which had been blown by Ken's predecessor, Norman Lamont. Having promised in the 1992 general election campaign that 'keeping control of spending will enable us to cut taxes while bringing the government's budget back towards balance', Norman had found that getting back towards balance actually meant putting VAT on gas and electricity. Then there had been the fiasco of leaving the ERM. Tory back-benchers had been less than gruntled by the tax on fuel. Some of them even rebelled, setting unhappy precedents which bedevilled the 1992–7 parliament. For the 1997 election 'the economy, stupid' wasn't going to be enough, but the Tory party sensed that it made sense to try to keep Ken on side during the campaign.

*

Tory victory at the polls in 1992 had been snatched from the jaws of Neil and Glenys Kinnock by branding Labour as the party which would raise taxes by £1,000 per head.

This time around, it was not just the Tory sheet anchor of economic management which looked frayed. So did another main strand of the party's traditional programme: law and order.

The Conservatives were confronted by a Labour Party no longer under the spell of a ragged army of bearded social workers wanting to counsel villains instead of locking them up. And the statistics were embarrassing to the party that had been in government for nearly two decades. The *Economist* summed it up: the recorded crime rate had doubled since the party took power in 1979. The Tories had introduced more criminal justice bills in six years than had been introduced in the previous sixty, but the flood of legislation had failed to stem the increase in crime. Latterly, Michael Howard's legislation had also contrived to worry good Tories with a concern for civil liberties. The English like to think their legal processes go back into the mists of antiquity. The new reforms could be traced no further than the tea bars at Conservative conferences.

The 1992–7 parliament ended with the Conservatives' law and order policy under attack not only from the social workers but from senior judges; from a couple of Conservative ex-Home Secretaries, Douglas Hurd and Kenneth Baker; from a range of Conservatives in the House of Lords; and occasionally, more in sorrow than in anger, from papers like *The Times* and the *Telegraph* which otherwise regarded the Eurosceptical Michael Howard as a good thing. The Lords' revolt was especially piquant because it seemed to involve Conservative peers doing a job that ought to have been done by the Labour opposition in the Commons but hadn't been. Under the Blair regime, political correctness demanded that Labour look tougher on crime than the Tories.

Judges fretted over the provisions of the Crime (Sentences) Bill which, in order to give effect to Michael Howard's conference rhetoric about locking up more criminals, limited the courts' discretion on length of sentences. And they fretted, too, over the powers being given to detectives by his Police Bill to bug conversations once thought to be confidential. One rule of thumb in the Thatcher years had been that Tory policies weren't really getting home unless the establishment was screaming foul. But at this stage in the game, for the Conservative government to go on offending the establishment looked, in Lady Bracknell's terms, more like carelessness than misfortune.

In the last six months before polling day the party became careless to the point of wilfulness. The Prime Minister had put off the election till the last possible date partly because he believed, reasonably enough, that each week saw the electorate becoming marginally more prosperous, and partly because he hoped that the strain of waiting would make Labour do something silly.

Silly stories indeed abounded, but few of them were the responsibility of the Labour Party. Government *bizarreries* became an accepted part of the Wonderland of 1997. The Portillo defence department, short of sailors to swab the decks, had to send one of Her Majesty's destroyers to sea manned – womanned – partly by Mrs Mops. Michael Howard's criminals hit the headlines yet again when it emerged that at some hospitals for the criminally insane the lunatics were literally taking over the asylum. There were the obvious jokes that Broadmoor wasn't the only government-run establishment where this was happening. On the legal side the news became odder and odder. The courts ruled that the Lord Chancellor, of all people, had acted illegally by increasing court fees. It was deemed that he should have had regard to the fact that this could deny poor people the age-old right to have access to the law.

Meanwhile the former transport minister, Steven Norris – he who had had to demit office because of irregularities in his private life – told a television audience of his doubts about Conservative roads policy while he was in office. A few months before, he had been writing in his punchy memoirs, *Changing Trains*, of his contempt for the spectacular acts of civil disobedience perpetrated by tree-climbing and tunnel-occupying protesters at the building of the controversial Newbury bypass, for which his department had been responsible. 'I doubt there are many more effective recruiting sergeants for the Conservative Party,' he wrote of them. Now he had evidently decided that the climbers' and tunnellers' hearts were in the right place after all. A sinner who repenteth doth not always bring joy to Central Office during an election campaign.

Right at the start of the campaign (with Central Office still at pains to woo the ethnic vote), Enoch Powell's successor as MP for Wolverhampton South West, Nick Budgen, announced that 'immigration is an election issue' and that he 'refused to be silenced'. With honourable friends like these, Conservative Prime Ministers wonder what need there is of Jeremy Paxmans.

On the silly wing of Labour Party, which had been expected to play into the Tories' hands, the Blairist thought police had done their work and the bruises scarcely seemed to show. Ken Livingstone expressed himself blandly as 'quite optimistic about the future of a Labour government'. Since it was impossible for the party to move any further to the right, he explained, 'what we may have, for the first time, is a Labour administration which could move sharply to the left when it gets into power.' For such faint praise, whips of all parties had learned, by 1997, to be grateful. Even Ken Livingstone's fiercer Old Labour colleague Brian Sedgemore was quoted as saying sweetly: 'Criticise the leadership? Me? We have become a religious movement.

We have a messiah and I will worship the messiah.' In Smith Square they had to fight back the tears when this sort of thing was fed into the Central Office computers.

As the weeks passed in waiting for the election, and the Labour meltdown refused to happen, it was all too predictable which party, with time on its hands before polling day, would behave badly. Conservatives with post-election leadership ambitions began to set out their stalls. The criminal law measures which distressed some of the Law Lords formed part of Michael Howard's campaign. The other Michael, Portillo, after a rather impressive period of being statesmanlike at defence, moved into candidate mode by promising the electorate a new royal yacht to mark out the clear blue water between the parties. And more army cadets in schools. A third campaigner for the leadership, Foreign Secretary Rifkind, launched on a programme of continental lecture visits to enlighten Europeans, and possibly the UK electorate, on his views on the EU.

Yet another contender, Stephen Dorrell, had a special problem. He was reputedly John Major's preferred candidate for the succession, and didn't seem to be aware just how much of a poisoned chalice this sort of status can be. John gave him special responsibilities as the thinking man's election campaigner. Sadly, thinking men can be tempted to prove that they are really quite blokeish at heart. Belatedly, Stephen decided to move nearer to the Eurosceptic camp. He did it clumsily, and lost credibility among both the 'phobes and the 'philes. Then he entered the thistly paths of Scottish politics and became over-excited about his loyalty to the United Kingdom without studying the small print of the carefully balanced Conservative Party line on Scottish devolution. The Scottish Secretary, Michael Forsyth, who had enough trouble on his hands, was not best pleased.

Stephen was removed from his special campaign duties.

The economy, law and order, the United Kingdom ... Another built-in advantage supposed to be enjoyed by Conservatives confronting Labour was simply the authority of their ministers. No more. During those final weeks before the election, as John Major's colleagues appeared at question time for what they knew must be their last appearances at the despatch box, they often behaved like a parody of a particularly crass fictional television version of life at Westminster.

Nicholas Soames, as Minister for the Gulf War Syndrome, solemnly described how the relevant medical evidence had been kept from him by his civil servants. 'Never complain and never explain,' said Disraeli. The Soames maxim was: 'Explain at length; complain about your officials; and never resign.'

Douglas Hogg, who as Minister for Mad Cows put up for months with insults about how he had shot himself in the foot over the BSE crisis, actually had to hobble into the Commons with a bandaged foot after an accident when he fell downstairs in his home. If this had happened in one of Edwina Currie's political novels the author would have been criticised for falling far below her normal convincing standards of realism. Douglas, on one foot, had to explain how *his* civil servants had failed *him*. They should have told him about a report which had effectively forecast the danger of an *E. coli* food poisoning epidemic of the kind which in fact then happened in Scotland. The Secretary of State for Scotland was not best pleased about this one either. The Prime Minister had to expend valuable pre-election energy preventing an interdepartmental punch-up.

Most surprising of all was the degree of carelessness in the most disciplined part of the machine, the whips' office. Demob-happiness? Or just weariness? Or the arrogance born of eighteen years in power? For John Major, watching gaffe after gaffe among the whips, it must have been like the captain of the *Titanic* finding not only that his liner was going down but that the lifeboats were leaky.

The whipping business is a rough old game, with the rules made up as you go along. A lot of it is bluff or double-bluff, designed to keep the enemy guessing and to keep the rebels on your own side guessing. But there are one or two basic rules that you don't break. The most important is that when agreement is reached 'through the usual channels' for sick or absent Members to be paired, the agreement must be honoured. Without some measure of pairing between government and opposition members, normal business is impossible. Invalids would constantly have to be brought in in ambulances. Ministers would never be able to go off to conferences they need to attend.

But just before Christmas 1996 the Tories broke the rule. They paired one of their number twice – once to Labour, once to the Liberal Democrats. It was cheating, of course. Worse, it was stupid, because it was bound to be found out. It was an even more blatant case of the chicanery which, when practised by Labour in the dying

days of the Callaghan government, moved Michael Heseltine to protest by snatching the Mace and wielding it around the Chamber. Now
Michael, as Deputy Prime Minister, was more relaxed when asked to
condemn the Conservative pairing whip, while the Prime Minister
himself airily dismissed the complaint as 'an arcane dispute'.
Altogether, the episode did nothing to enhance the prestige of what
is supposed to be the natural party of government.

And even stranger things than this had been happening in the whips'
office, adding depth to the picture of an administration that had run
its course. Particular oddities arose over – what else? – the Neil Hamilton case.

Back in 1994 the allegations about Neil Hamilton were considered
by a Commons committee under the chairmanship of Sir Geoffrey
Johnson Smith. The whips would have been less than human if they
had not taken a keen interest in the committee proceedings. The whip
principally concerned was a newcomer to the office, David Willetts
– new to whipping but with an impressive track record in and around
Westminster. He had served in the No. 10 Policy Unit in the Thatcher
years and before becoming an MP in 1992 had been director of studies
at the Centre for Policy Studies, the organisation which was effectively
the keeper of the conscience of the Thatcherite revolution. David, in
other words, was one of the party's thinkers. Cynics were to say that
to appoint thinkers to the whips' office was a serious break with
tradition, and bound to end in tears.

Being of an analytical disposition, Willetts wrote down his assess-
ment of the situation that had arisen in the committee investigation
of the Hamilton business (which was the subject also of a High Court
action). The committee, he reckoned, had two options. He summed
them up in telegraphic form in the whips' book: As chairman, Sir
Geoffrey could '(i) argue now *sub judice* and get committee to set it
aside or (ii) investigate it as quickly as possible, exploiting good Tory
majority at present. We were inclined to go for (i) but he wants our
advice.'

All this was classic whips' office *realpolitik* and would never have
attracted attention had the Hamilton case not by now developed its
own momentum. But it worried the Standards and Privileges Committee when they had a sight of the entry in the whips' book and they
asked both Geoffrey and David what had been going on. Had the

whips been trying to influence the outcome of what were supposed to be quasi-judicial proceedings? Geoffrey denied impropriety. He also denied 'wanting advice'. The committee's members waited with interest to see how the thoughtful David Willetts – by this time promoted to public services minister – would explain.

They were not disappointed. Nor were the viewers on television who watched David squirm under questioning at a public session of the committee. 'Exploiting a good Tory majority' did not, he told the committee, mean what they might think. It was 'my way of describing how committee members would see it as not being in the House's interest for an inquiry to be dragged out unnecessarily'. There was even more interest in his explanation of the phrase 'he wants our advice'. If members looked at their dictionaries, David told them, they would find that there was an older meaning of 'want' – to be in need of. Whips, as always, knew what was needed. One of his Conservative colleagues placed his dilemma before him directly and cruelly: 'Either you were deceiving your colleagues in your original memorandum or you are trying to deceive this committee now.'

It was not one of the great moments of triumph for the natural party of government. Yet another member of the Major administration had to be written off.

*

Around this time the Conservative spin doctors had told Downing Street – not specifically because of the ramifications of the Hamilton case – that the clever thing would be to call a quick election before Christmas 1996. The Prime Minister couldn't rely on his prospects improving, they told him. A low turnout in a December poll might help the party. Apart from anything else, it would remove the need to go ahead with the by-election due to be held at Wirral South.

They were over-ruled, and the by-election in Wirral South went ahead in February. It provided a disastrous launch pad for the general election campaign – and this in Tory heartland: a middle-class sub-urban constituency where all the right issues – family values, taxation, grammar schools – might have been expected to play best. It was hard for the spin doctors to find any comfort in the outcome. The swing to Labour was 17 per cent, and the turnout was outstandingly high; this was no case of disgruntled Tories staying at home, but prepared

to reappear at the general election. The result could only be explained
by traditional Tories switching, in droves, to New Labour. It was an
unhappy start to the year of the general election. And as the daffodils
inexorably came into bloom to remind voters that the election couldn't
be put off much longer, carelessness within the party swelled into a
crescendo.

Take David Heathcoat-Amory – another thinker, and one-time
Treasury minister, who had moved to the back benches to leave him
free to denounce the government for its lack of Eurosceptical fervour.
He rounded on Ted Heath. Ted, he said, lacked credibility. No surprise there, coming from a Eurosceptic. But the grounds on which
he based this judgement unwittingly summed up the chaos in the
party: Ted, he said, 'didn't speak for any faction or group'. Er, quite.
A Freudian slip, maybe, but when Tories talk in terms of membership
of a faction as the stuff of credibility it is time to be gazing longingly
at the drawing-board.

Then there was Lord McAlpine, once Conservative Treasurer, confidant of Margaret and now an activist in the Referendum Party, who
brought out a book of memoirs during the run-up to the election.
They were a fascinating but unhelpful piece of pre-election reading.
The timing of publication, he explained, not unreasonably, wasn't his
fault: he had assumed that the government would be sensible enough
to go to the polls much earlier.

At about the same point in the run-up to the campaign, incidentally,
the Referendum Party suddenly found itself with its first MP, after the
Reigate Conservative association deselected George Gardiner. The
association had put up with his Euroscepticism but drew the line at
his description of the Prime Minister as 'Ken Clarke's ventriloquist's
dummy'. So George switched parties. There was more to this than
European policy; George's friends blamed his plight on the 'Toffee-
Nosed Tendency' of Surrey suburbia. A lot of interesting factors were
at work in the 1997 election.

In the gallery of unhelpful remarks there had to be a special place
for David Evans, not regarded as one of the great thinkers of the
party but a major sponsor, it will be remembered, of the Redwood
leadership bid. He certainly had enough experience of the world to
know that nowadays you are liable to have your words recorded elec-
tronically and flung back in your face. As with a famous Portillo

indiscretion, the Evans incident happened in one of those tricky encounters to which MPs expose themselves when they agree to talk to the young.

David Evans's meeting with sixth-formers at Stanborough School in Welwyn Garden City was intended, as he explained afterwards, to be private and light-hearted. Anyone could have told him that you are courting disaster to try to be private and light-hearted when your party is divided and there is an election coming up in a few weeks. He was light-hearted about his colleague Virginia Bottomley: she was 'dead from the neck upwards', he told the sixth-formers, and she was in the Cabinet only because they needed a woman there. He was even more light-hearted about his Labour opponent, 'a single girl who lives with her boyfriend and three bastard children'. Moreover (being a school inspector) she 'didn't have a proper job'.

All this was being recorded on a tape which was duly leaked to the Labour Party. David Evans was luckier than George Gardiner in being backed by his constituency when the story exploded. He was quietly rebuked by the Prime Minister, gracefully forgiven by Virginia Bottomley, and defended by the *Daily Telegraph*, in a leading article headed 'Thank Evans': unlike the 'prissy ideologues' who were now criticising him, the *Telegraph* said, David was in touch with the real feelings of very substantial numbers of his fellow-countrymen.

There were a number of lessons to be drawn from the Evans episode. One was about his naïveté in not knowing that school teachers these days go around with tape recorders. Another lesson was simply about good manners. Yet another, which goes beyond good manners, was about political realism. There is nothing new about Tories with old-fashioned views about women. Or about racial minorities. (When asked to express a considered view on penal philosophy to the sixth-formers, David Evans suggested castration as the remedy for 'black bastards' who commit rape.) Anybody who has ever visited a Conservative club in the seedier suburbs, or indeed a golf club in the leafier suburbs, knows that these kind of remarks are the small change of conversation. Many would add that for really nasty racial innuendo you have to go to some of the watering holes patronised by trade unionists when they discuss immigrant blacks, or slanty-eyed people who make cheaper computers than we can. Prejudice is a fact of political life. But there was a time when Conservative MPs didn't say

things like this to school pupils. Call them old-fashioned, call them
hypocritical, but there had been a sense of propriety among Conservatives a generation earlier which counted for something when they
faced the electorate. The proprieties – like the convention that ministers resigned when they or their officials were caught out doing something awful – now seemed to belong to a dim, distant, pre-Major age.

All these things featured in the calculations electors made when
they went to the polls on 1 May 1997.

PART II

A Month in the Country
Campaign Diary
30 March–30 April 1997

JULIAN CRITCHLEY

I have something in common with Maurice Chevalier, and it isn't little girls. 'I'm just glad I'm not young any more.' I have been a Tory candidate at the last ten elections, eight of which I have won. Were I a boxer my record might read 8:2:0. I have been an MP in two incarnations for thirty-one years and have never held office; yet I would not have a missed a moment of it. But I am not standing this time, ill health from which I have suffered from the past five years having obliged me to retire to Shropshire, a knight of shire and not of suburb. This time I shall sit on my hands and do nothing more than write about the campaign as it unfolds. For the first election since Harold Macmillan swept to power in 1959, I shall be keeping my tattered blue rosette (time, chemical reaction and Mrs Gorman have turned it pink) safely in my desk drawer. Thank God, I will be a spectator and not a participant.

If any MP tells you he enjoys elections, he is not telling the truth. MPs hate elections. The call of the bugle drags them from the comfortable womb that is Westminster, where constituents are kept at bay by a handpicked corps of policemen, and competent secretaries deal with one's correspondence, and returns them to the mean streets of their constituencies. It presents a challenge both to their physical stamina and to their reserves of nervous energy. They are faced with three to four weeks of unaccustomed physical activity, speaking nightly to a handful of the faithful in draughty village halls, and spending the days canvassing their unheeding voters.

Candidates, on the other hand, love elections. They have, after all, waited anxiously since their adoption, spoken to small meetings of party activists, and bombarded the local press with handouts purporting to show knowledge, competence and concern. They have tramped the streets in search of recruits; they have even attended party conferences at seaside resorts out of season in the hope of being summoned to the rostrum to perform. A general election might transform their lives, taking them out of dead-end jobs to seats at the very back of the government's back benches. Candidates live in hope. A small swing in their direction might bring with it the gift of the magic initials 'MP', a reasonably handsome salary, and, if one is so unwise as to make one's wife one's secretary, a fat sum in expenses. I employed my wife as secretary for all of six months, but I soon learnt that there are demands that one can make on secretaries that one cannot make on wives, and vice versa. I do not recommend it.

Safe in my book-lined study in Ludlow, I shall watch the progress of my two successors (the Aldershot constituency has been cut in half) as they shake the reluctant hands of bewildered electors, address the party faithful (all thirty of them) in draughty village halls, and attend, if they are wise, the two meetings that feature all three candidates. Usually, one such 'open forum' is held by the churches; the other by the National Union of Teachers. In such meetings the Tory candidate is invariably cast as Satan, and is at somewhat of a disadvantage. If he defends fox-hunting, he is roundly abused by teenage girls who have never seen a hound. As for the teachers, I used to annoy my hirsute audience by reminding them that the low status that teachers enjoy is due in large part to their habit of striking, and that teaching is the only profession run not by the wisest and most senior of its members, but by the youngest and worst qualified. Such assertions did wonders for one's flow of adrenalin. The churches' meeting was, if anything, worse. The Labour and Liberal candidates invariably took a strong moral stance, leaving me to take a more pragmatic view. Happily, I have never been in favour of capital punishment or flogging, but believe that abortion is none of my business; it is, surely, for the woman to decide. This view would be greeted by Catholic hysteria. At these sorts of ill-structured meetings, usually with an incompetent parson in the chair, the Tory came cast as the villain in favour of inequality, heedless of the problems of the poor, and as self-seeking as Mr Max Clifford. No doubt at the coming election, the first stone will be thrown at Tory candidates who will be universally held responsible for 'sleaze', however defined.

I have sat at the feet of four Tory prime ministers. Harold Macmillan was easily my favourite. Badly in need of dentistry, wearer of a Guards' tie and a shabby cardigan, he was wise beyond the call of his party. Some of its members thought him 'pink'. The more intelligent adored him. He used to address the 1922 Committee as if we were a university historical society.

Alec Douglas-Home was decent but dull, and no match for Harold Wilson at his best. Reggie Maudling once told me that, nice as he was, 'Alec never really understood a word I said.' He used to address the 1922 Committee as if we were a county agricultural show.

Edward Heath was a desperately unlucky prime minister. Defeat in 1966 was inevitable. But, thanks in part to Enoch Powell and in part to Roy Jenkins's chancellorship, he won in 1970, and succeeded in taking us into Europe, an achievement for which he will long be remembered. He lost in February 1974, in part because he picked the wrong date, in greater part, because of Enoch Powell's call for Tories to vote Labour. He has mellowed, and now even has a good word (one) to say about Margaret Thatcher. He used to address the 1922 Committee if we were the Bexley Rotary Club.

I soon learnt to dislike Margaret Thatcher intensely. Surrounded by a court of flatterers, she had little patience with those who felt differently from herself. As the years went by, and her electoral successes multiplied, she began to believe in her own star ('I have changed everything') and then to become, as Alan Watkins once wrote, 'funny', an expression much used in Watkins's native Wales. By 1990 the party had had enough of her. A combination of Geoffrey Howe, Michael Heseltine and her own Cabinet gave her her cards. She has yet to forgive her successor. She used to address the 1922 Committee as if she were the headmistress of a less than satisfactory Girls' Public Day School Trust establishment.

Although I did not vote for John Major in 1990, preferring my old friend Michael Heseltine, I have been for the last four years or so an absent loyalist. John Major may have been 'invented' by the Tory party in order to stop Heseltine, but he has suffered unfairly at the hands of his enemies. Sniped at by Lady Thatcher, slandered by the Eurosceptic wing of the party, and abused in private by the 'bastards' within his own Cabinet, he has striven manfully to keep the Tory party united. He saw the sly Redwood off without much trouble, but has had to endure the likes of Cash, Gorman, Gill, Lamont and Tebbit – I cannot bring myself to list any more of them. He addresses the

1922 Committee if it were an assembly of decent and intelligent men and women with A-levels, which it is plainly not.

I hope the Tories win on 1 May, but I have my doubts. With a view to buttressing the Conservative cause, in the 15 March issue of *Punch* I advocated a debate between Major and Blair, to be shown on television. I am glad Central Office seems to have taken up my suggestion. Such a television spectacular would play to Major's strengths. He is infinitely more experienced than Blair, is at his best in a one-to-one situation, and could come across as a 'safe pair of hands'. Blair, with his youthful good looks and puppy-like desire to please, could appear to be a boy sent on a man's errand. In the past, premiers have never debated with leaders of the opposition for fear of giving the latter publicity. But desperate times demand desperate measures. Major's task is to get out the Tory vote which threatens to sit on its hands. He won't do that by lugging his soapbox from one provincial town to another. He has to demonstrate before a World Cup audience that he has both the personality and the policies to carry the day. If he fails, we can only look forward to at least ten years of Labour government. On the other hand, he could change the election climate overnight.

If the Conservative Party is defeated on 1 May, life within it will not be worth living. I could not remain in a party led by Michael Portillo, or the unctuous Howard. But time has thankfully come between me and the possibility of crossing the floor of the House.

1 April

Sir Larry Lamb and Mr Kelvin MacKenzie, former editors of the *Sun*, must be tearing their hair out. The announcement by the incumbent editor of the 'currant bun' (those who work for the *Sun* call it 'the Comic') that his great newspaper is to come out in favour of Tony Blair marks the passing of 'Essex man'. As a Tory, I can't help hoping we shall not see his like again.

Essex man, the second-generation working-class voter, whose father left the London docks for the drab lands of Essex, sustained Mrs Thatcher in power during the 1980s. His evolution can be illustrated by Mr David Amess who, having held Basildon in 1992 for the Tories, has now quit the seat for the blue-haired gentility of Southend.

The Tory party establishment always looked askance at Essex man, a name bestowed upon the Conservative-voting working class by Simon Heffer and myself. He would eat his peas off a knife, wore grey leather shoes, and had all the raucous prejudices of a Mr David Evans (Luton man). He was above all else a passionate Thatcherite, liable to prostrate himself at her feet were he fortunate enough to pass her in one of the endless corridors that make up the Palace of Westminster.

The *Sun* is Rupert Murdoch's flagship. Clearly its editor would not have changed his shirt without the approval of his multinational boss, and indeed he admitted as much on the BBC. Does a Blair victory then mean the rehabilitation of the Dirty Digger? In Good Queen Margaret's golden days, No. 10 Downing Street was Rupert Murdoch's first port of call on his arrival in Britain. Since John Major became Prime Minister, he has not set foot in the place. When Tony Blair was asked if the *Sun*'s change of heart meant a free hand for Murdoch, he replied to the effect that his government would not impose more restrictions on cross-media ownership. The Labour leader called simply for the proprietors to behave 'responsibly'. Pigs might fly.

Whether newspapers influence people, or people newspapers, is a riddle without an answer. But what is true is that no Tory prime minister this century has suffered from so hostile a press as has John Major. Conrad Black's *Telegraph* has set the paper's columnists against the government – especially over Major's attitude towards Europe. Dominic Lawson, the editor of the *Sunday Telegraph*, has adopted a tone almost universally hostile to the Major administration, the attack tediously led by a Mr Christopher Booker. *The Times* has been consistently critical of the government, although it is not yet clear whether its leader-writers will come out in favour of voting Tory. The *Mail* has been favourable to the government, but not to John Major; so, too, has the *Express*. What does that leave? The *Guardian*, *Observer* and *Mirror*, all of which are pro-Blair. Only the *Star* sits uncomfortably on the fence.

This unattractive coalition is one of the main reasons why John Major is embarking on an election campaign so far behind in the public opinion polls that it is hard at the time of writing to find even a Tory MP who does not think that defeat on 1 May is inevitable. Many Tory MPs, including some ministers, had tried to persuade John Major to introduce laws that would safeguard the privacy of the individual and outlaw such practices as long-lens photography and the recording of private telephone conversations, such as the 'Camilla tapes'. Major's spin doctors bent his ear. How, they asked, could he hope to win an election having offended what the pompous would call 'the freedom of the press' or 'the public interest'? Major took their advice and entered the 1997 election with less newspaper support than any Tory prime minister since Palmerston. Our largely foreign-owned press has never forgiven Major for not being Margaret, while the Australian-American Rupert Murdoch and the Canadian Conrad Black were opposed to all things European and therefore 'foreign'. Ironically, had Major acted to curb the worst excesses of the press, he would have been not only loved by the populace but greatly respected for doing so. He should have had the courage of Stanley Baldwin's convictions. Baldwin, you will remember, was the target of the newspaper proprietors in the 1920s and 1930s. Goaded beyond endurance, he rebuked them, in words written by his relation Rudyard Kipling, for presuming to exercise 'power without responsibility, the prerogative of the harlot throughout the ages'. The speech struck a chord very much in Baldwin's favour.

As it is, we have to endure six weeks of soundbites, photos of Norma Major trying not to look bored, and of the sight of the Prime Minister clinging to his magic soapbox like a small child with his comfort blanket.

2 April

What has John Redwood been up to in Wolverhampton? The answer must be 'no good'. The self-appointed leader of the Tory right is clearly not content to canvass his allotted patch of Wokingham, his Berkshire constituency. Redwood has his eye on the future. He wants to take advantage of a Conservative defeat at the polls, and then to present himself as the 'saviour' of the party. To that end he has been getting himself about. Earlier this year, and without my leave, he turned up in my constituency, Aldershot, where he bored the members of the Conservative Club. Friends tell me that he has been busily engaged in making friends in any constituency that will put up with him. But why Wolverhampton, the only town in England with a statue to Mr Enoch Powell?

He was in that grim city at the invitation of Mr Nicholas Budgen, the successor to Enoch. Nick, as he is invariably known, is something of a card. He wears Oxfam suits, rarely buys anyone a drink and, as did a younger Enoch, rides frequently to hounds. It is only then that he can be glimpsed wearing a pink coat. Budgen wants to play the race card.

The body of the Tory party, slightly corpulent after eighteen years of rich living, bears two scars. One is race, which has almost healed; the other is Europe, which is still suppurating. John Redwood, the Darth Vader of the party, has already challenged John Major unsuccessfully for the leadership of the party. With his shy, sly smile he is often to be seen on the television warning us against the common currency in particular and foreigners in general. He was, for a time, in the Cabinet, as Secretary of State for Wales, fleeing the Principality nightly in order to grace the marital bed.

Last week Penguin published a book by Redwood in which he rehearses yet again his arguments against further progress in Europe. After a heated meeting with Alistair Goodlad, the government's Chief Whip, he promised to soft-pedal the *éclat* that was bound to accompany its publication. No doubt he sat in Harrods, a lonely figure, waiting to sign copies. But the publication comes at a difficult moment for John Major, who is sitting uncomfortably on the European fence.

The Prime Minister, too, was in Wolverhampton last week, where he refused to play the race card *à la* Enoch. Redwood, Budgen and a handful of west midlands Tories took the opposite view, and by falsely accusing Labour of opening the floodgates of immigration, deliberately stirred up old, and once forgotten, hatreds. Enoch Powell's 'rivers of blood' speech, from which his political career never recovered, actually helped Ted Heath to win in 1970. But Enoch's opposition to all things European and his plea to the country to vote Labour lost Heath both the 1974 elections. Now Enoch is frail and aged; but, like John Brown, while his body lies a-moulderin' in the grave, his spirit goes marching on. Has Redwood travelled to Wolverhampton to breathe life into Enoch's political 'corpse'?

Redwood, who is regarded by many of the colleagues with dislike, seems to think that, having already challenged John Major for the premiership, he has prior claim upon it in the event of a Tory defeat. But there are bigger beasts in the Tory jungle who actively seek the prize. Is it too much to hope that until 1 May John Redwood might spend his time among the Wates houses and executive estates of his patch in Berkshire? He will have his work cut out. It could be that he is not much loved there.

It will be fascinating to watch how the Tory right behaves during this long campaign. Redwood, if his visit to Wolverhampton is any guide, will be the most provocative. He is a Fellow of All Souls, as is William Waldegrave. But academic qualifications are not all that is needed to succeed in politics. Michael Heseltine got a second, thanks to intensive coaching by his friends, a result which the dons of Pembroke said 'was totally undeserved'. I remember once at lunch in the Commons sitting next to Quintin Hailsham. I suggested, somewhat rashly, that Enoch Powell was the most academically distinguished Tory. At this Quintin exploded. '*I* am the most academically distinguished Conservative!' he cried. Who am I to dispute the matter? Enoch's brains did not guarantee him a political career of any real distinction. Neither, I suspect, will Redwood's.

Success in politics is the result of many things, of which academic cleverness is only one. Balfour was a philosopher, but it did not prevent him from being ousted by Bonar Law, who was not. Macmillan and Butler were both intellectually distinguished in a party that pretended to mistrust 'brains'. Macmillan became Prime Minister only because he hitched himself to Churchill's star, and was able to show his abilities while resident minister in Algiers towards the end of the war. He also made the most of the Suez fiasco. Butler never wanted anything, even the premiership, badly enough. Iain Macleod, who earned £2,000 a year before the war playing bridge, died too early to fulfil his promise. The real factor that determines success is luck, being in the right place at the right time. Politics is a lottery.

The Tory right feels that its time has come. Heath was the last of the Tory prime ministers who could trace their elevation back to Winston Churchill's premiership in 1940. Margaret Thatcher was something of an aberration; she appeared to be of the right, but her bark was far worse than her bite. Major is a One Nation Conservative. But it appears that his days are numbered. A much diminished Tory opposition will revert to the right, and the leadership of the opposition will be fought out between the major right-wing figures. Hence John Redwood's totally unnecessary visit to insalubrious Wolverhampton. He may yet visit Brussels in order to put the cat among the Commission's pigeons.

3 April

The powers that be within the Tory party have bowed to the inevitable. They have accepted that the Beckenham and Tatton Conservative associations have the right to pick Piers Merchant and Neil Hamilton as candidates if they so wish. Merchant is a fool who seems to have been set up by the *Sun*, the political correspondent of which admitted that the seventeen-year-old 'night club hostess' with whom Merchant is alleged to have had an affair had received money from the newspaper. He was careful not to say how much. As for Hamilton, who has strenuously asserted his innocence, he will be adopted later this week, sustained by his good looks, the susceptibilities of the ladies of Tatton and a belief that someone is innocent until he is proved guilty.

Conservative Central Office has always been viewed with suspicion by Tory party constituency associations. They guard their independence jealously, especially when it comes to picking candidates. Having accepted a list of names of potential candidates from Central Office, they then feel free to pick and choose. In my own case, after I had been adopted as prospective candidate for Aldershot in 1969, Central Office intervened twice: first to try to persuade the local Tories to interview the young Churchill (who, incidentally, is sitting out this election, unable to find a seat), and, secondly, when that dodge proved unsuccessful, in an attempt to persuade the Aldershot association to take John Davies, then head of the CBI. That failed, too.

But in 1997 the desire to keep Central Office at arm's length has been joined by another factor: hatred of the press. The burghers of Beckenham did not want to be dictated to by the *Sun*, a rubbishy and unscrupulous newspaper that had just come out in favour of Blair and which had, they suspected, choreographed the discomfiture of their MP – however foolishly he had behaved. In Hamilton's case the *Guardian*, which was not the favourite reading of the Tories of Tatton, had clearly been waging a campaign against Hamilton under the general heading of 'sleaze'. The good ladies of Cheshire were not going to be bullied by the *Guardian*. How short-sighted of Heseltine, Townend of all people, and others who went public demanding that Hamilton stand down. They changed their tune within the space of a weekend: another U-turn.

4 April

I was rung last night by an Emma Somebody from the *Today* programme asking me to comment on the news that Lady Thatcher had decided to campaign for the Conservatives. Unknown to a considerable section of the electorate (it is seven years since she was premier, ten since she last won an election), 'the Great She Elephant' has foisted herself uninvited upon Conservative Central Office. The press carried no news of this development. It appears that the Thatcher Foundation has made Central Office an offer it could hardly refuse. Margaret's itinerary, and no doubt for whom and where she speaks, will be the responsibility of her Foundation. But with friends like her, who needs enemies? She has spent much of the past seven years sniping at the government's European policy in general and at John Major in particular, and will make mischief wherever she goes.

Gerald Howarth, the Thatcherite Tory who is contesting Aldershot, tried a year or so ago to invite Margaret down to what was then still my constituency. He did not tell me of this; I learnt the news from the president and chairman of my Conservative association. I quickly wrote Howarth a stiff note reminding him that despite my infirmity I was still the MP for Aldershot. Once he was adopted, I wrote, he could invite whomsoever he wanted.

Margaret Thatcher has been a thorn in the side of John Major ever since she realised, somewhat belatedly, that 'dear John' was no Thatcherite. Her Eurosceptic views, which border on nationalism of the crudest sort, made her an opponent of the Maastricht Treaty, and, in conjunction with extinct volcanoes of the Norman persuasion (Tebbit, Lamont), she did her best to undermine government policy. Her autobiography contains chapters that are less than enthusiastic about the progress and policies of the Major government. In fact, in the days running up to the announcement of the election, she – along with the 'soar-away' *Sun* – appeared to have transferred her affections to Tony Blair. By the time the date was fixed, however, she had backtracked, and had begun to attack the Labour Party.

There are two dangers attached to Margaret's speaking tour. One, is she still an electoral asset for the Tories? I do not think so. It is seven years since she was ousted, and I believe her to be no more popular today than she was then. She could rally some of the party activists, who would attend her meetings anyway out of a mixture of admiration, loyalty and nostalgia, but she would have little or no appeal to the voters at large. And she would take care to speak only for her friends: Howarth, who was the last Tory to carry her bags, 'Little Norm' Lamont, who has bundled Robert Banks out of his Harrogate nest, Michael Portillo and Michael Howard. She might even speak for such passionate Eurosceptics as Bill Cash, thus giving him a kind of legitimacy that he has done nothing to deserve. Would she lend what authority she has left to 'Mother' Teresa Gorman?

In fact, she will flatter the slate of right-wing candidates for the leadership who are waiting anxiously in the wings, hoping against hope for a Labour victory. Whom does she favour? Once it was Portillo, although I doubt if he is good-looking enough to last the course. Physically, he has nothing in common with the 'pretty boys' – the John Moores, Humphrey Atkinses and Peter Lilleys – who have caught her eye in the past. Michael Howard has emerged recently as the hardest of the hard men, challenging the judiciary in its right to pass sentence. She might even be tempted to invite 'Big Norm' Tebbit to accompany her on her pilgrimage, his task to act as warm-up man to what may well be empty houses. He will spill his acid on to the platform.

More to the point, the press will be sure to attend. The hacks will be at the back of the hall, marked out from the ranks of the respectable by their dirty mackintoshes and grubby notebooks. Their task will be to watch for any statement made by Margaret that could be interpreted as being less than loyal, and, with their proven capacity to make mountains out of molehills, will amplify Margaret's mischief to a mass audience.

The resurrection of Margaret (even allowing for the fact that the initiative came from her, and not from Central Office, which has had to put its best face forward) has thrust the emphasis of the Tory campaign away from the future and back to the past. The Thatcher years were marked by two busts and one boom; Major's difficulties have been compounded by the need to raise taxes in order to keep public spending under control. Hence the Labour jibe of broken promises on tax. But the recession, caused by the combination of Nigel Lawson and Margaret Thatcher, was the direct cause of the slump. Margaret Thatcher is dead; she should learn to lie down.

5 April

On the dissolution of Parliament on 8 April, sixty-two Tory MPs will retire to shire and suburb, leaving the Conservative Party quite unrecognisable. Twenty-four Labour MPs are also to retire, along with six Liberal Democrats. I want to bid farewell to some of those who have stood the test of time.

With these departures the Conservative Party will lose its ballast – the 'sound' Tories who put loyalty first and who came to Parliament not as professional politicians but as men of the world. They could not be bought. Their successors will be grey men brought up within the confines of political research or Conservative Central Office, or inexperienced local councillors. A large number of the new intake will be public relations men. At long last the 'players' will have replaced the 'gentlemen'.

The Tories who are to quit include Kenneth Baker, a literate Conservative who nailed his colours to Mrs Thatcher's mast. He went down with her ship. Under John Major he remained on the back benches; a wasted talent. As a former Cabinet minister he is likely to go to the Lords in the Prime Minister's dissolution honours, and make a lot of money elsewhere.

If I might use wine terminology, not all those who will quit are 'first growth'. John Carlisle, the right-wing MP for Luton North, is *vin du table*. What with David Evans in the South of that unlucky borough, the burghers of Luton have not enjoyed the best of good fortune. I hope that Carlisle, who is somewhat to the right of Genghis Khan, will take up residence in a cardboard box in Luton Airport.

John Biffen, the Sage of Shropshire, and the most successful Leader of the House since the war, will, like Baker, go to the Lords, where he will sleep gently upon the red benches and enjoy a luncheon of

Defenestration: Margaret Thatcher leaves
10 Downing Street, 28 November 1990.

Above left: 'Little Norm' leaves the emergency cabinet meeting on 17 September 1992, the day after Black Wednesday. *Above right*: 'The biggest beast in the Tory jungle' – Michael Heseltine, 1995. *Below*: 'I shall of course be registering the biscuit in the Register of Members' Interests' – Neil and Christine Hamilton, October 1994.

The leadership election, 1995. *Above*: 'The rose garden putsch' as John Major addresses the Downing Street news conference. *Below*: 'The urban fox' John Redwood, surrounded by his chums, declares himself a candidate.

Early morning, 2 May 1997. *Above*: At the Putney declaration, David Mellor invites Sir James Goldsmith to 'get off back to Mexico', while (*below*) 'the Great White Shark' Michael Portillo is beached at Enfield Southgate; the victor Stephen Twigg applauds.

Late morning, 2 May 1997: John Major sets
off for The Oval, via Buckingham Palace.

The leadership campaign,
1997. *Above*: Peter Lilley
with his main supporter
Gillian Shephard.
Left: Ann Widdecombe,
dropped from the Lilley
campaign after she had laid
into a rival candidate, her
former boss Michael
Howard. *Above right*:
Kenneth Clarke and John
Redwood, uniting to lose.
Below right: 'Just William'
Hague arrives at his press
conference, 18 June.

'King Billy'.

cottage pie and suet pudding, served by ancient retainers. ('Now eat up, Master John . . .') Although his path was crossed by Enoch at an impressionable age, the party will sorely miss his intelligence and sense of fun. To use the jargon of the wine trade, Biffen too is *premier cru* – and of a good year, 1961.

Steve Norris, the party's chief *garagiste*, will be found on the forecourts of the East End. Irrepressible as ever, he will probably make, and lose, a second fortune, but if his autobiography is any guide he will bounce back yet again in a few years' time by joining the cast of *Eastenders*, to the ladies of which he will be their second-hand Escort. *Cru petit bourgeois* (1974 was not a good year).

The party will lose prematurely two of its former chief whips, who, in their time, held the keys to the kingdom and the dark secrets of the party in the palms of their sweaty hands. Richard Ryder suffers from a bad back. Had this not been so, he would most certainly have been Cabinet material. Tim Renton has his pen to rely on. He is the author of parliamentary novels which are neither as clever as Hurd's nor as dirty as Edwina's. He, rather than Edwina, could settle down to become the Trollope of the Tory party.

Douglas Hurd is the party's most grievous loss. He was a most distinguished Foreign Secretary whose robust pro-European views did something to stem the tide of Euroscepticism. He will spend his declining years commuting between the City and the House of Lords, feathering both nests.

Michael Jopling, 'Joppers' to the party, is to retire to the country. As Margaret Thatcher's Chief Whip in the early 1980s, he steadied the ship, despite his doubts about the Lady's zeal. Rich and landed, he at least will not be obliged to buy all his own furniture. He will drive to the Lords on his motorbike, his pretty wife clad in black leather and perched upon the pillion, at the sight of whom many of the older peers will have to be helped into the Chamber. *Deuxième cru*.

John Patten will not be missed. At best a 'third growth', he will probably teach geography at some secondary school in a deprived area of a northern city. On the other hand, he might be appointed manager of Hartlepool United.

Paddy Mayhew will be almost as serious a loss to the party as Douglas Hurd. Grand, as all Tories once were, and, even as a young man at Oxford, the possessor of a ducal voice, he has striven mightily to bring sense to 'poor mad Ireland' (Yeats). He was set an impossible task. *Tête de cuvée*.

Sir Cranley Onslow will retire to his farmhouse in Sussex. 'Cranners', as he was sometimes known, was for a long time chairman of the 1922 Committee of Tory back-benchers, succeeding the egregious Edward du Cann and being replaced in his turn by Sir Marcus 'Compo' Fox. Cranley is an old-fashioned Tory squire who spoke for the 'sounder' Conservatives – those who never rocked a boat, or took lunch at the Savoy with Mr Ian Greer. *Premier cru*.

The flight of the knights gives me much cause for alarm. Sir David Mitchell will serve behind the bar at El Vino (the family firm), leaving the clan to be represented in Parliament by his promising son, Andrew, already a junior minister. David will find comfort, as always, in a decent claret. Another 1964 *premier cru*. Sir Hector Monro, called by the irreverent 'the Monarch of the Glen', will vanish into the Highland mists. Sir Anthony Grant, dubbed 'the Squadron Leader' (because of his Second World War moustache) will open a Chinese restaurant near the museum at Hendon Airport.

The Rt Hon. Michael Alison, known as St Michael Alison because of his piety, will enter a silent order where he will pray for the sins of his colleagues – some of whom need all the help they can get.

The formidable Dame Elaine Kellett-Bowman will be much missed. A feisty lady with a good left hook (allegedly she once punched Emma Nicholson in the stomach), she has been the doyenne of the Tory women MPs. Shrill of voice and short of temper, she carries a small black book in her bag in which she enters the bets her rash colleagues are encouraged to make with her while dining. I have been keeping her for years.

George Walden, a very clever Tory indeed, is to quit politics. We cannot afford to lose so able a man, and a moderate to boot. A *premier cru* (1974); the government should have made greater use of his talents.

I will mention only a few more. Why Richard Needham, an Irish peer, is giving up, I do not know. The smoking room will be much the poorer without him. Sir Wyn Roberts is a delightful Welshman who has never stolen a leg of beef. He is to retire to the Principality.

As for my enemies – I would like to think I have none, but that cannot be so. Sir Fergus Montgomery, Margaret's first parliamentary private secretary, is to return to the north-east, where he will open a hairdressing salon for the likes of Gazza. He tells me it will be called 'Short Back and Sides'.

I have barely scratched the surface. I should conclude my list of Tories by saying farewell to Paul Channon, who twice married a Guinness and, as the son of 'Chips' Channon, has as much material of his father's unread in his cellar than has ever been published in his famous diaries. Does he know that he is sitting on yet another fortune?

The most prominent Labour MP to quit is Roy Hattersley, whose proud boast it is to have earned £100,000 a year writing for the newspapers. No doubt he will continue to appear in magazines as diverse as *The Weightwatcher's Guide* and *Playboy*. Had the cards fallen differently, he might have become Prime Minister. Andrew Faulds will leave Westminster to become a strolling player, while Peter Shore will retain his age-old hostility towards all things European. Alf Morris, who has done more for the disabled than any other MP, will kick away no one's crutch.

As the old Tories fade away, Labour will be reinforced by a motley crew of social workers, polytechnic lecturers and local government officers, who will combine to give Blair a hard time. The hand-made shoe and the military title will become things of the past. Only the resurrection of Mr Alan Clark, who believes that no bottle of claret is worth drinking if it costs less than one hundred pounds, will provide an echo of what the Tory party once was.

I should also say farewell to David Steel and Russell Johnston, two civilised Liberals who never credited cracks in paving stones as having any deep ideological significance. They will both be missed.

6 April

In 1992, when I retired from active parliamentary work due to ill-health, we came to live in Ludlow, a small Georgian/mediaeval town on the borders of Shropshire and Hereford. Its Member was Christopher Gill, a meat processor and pork pie manufacturer. It was over two years before he took the trouble to call upon us in Mill Street. During that time, we had gone quite frequently to London, where we stayed at Prue's flat in Olympia. My experience in Parliament in this period was a miserable one. The extrusion of a spinal disc (between the fourth and fifth vertebrae) had spread paralysis down my right leg, already withered by an attack of polio in 1949. I could no longer walk without the aid of crutches, and even with them could manage only a few yards. I could not stand for any length of time, or sit in comfort. My condition was such that I was given a full disability allowance of £187 a month, and a much-coveted and useful orange disabled driver's badge. I was therefore a very infrequent visitor to the Commons, voting only when the chips were down. To add to my misfortunes I was diagnosed as suffering from prostate cancer in June 1993.

Christopher Gill, who succeeded Eric Cockeram in 1983, held the Ludlow seat in 1992 with 51 per cent of the vote. He is a Eurosceptic, who in June 1995 acted as the organiser of John Redwood's campaign to wrest the leadership from John Major. He is on record as having said that he would vote to take Britain out of the European Union, and for several months in 1992–3, as one of the Maastricht rebels, he lost the Tory whip. In view of all this, could I bring myself to vote for him? I have been a passionate pro-European ever since I joined the House in Harold Macmillan's day. I decided that there were no circumstances in which I could vote for Gill (I would sit on my hands in the 1997 election) and announced as much. The story was immediately picked up by the papers, some of which ran it under the misleading headline 'Tory MP says he will no longer vote Tory'.

When I went down to the House to vote for John Major in the leadership poll, Prue propelled me up the committee corridor in my wheelchair. As I approached the door of Committee Room 14, where the ballot was taking place, Gill rushed towards me, crying loudly 'You're no gentleman!', a reference presumably to my decision not to vote for him. Struggling to get to my feet and make use of my crutches, angrily I told him to fuck off, which, on reflection, was very rude. I should rather have struck him with my crutch. The members of the press who were hanging about the committee corridor picked up my expletive, and published the fact that 'an ailing Julian Critchley' had roundly abused his colleague (though Gill was, at the time, no longer a member of the parliamentary party, having had the whip withdrawn). It was a silly spat, and I should have known better, but it led to open warfare.

It is thus with some interest that, twenty months later, I follow the campaign in Ludlow. It was rumoured that Gill had had a rough time at his annual general meeting, but that his anti-European views had the support of his officers and particularly of his chairman, Michael Wood. There are many Tories who are unhappy with Gill. He is pretty second-rate, and although 'Europe' has undeservedly become unpopular as a result of hostility in the press, there are still many Tories who are uncertain whether or not to vote for him.

At the start of the campaign, the journalist Tony Howard – who has a house in Ludlow and is, in consequence, well informed – wrote a column in *The Times* in which he recounted with some glee a chapter of accidents that had befallen Gill. He related how Gill had turned down an invitation to appear on the platform with the other candidates in Ludlow on the grounds of a prior commitment to speak in Bishop's Castle. There was much huffing and puffing in the local press, Ludlow being a largely Liberal town. But worse was to follow. Gill duly arrived at Bishop's Castle, a town in the back of beyond which, until the Great Reform Bill, returned four Members to Parliament. The slate of candidates, Tory, Lib Dem, Labour and Green, took their places on the platform after a civic ceremony of the kind that only such an ancient borough could lay on. Gill then promptly walked out, claiming that the cost of the meeting would count against his election expenses. The other three, to whom the same handicap applied, sat firm. So to boos, hisses and catcalls from an unusually large audience, Gill ignominiously beat the retreat. The county's papers were besides themselves with indignation. Gill's campaign, to quote John Major's *bon mot*, certainly did not 'peak too early'. Still, whatever one thinks of him, Gill is in a strong position. He might suffer slightly from Tory abstentions, but for as long as the anti-Tory vote is split two ways (there is little difference between Labour and the Liberal Democrats), he should come through the middle and be returned to Westminster – where he will no doubt once again raise John Redwood's tattered banner.

I have met the Liberal and Labour candidates, both of whom have had the courtesy to call upon me in my house in Broad Street. The Liberal, a barrister, seemed a charming man; the Labour candidate, a clever and just as charming young woman, said that in the past she might have described herself as 'left wing' but events had made her a 'pragmatist'. I would think she has a political future; she works at present raising money for a children's hospice near Oswestry. Neither was so impolite as to solicit my vote, but we had an interesting discussion about politics, local and national.

The most popular MP for Ludlow in recent years was the late Jasper More. The Mores have represented the southern half of the county for nearly four hundred years – they were originally Parliamentarians, and my mother's family must have touched their hats and voted for the Mores over the centuries. I spent the night at their Palladian house, Linley, in the 1980s, the first member of my family to have done so. Jasper was a lovely man, a library squire and the author of a delightful book called *A Tale of Two Houses*. After he died I had lunch with his widow Clare, who was a Hope Edwards and a formidable woman. She told me of an incident that had occurred a few days previously. The bell had rung and, descending a long staircase to open the front door, she saw on the gravel Norman St John-Stevas and a boyfriend, both clad in identical apple-green blazers. 'Ah,' said Clare, 'the House of Lords Archery Club, I presume.' It appeared that Norman wanted to buy her great house.

7 *April*

For the run-of-the-mill candidate at a general election, the whole grim process is hell. Stranded within the boundaries of his constituency, news filters in to him as into a city besieged. He has no role save that of Sister Anna: that is, to carry the banner, whether it be blue, red or, in the case of the Liberals, yellow. He puts himself at the head of a tattered army of political extremists whom he will harangue at intervals in the hope that a largely unheeding electorate will eventually send him to Westminster.

I have fought ten elections of which I have won eight, so I know what I am talking about. The process of electioneering is ghastly because it is an activity which, although strenuous and psychologically demanding, is largely bogus. Nowadays no candidate is worth more than a couple of hundred votes. His electorate, which can number 70,000, seems utterly unresponsive to his blandishments, and goes about its way apparently careless of the result. Its collective mind, if it can be so described, is already firmly made up.

The average voter does not decide how to vote as part of a rational process in which the pluses and minuses of the contending political parties have been carefully weighed in the balance, although there is a small minority that changes its mind from one election to another, and who may decide the result. Thirty per cent of the voters stay at home on polling day and watch the telly; the other 70 per cent disregard the beauty competition laid out for their delectation by the three political parties (and Sir James Goldsmith). Many black people do not vote; most Asians do. As the latter run the majority of the newsagents' shops in the country, they are increasingly inclined to vote Tory. Most people vote the way they have always voted; change is effected when a proportion of one side or the other refuses to vote.

Thus the voter, certainly at the constituency level, remains cheerfully impervious to the spin doctors of the rival head offices in London, as the method by which they determine how to vote has already been applied: a combination of family circumstances ('my father voted Tory; so do I') and sense of economic well-being – hence the importance of the so-called 'feelgood factor' – balanced in the voter's mind by the belief that one party should not remain in power indefinitely, however good or bad its record may be. That would not be 'fair play'.

The candidate's frustration is increased by his inability to get to grips with the electorate. His occasional speeches are delivered in draughty village halls to small groups of his committed supporters, who would be much better engaged tramping the streets of his constituency in search of converts. In 1987, I made ten speeches. They were attended in Aldershot by my friends and their whippets; in the smarter villages like Hartley Wintney by more of my friends, this time escorted by their well-behaved golden Labradors. Heckling is a dead art, which is a pity. The presence at the back of the hall of a stout party crying 'liar' at intervals does wonders for the flow of one's adrenalin, and turns an otherwise depressingly dull occasion into a cheerful bear garden. But the old fashioned election meeting for which the town hall would be packed to the rafters is long dead. It has been killed by television.

The fact that the diesel locomotive is more cost-effective and user-friendly than steam locomotives does not stop me from being a 'steam buff'. By the same token, I very much regret that the 'soundbite' so beloved by the new breed of spin doctors who have latched on to the political parties has helped to bring about the end of the classic election-time public meeting. The days when David Lloyd George was obliged to flee the Birmingham Town Hall by the back door and in the uniform of a policeman have long passed; but in 1959, when I fought and won Rochester from the sitting Labour MP Arthur Bottomley (and five years later, when I lost the seat to Mrs Anne Kerr), the public meeting was still in existence.

Rochester and Chatham was a crucial marginal which the Tories had to win in order to form a government. To achieve this necessary victory we were visited by the party's finest platform speakers (who talks of 'platform speakers' today?). The best of them, by far, was the Radio Doctor, Charles Hill, who later ran both the BBC and independent television. He served up a rich broth of assertion and humour in the town hall to an audience of some four hundred, drawn from across the political spectrum, scoring round the wicket whenever anyone was foolish enough to heckle him from the back.

The heckler provided the necessary yeast which could, if the speaker/candidate had his wits about him, work in favour of the platform. Charles Hill, who kindly congratulated me on my five-minute introduction, later took me on one side. In that gravelly voice that only the elderly will remember from the wireless, he told me not to take on the first heckle. 'Wait until they are all shouting at you, and then pick the one which is easiest to answer.' What good advice; and, as the speaker had the benefit of a microphone, the heckler would be at some disadvantage.

In 1964 when I was defending my majority of 2,000 against Anne Kerr, Harold Wilson, then very much at his best, spoke at Chatham Town Hall. The meeting was packed to the gunwales, and 'Little Harold' made a superb speech. But he made an elementary mistake: he asked a rhetorical question. 'Why', he thundered, 'do I speak about the Royal Navy?' Quick as lightning came the response, this time from the then chairman of the Young Conservatives: 'Because you're in Chatham.' The audience collapsed in laughter.

This election will be much duller. John Major will make a progress from one provincial town to another, speaking from his soapbox and shouting inaudibly into the wind. He will be abused by a handful of yobs. What has he to hope for? A three-minute report on television news.

Michael Heseltine is the master of a dying art. He is the best platform speaker in politics today, a fact that he has often demon-strated at Tory party seaside conferences. (There are two schools of Tory conference speakers: the Heseltines, who attack, often amus-ingly, the pretensions of their party's opponents, and attempt to lift the eyes of the activist to the world beyond Brighton or Blackpool; and the Portillos and Lilleys, who surreptitiously undermine their own side and play upon the dinner-time prejudices of their audience.) No doubt Michael Heseltine will address major public meetings, and do so very well. But the question must still be asked: 'Who is likely to turn up?' Who would leave their fireside and brave the east wind to listen to members of a party's third eleven, while, if they so wish, they can stay put and watch the first eleven slagging each other off on *Newsnight* and, if they are fortunate, a one-minute clip of Michael haranguing the electors of Bradford? The likelihood is that Michael will be reserved for television appearances where he will be asked to defend the indefensible (sleaze). No doubt he will do so very well.

As television has taken over the election, the logic would suggest going the whole hog, and adopting the American practice of debate on the air between the two principal candidates – as I suggested back in the middle of March.

Thus events have made the parliamentary candidate largely redun-dant. He has become the means not the end. He rarely sees or crosses swords with his opponents – or, indeed, his colleagues. When I won, and later lost, Rochester and Chatham, its status as a key marginal meant that we were visited in turn by one Cabinet minister after another. Even Harold Macmillan visited me. We drove together through the town. I sat silently beside him. 'Beastly things, elections,' he observed, baring his bad teeth. He spoke briefly to a crowd of bewildered housewives. 'Don't let Labour ruin it' was his message, but his words were carried away towards Faversham by the wind. Aldershot, on the other hand, was considered by our masters a safe seat, and we were left to our own devices. No Great Man ever set foot in the constituency, and we were left isolated from the national campaign.

There is one thing and one thing only that unites Labour and Tory candidates: namely, their passionate dislike of the Liberals. I have found in Aldershot that they invariably fight dirty, in my case per-sonalising the campaign by attacking me for non-attendance in the constituency during the past five years. It was Harold Macmillan, the wisest of men, who said that an MP's task was to be the Member for Aldershot in Westminster and not the Member for Westminster in Aldershot. But try telling that to Liberal Party activists whose obsession with cracks in the pavement, which is surely the responsibility of local government, is habitually used as a weapon against the sitting MP.

The Liberals are also rotten losers. In Aldershot in 1992 they came a poor second (Labour invariably came third). My victory was greeted by boos and by personal attacks, the traditional speech of thanks to the returning officer being used by a second-rate candidate as an opportunity to launch yet another broadside. The reason for Liberal misbehaviour is, of course, their inability to attract many people of merit to their banner.

For the twenty-seven years I represented Aldershot in Parliament, my wife and I lived in nearby Farnham, where we were lucky enough to buy on mortgage for £13,000 a large house in Castle Street. Initially this gave some offence, as I was expected to live in or near the constituency, but Aldershot is pretty grim and Farnborough not much better. As my predecessor, Sir Eric Errington, lived in London and Anglesey, the aggrieved had little about which to complain. Farnham, in any case, shades imperceptibly into Aldershot; but it is a much prettier town, where every Georgian door was painted a pastel colour, and even the policemen talked posh.

The candidate's day begins early and ends late, even in a safe seat. As I had previously won and lost a crucial marginal, I found it easy enough, certainly in my earlier days, to surprise the somewhat sluggish Aldershot Tory machine with my energy. As the years passed, that energy began to flag, and by 1992 I was crippled and fought the election at less than half speed; even so, I polled the highest number of votes ever, a comforting fact for which I feel there is no rational explanation – save, perhaps, that candidates count for nothing at all.

In the seventies and eighties, though, I carried the Tory banner, despite my latter-day anti-Thatcherism. Ian Gilmour and I decided not to mention Margaret Thatcher in our election addresses; instead I mentioned Iain Macleod, Ted Heath and Harold Macmillan. I would breakfast on toast and coffee at eight o'clock while listening to *Today* on Radio 4; this would alert me to the principal national political developments. That apart, I could only keep up with the campaign by glancing quickly at *The Times* in the morning and slumping exhausted in front of *Newsnight* on the telly in the evening. Sooner or later *The Times* and *Telegraph* would each send a reporter to Aldershot to write a short column on how we were doing in the heathlands of north-east Hampshire. In 1992 we were visited on behalf of *The Times* by one Kate Muir, who wrote a snide piece ridiculing my bulk and my crutches. Still, I had my revenge: it is always foolish of one journalist to attack another, and I reviewed one of her undistinguished books without once mentioning her name.

After breakfast, I collected my motor car from the yard of the local Farnham police station, which was round the corner from the cottage in which we were then living. As Tory MP for Aldershot, the home of the British army and the base of the much-hated (by the IRA) Parachute Regiment, I was permitted to garage my car alongside a fleet of police vehicles. It appeared that my name had been found on an IRA 'death list'. Even so, I used to look carefully beneath the engine with a mirror on a long stick, provided by the House of Commons. Once the election was over, I was duly refused permission to take up 'valuable space'.

Tory HQ in Aldershot was a suite of two rooms (one tiny) provided by the Aldershot Conservative Club, whose large, red-brick building occupied a prime site in the middle of Aldershot. When I arrived Mavis Banham, my election agent, would be already at work. She spent most of the day on the telephone, organising groups of 'workers' to canvass their wards. It was my task to accompany them, press the flesh and answer questions or take up any problems.

After the dissolution, I was no longer an MP, and so could not use House of Commons writing paper and free postage. New paper had been prepared, which bore a deceptively youthful picture of me (taken in 1970) in one corner and the legend 'Tory Candidate Julian Critchley' across the top. My secretary, Angela Bayfield, would write my letters. The treasurer would arrive to announce the latest figure for the fighting fund. We always worked an election in front, as it were – for example, the money raised for the 1992 election was spent during the 1997 campaign – although this point was never made clear to our donors. Leslie Dann, a delightful seventy-year-old who had stuck by me through thick and thin, would sit at the table all day, writing letters to subscribers and adding up the shower of small cheques that would arrive by return of post. A flock of visitors would arrive during the day, demanding canvass cards and gossiping about the merits or demerits of the three candidates.

On the morning of the Monday of the first week of the campaign, warmly wrapped up and sporting a large blue rosette like a bullock, I would be driven out of the club's car park standing sheepishly in the back of an aged Land Rover covered with posters bearing my youthful image and a general exhortation to 'return Critchley'. I felt an absolute ass. But I soon got used to the exposure and continued to wave bravely for three weeks at unheeding electors. This vehicle was driven by my minder, whose task it was to collect me early in the morning and return me late at night, dizzy with fatigue. His real purpose was to keep me out of mischief; if the candidate is propped up in the back of a Land Rover, or admiring an elector's dog (whatever you do, do not kick it), he cannot do anything that will get his name in the papers.

As the constituency grew in population through the years, it shrank in size until the smart outlying villages were no longer within its boundary. With this contraction we lost votes and, more importantly, money. One consequence of this was that my minder, at one time invariably a retired officer of field rank, came to be a less senior officer. In 1992 this role was filled by a Brigadier Mike Patterson, late of the Catering Corps (which had its HQ in Aldershot). He was a nice bloke, but he had never forgiven me for a joke I had once made in the *Telegraph* when I described the Remembrance Day march-past during which, 'terrible with banners', the white-capped cooks and bottlewash-ers swung past the rostrum on which stood the current Mayor of Rushmoor (the name given to Aldershot and Farnborough combined). I claimed that the banners bore the words 'Diner's Club', a firm that operated from a glossy building in Farnborough. But if Mike Patterson never forgave me, his pretty wife, Diana, did.

The diminution of the constituency undoubtedly changed its character. First, I lost Odiham with its helicopter base, and its long and very handsome Georgian high street. Next to go was Crondall (pronounced 'Crundell' by the toffs), a village so smart that it had two retired admirals living in it. Nothing annoyed its inhabitants more than having their telephonic address changed to 'Aldershot'. My most serious loss was the small town of Fleet, home of retired colonels and their ladies. By 1992, I was left with Aldershot, a working-class town full of retired NCOs, largely middle-class Farnborough, with its scientists and air show, and the fast-growing 'town' of Yateley, which is Wates country full of first-time house buyers and many Liberals. The more salubrious part, the rich villages of Hartley Wintney, Rotherwick and Mattingley, had been hived off into the new constituency of North Hampshire, which has adopted as its candidate for the 1997 election a Tory moderate, James Arbuthnot, who is already in Parliament and a junior minister. Politically, he is more my cup of tea than Gerald Howarth, who takes over from me in Aldershot.

Each morning we were given an itinerary. The morning would be spent canvassing in the better part of Farnborough, adjacent to the abbey and the school which my daughter Melissa had attended. The Empress Eugénie had retired to Farnborough after Sedan and the death of the Emperor Napoleon III at Chislehurst in 1873. The abbey had attached to it an almost full-sized replica of Les Invalides in Paris in which were buried the three members of the Imperial family. It gave a touch of class to Farnborough, otherwise famous only for the air show and two unusually named public houses: the Tumbledown Dick (after Richard Cromwell) and the Prince Imperial, who died fighting for England in the Zulu war. (Queen Victoria once described the swarthy lad as 'looking like an hairdresser'.) I knocked gently on front doors in roads named after long-forgotten courtiers of the Second Empire. 'Yes,' said the majority, 'we will certainly be voting for you, Mr Critchley.'

Lunch was usually a meagre affair, taken in the saloon bar of the nearest public house. Sometimes we sat at a table and ate fish and chips (how dreadful is most pub food today, bought in and thrust beneath a microwave); at other times we sat on bar stools and ate a 'ploughman's lunch'. To me a general election campaign is summed up by the taste of bread, cheese, marge and Branston pickle. I introduced myself to the landlord, and shook the hands of customers. 'We only see you at election time,' was a frequent comment. Voters are inclined to confuse the function of their MP with that of a traffic warden.

In the eighties, I would then return home and put my feet up for an hour or so, returning to the fray in the latter half of the afternoon.

Then we would join up with a small band of supporters and walk up and down the shopping precincts of Farnborough, Kingsmead and Queensmead, cheerfully greeting bewildered housewives who clearly wanted nothing more than to be rid of us. Nobody was ever rude; they were simply embarrassed. They did not have to meet me in order to cast a vote. If one is young, that is, under forty, one is encouraged by Conservative Central Office to run from house to house in a desperate attempt to garner votes (most people were thankfully out). As I grew stouter, I would leave the running to a handful of Young Conservatives, while I engaged in conversation any unfortunate who happened to be passing by.

If there was to be a public meeting that night, I would return home at about seven and eat a good dinner and drink a half bottle of wine. At a quarter to eight my minder would arrive, and we would drive fifteen miles or so to Mattingley, one of the outlying villages remaining to me. We would meet in the hall. There would be an audience of thirty or so, and as many Labradors. Mattingley was, and is, a rich village where the houses fetch £200,000 or more, and the bulk of the audience was known to me. I made my usual brief speech, and answered questions. The whole affair lasted an hour, and I was then taken back to a friend's house where we would sit in the drawing room of the Cordingleys (pretty furniture, some Worcester in a cabinet, rarely any pictures of merit) and drink coffee and brandy. The election, we concluded, was 'in the bag'.

As time passed I became less and less enthusiastic about holding public meetings which attracted only one's own supporters. It would have better had they been out on the knocker, converting the doubtfuls on their canvass cards into certainties. But the villages were used to having a public meeting, and regarded one as their due. And sitting down in relative comfort, dog safely beneath the chair, was less strenuous than walking the darkened country lanes in search of converts.

I would be driven home, arriving in time for *Newsnight*; then I went to bed, where I slept long and well. The traditional three-week campaign seemed to stretch interminably ahead of me.

Fighting elections is hard work, combining as it does unaccustomed physical activity with the psychological strain of leadership. It is also exhausting being nice to people all day. What does it all achieve? The language of elections is the language of war: campaigns are fought, elections, won or lost, and the task of the candidate is to carry the party's banner. I don't think it makes any difference to the votes cast. Candidates have spent the whole three weeks in hospital and still been elected. What you are really doing, in a 'safe' seat at least, is not garnering votes – they will be cast willy-nilly – but conducting a love affair with your own party. At Westminster you tend to lose touch. At elections you are given a chance to rekindle old friendships and make new ones among the ranks of the party activists. I might have been out at all hours and in all weathers (February 1974 was frightful), but I was accumulating credit in the bank, credit that stood me in good stead when I got into trouble, notably for writing anonymous articles in the *Observer* and for voting for Michael Heseltine in 1990, which prompted an attempt to deselect me.

There was, however, one more immediate undoubted benefit. By the end of three or more weeks of physical activity and snatched meals, I would have lost a stone in weight and come to resemble more closely the photograph of myself which adorned the bills that the local Tories had bravely stuck in their front windows. But weight removed so rapidly rarely stays off, and two square meals a day for four days a week in the Commons dining room in the company of friends soon put it all back.

8 April

Today I lost the precious letters after my name. The dissolution of Parliament went largely unnoticed, but those of us who are not standing at the election can no longer call ourselves MPs. Nor, indeed, can anyone who is. It is twenty-seven years since I was elected for Aldershot as its Conservative MP. Now I am back in the real world, and I do not even know the cost of a first-class postage stamp.

MPs enjoy many perks, not the least important of which is free postage. Writing paper and envelopes of various sizes were there for the taking, each and every one duly franked with the Queen's head. We were supposed to use them only on parliamentary business, but I must admit there were occasions when, to save time and trouble, they were used for other purposes. I shall now have to find 26p to write to my friendly bank manager first class, and 20p for my friends.

This is the second time I have lost my 'magic initials'. In October

1964 I lost Rochester and Chatham to Mrs Anne Kerr, and was out of the House, earning my living in part by freelance writing and in part by becoming the editor of *Town* magazine, owned at that time by the young Michael Heseltine. In those days one's parliamentary salary was £1,750 a year, and it, too, stopped on dissolution. Today, the salary is £43,000 and is paid until polling day. From then on it will be life on a pension, the size of which depends on the length of parliamentary service. I will be on less than half pay, but the pension is indexed.

So far, I do not feel very different. After thirty-one years as an MP I suppose I shall always be known as having been one. After four months I can no longer pay my secretaries out of my 'winding-up allowance', but I can pay them redundancy money, thanks to the accident of the date of dissolution: as it was in April, we are entitled to a quarter of one year's secretarial allowance. My motor car allowance has gone, but I will no longer need to drive to Westminster and back, or to Aldershot. I made my farewells there three weeks ago, and I very much doubt if I will ever set foot in it again.

Will I miss it all, the cut and thrust of political life, the friendships made, the enemies cosseted? Certainly I shall miss the constituency, although recent ill-health has kept my visits to a minimum. An MP feels a pride of possession; he is 'the Member' and he imagines that all those broad acres, to say nothing of the mean streets, are somehow 'his'. And I shall miss the womb that was Westminster. Once the elections were over, I would take refuge in my office, protected by a handpicked corps of Metropolitan policemen, my constituency correspondence in the competent hands of my long-time secretary, Angela Bayfield. What I enjoyed most was the gossip: well-informed, witty and invariably malicious. The best person to have lunch with was Alan Clark, whose resurrection as MP for Kensington and Chelsea is proof of life after death, if ever it was needed.

I shall now have to earn my living by my pen. I have two wives to keep in a style to which they are accustomed, and can manage to do so only if I can keep on scribbling. I cannot boast, as has Roy Hattersley, of making £100,000 a year from my pen, but, despite my disabilities, I have in the recent past almost matched a half of that sum. The Public Lending Right brings me £1,200 once a year. I could try my hand at a serious political novel; not the sort Edwina Currie writes, in which Ministers of the Crown lick chocolate spread off the private parts of their inamorati, but a serious novel with a theme. The decline of Parliament, perhaps? But my bread and butter will come from my occasional journalism and book reviewing. Will the absence of the letters 'MP' after my name make a difference? Only time will tell.

I can see myself in a year or two, sitting on the pavement in Ludlow, playing my guitar, a flat hat on the ground beside me. I will face competition. Ludlow already has a beggar whose Alsatian dog had pups, and, for a time at least, he lived like a lord. My music will be sad and Spanish (out of respect for Michael Portillo, the newly elected Leader of our Great Party), and I will display a card proclaiming 'Ex-MP with two wives and a fractious opposition to support, please give generously'. Will it come to that?

9 April

I settled down to the ITN news at 5.40 p.m. yesterday only to watch with amazement the clash between Neil Hamilton, the 'Black Knight of Tatton' according to the *Guardian*, and his 'White Knight' opponent, the television reporter Martin Bell. Why on earth did not the local Liberal and Labour parties, in cahoots with the London media, as they must have been, choose Kate Adie instead?

Bell, who appeared dressed in a crumpled white suit, has been divorced twice. I have nothing against divorce, regarding it in the same light as I do abortion, namely as a necessary evil, but it does seem just a little unfortunate that the 'White Knight' should have been matrimonially so unlucky – the more so, because Neil Hamilton's staunchest ally seems to be his wife, Christine. Lynda Lee-Potter, writing in the *Mail*, claimed that 'with more women like her we would not have lost the Empire'. Silly Miss Potter, but one knows what she means. Christine Hamilton is in the long line of distressed Tory wives who have stood resolutely beside their husbands.

It appeared that Bell, who looked like an unmade bed, had left his modest hotel in the constituency, flanked by his media circus, in order to give a press conference. To his dismay he was immediately confronted by none other than Mr and Mrs Hamilton, dressed to the nines and ready for battle. The press conference became a joust. The

Hamiltons – two old pros versus one green amateur – stole Martin Bell's thunder. To Christine Hamilton's demand to know whether Bell did not believe a person to be innocent until proved guilty, Bell lamely replied 'yes'. Neil Hamilton than asked the 'White Knight of Bosnia' whether he (Bell) was prepared to give him (Hamilton) 'the benefit of the doubt'. Bell cheerfully agreed to give Hamilton such an undertaking. Game, set and match to the Hamiltons.

That evening Neil Hamilton's constituency party adopted him as their candidate by 182 votes. It was a pyrrhic victory perhaps, but a victory nonetheless. The *Guardian*, which continued to lead the crusade against Hamilton, attempted to take the gloss off the Tory candidate's victory by publishing, yet again, a resume of the 'charges' brought against him. Under the headline 'Martin Bell's Letter to Neil Hamilton', presumably speedily concocted later that day, Bell wrote: 'As I said to you today I am prepared to give you the benefit of the doubt on the unproven allegation which remains outstanding against you . . .' Bell then went on to list Hamilton's 'wrongdoings', which, he asserted, 'make you unfit to become the MP for Tatton. You accepted gifts, hospitality and payments in kind from Mr Al Fayed, thus breaking the rule that MPs should not be for sale. Specifically you accepted a free holiday in Paris, a second free holiday at the Ritz, a third free holiday in Balnagown, and free hampers from the owner of Harrods.' There followed a list of further wrongdoings, among them failure to declare various payments, including £20,000 from the lobbyist Ian Greer. And, continued Bell's letter, 'You lied to Michael Heseltine and to Sir Robin Butler.' It is these charges for which Martin Bell is now not prepared to give Hamilton the benefit of the doubt, despite what he said yesterday.

I admire Hamilton's courage, and that of his wife, and have said so publicly. But I think he should have stood down. His adoption as Tory candidate for Tatton, and the arrival of the egregious Mr Bell, will put the election result in jeopardy in what should be, even if there were to be a Labour landslide, a safe Tory seat. What is worse, it keeps the sleaze issue well before the public for the duration of the election campaign.

Hamilton is a good-looking man, smooth, well-mannered and clearly popular among his active supporters. But what will the Conservative voters do? At best they will sit on their hands. What has worked in his favour is the passionate hostility of many of his party activists to what they see as interference on the part of a hated media. And how many Tory activists take the *Guardian*? The *Sun* paid a seventeen-year-old 'night club hostess' £50,000 to ensnare Piers Merchant, but the Beckenham Tories hate the *Sun* more than they do the 'New' Labour Party. There is widespread umbrage that an unelected media should presume to dictate to the voter the way in which he or she should vote.

Electors might profitably reflect on the wider environment in which politicians now operate. It was evident long before Michael Portillo's recent speech that the notion of a 'station in life', and of social hierarchy, had disappeared. The monarchy has been demystifed and even made subject, albeit at the sovereign's wish, to income tax. Grandees, whether archbishops, prime ministers, university vice-chancellors, red-robed judges or landed dukes, no longer impress in the way they once did. Traditional respect for rank or office has evaporated. Where authority in matters of faith and morals is still asserted from above, it is often disputed or merely disregarded from below.

We have all lost a great deal, as well as doubtless won a little, from these curious changes. In a confused world, ancient words have lost their meaning. Faith has been relativised, religious education in schools diluted and neglected; standards of conduct have lost their former objective foundation. While much instinctive moral decency remains, the anvils of the churches have taken a beating. Nor has liberty been matched by any very solid fraternity. Even if the average working citizen contributes £13 a week to the welfare state, the unemployed remain for him, more or less automatically, 'scroungers'. As for equality, a new pecking order is in the process of construction: he who walks tall, enjoys 'street cred', is the one with loadsamoney, while media personalities, playboys and sporting heroes occupy the new high ground.

For an emblem of this topsy-turvy world we may perhaps look to the National Lottery. It is a curious institution. With odds against winning of fourteen million to one, the working class and the underclass are encouraged to spend in pursuit of the remote chance of unimaginable riches. The money raised is then spent on a series of middle-class good causes. Is it not a confidence trick? This is not what was meant by the redistribution of income. *Liberté*, *Egalité*, *Fraternité* have given way to *Luxe*, *Calme*, *Volupté*.

In such a setting as I have described here, one characterised by sleaze and greed, life has become particularly difficult for political leaders. They are subject to low public esteem, to intrusion into their professional life by leaks of confidential memoranda, and to trial by media of all aspects of their lives. Furthermore, their working conditions are poor (although much improved in my lifetime): their tenure insecure, their families often separated from them for long periods (as I know to my cost). The Westminster model which the Victorians admired no longer impresses. Parliament itself seems due for reform. Politicians therefore need, more than most people, sympathy, tolerance and the understanding of the cynical electorate.

It is a sad spectacle when ministers cling to office over-tenaciously; and finally surrender it with so little grace, as if the portfolio were a personal perquisite. It is a long time now since we saw the dignity and self-sacrifice of Peter Carrington who offered himself as a scapegoat for Galtieri's occupation of the Falklands. But among the elite, and in the media, and on the streets of contemporary Britain, we now live in what has been called a 'culture of contempt'. Not even the monarchy is exempt from this abrasion; not even an archdeacon can resist the temptation to pass judgement on the suitability for his role of our future King on the basis of media surmise, cloaked as truth. It is in this depressing context that we must watch the contest between Hamilton and Bell.

11 April

Lady Thatcher is back on the warpath: a sight to put the fear of God up the pluckiest voter. (One can judge her mood by her dress: when she is wearing bright blue and a string of pearls, watch out.) On Wednesday she paid a visit to my old constituency, Aldershot, whose newly adopted prospective candidate, Gerald Howarth, is a devoted Thatcherite – so much so that he once carried her handbag as her parliamentary private secretary. She paid a visit to a local hotel; to the Conservative Club, where there are more slot machines than members; and to Aldershot's football club, which hovers at the bottom of every league. (At one election I spent the afternoon watching Aldershot play, but they moved so slowly that I fell fast asleep. So did most of the other spectators.) In Christchurch, Hampshire, she could not resist a crack at the European fisheries policy. 'They are taking 80 per cent of our fish!' she cried. Whether or not that figure is accurate is not the point; it was under her leadership that Britain agreed to the Common Fisheries Policy. Margaret has a conveniently short memory.

I am afraid lest Lady Thatcher go off at half-cock. Seeing her on television, it appears that age has taken its toll: she resembles an elderly bird of prey, and her voice has risen by two octaves. Since she was defenestrated in 1990, she has gone what the Welsh call 'a little funny', and, given the encouragement of an audience of pensioners, she could easily launch into an attack not only on 'dear John' (as he once was), but on the government's entire European policy (such as it is). Her Foundation, financed by excessively large lecture fees and the profits from her largely unreadable autobiography (many hands made heavy work), has acted as a centre of right-wing opposition to the Major administration. In the press she is sustained by the Johnson Brothers, Frank, Boris and Paul. She thinks the world of Michael Portillo, and was none too 'sound' when it came to John Redwood's challenge to John Major's leadership, two years ago. She hates Michael Heseltine with a passion born of humiliation.

Now anxious apparatchiks at Conservative Central Office are asking: Is she safe out without nurse? Would not the media concentrate their attention upon her rather than upon the leader of the party? After all, we got rid of her in 1990 because we feared we could not win with her in '92. What with Hamilton and Co., and Tim Smith, have we not got troubles enough?

I wonder whether Tory wives would not make better candidates than their errant husbands? Christine Hamilton is worth two of her spouse, and in recent years we have become accustomed to stalwart Conservative women, sometimes more Pimlico than Sloane, standing bravely alongside their men, while the representatives of the media push woolly sound-catchers in their faces and demand answers to impertinent questions. Who comes to mind? Mrs Mellor and her extended family; Mrs Yeo; Mrs Tim Smith; Mrs Merchant. There may well be more. And yet it is the Labour Party that is recruiting women to stand as candidates at the election, far more than the Tories.

Let the 'little woman' come forward. Not all of them would write such bad novels as Edwina Currie or have the architectural know-how of Teresa Gorman.

12 April

Who in God's name thought up the ridiculous idea of hiring an actor in the costume of a chicken to follow Tony Blair? Tim Bell? Peter Gummer? Or the egregious Saatchi brothers? Spin doctors are parasites upon the body politic, dressing up their commonplace suggestions in the jargon of PR. I suggested a debate between Major and Blair in *Punch* four weeks ago. Negotiations between the parties broke down, each side blaming the other. Now I see that the *Times* leader has come out in favour of a debate. Imitation is the sincerest form of flattery.

Until today, nobody had ever heard of Angela Browning, the Conservative MP for Tiverton. She is a junior minister of agriculture under Douglas Hogg. Does she choose his curious hats? If so, it is the most useful thing she has managed to do during her first term in Westminster. Now she has come out against a single European currency in her election address, stating that a common currency, and the requirement in the Maastricht Treaty (for which, incidentally, she voted) that some of Britain's gold and currency reserves be transferred to a central bank in Frankfurt, 'would mean the end of the sovereignty of the nation-state'. In one sense she is right; but the nation-state, as we know it, is in any case obsolete. Isolation for Britain would not be splendid. Europe would have the ecu, Japan the yen, America the dollar. Sterling would become the victim of every currency speculator. Outside Europe, we would slowly wither on the vine.

Miss Browning, who has all the noisy charm of a jolly hockey stick, must have known of John Major's instruction that ministers (however junior) should stick to the party line of waiting until the terms are known, as they will be after the intergovernmental conference in June. She disregarded the Prime Minister's wishes, and, naturally enough, left John Major vulnerable to the charge of weak leadership and indecisiveness. Angela Browning could be the one pebble that started an avalanche. If the Tories lose the election on 1 May, the debacle could be traced back directly to one silly woman, not clever enough to understand the complexities of the issues involved. For, sadly, Angela Browning is not alone. Over a hundred or so Conservative Eurosceptics have already announced their intention of rewriting government policy on Europe, defying John Major and pledging themselves in their election literature never to vote for a common currency. Faced with such a revolt, the Prime Minister had limited his diktat to ministers serving in his government. They were obliged to toe the party line, and most certainly not to accept money from a Yorkshire businessman called Sykes who promised to make a gift of a large sum of money to any Tory willing to stand out against the ecu.

William Hague, the baldest young man in captivity, who is Secretary of State for Wales, told the BBC that 'Conservative candidates are free to set out their views in their election addresses'. True enough. But he went on: 'Candidates are setting out what views they would take at the conclusion of the debate about the single European currency.' At the conclusion of the debate? Are MPs not expected to exercise free choice after listening to the arguments deployed by their own front bench? If Hague, who is at best a rabble-rouser, had his way, parliamentary debates would be of no importance whatsoever, as MPs would vote according to their already declared prejudices.

Perhaps the worst example of the crass nationalism of the right is a leaflet put out by one Rupert Matthews, Tory candidate for Bootle (thankfully a Labour seat). In it he shows three photos. The first is of his grandfather on horseback (the 17th Lancers); the second, of his father in Royal Air Force uniform; the third, of the candidate himself, grinning from ear to ear. The copy reads as follows. 'For generations the people of Bootle have fought to keep Britain free and independent. Now powerful people in the Establishment want to sell out and push Britain into a Federal Europe ... Don't let them get away with it.' It comes to something when Tories talk of 'the Establishment' in those terms. And what does he mean by 'Federal'?

The list of Eurosceptic Tory MPs includes Gerald Howarth (my successor at Aldershot, who is likely to hold the seat); Robert Blackman, a candidate in a Tory-held seat; Billy Wiggan of Burley (a Labour seat, so thankfully we shall not see him); John Todman, candidate for Cheltenham (as he is white, unlike John Taylor at the last election, he might take the spa from the Liberals); Graham Bradley, candidate in Altrincham (another Tory seat); Paul Bartlett of Coventry North

West (we shall not see him either); Adrian Rogers in Exeter (a seat at present held by the Tories); Oliver Letwin (who at least has brains, and is candidate for West Dorset, which the Tories will probably hold); Vivian Bendall, the taxi-drivers' friend, who will probably lose Ilford North; and many, many others – including, of course, Christopher Gill in my home town of Ludlow.

I sent Prue to Gill's adoption meeting, which was held yesterday evening in an upstairs room at the Feathers Hotel. A hundred people were present and Gill, despite his record, was adopted unanimously. His speech was pedestrian, aimed at the lowest common denominator of his audience. What was of interest were the leaflets that were distributed in his name. One read:

> The question every voter must ask is which candidate can be abso-
> lutely relied upon to defend Britain's freedom and independence.
> The choice is between:
> – the Liberal Democrats who support total integration into the
> European Union [not strictly true];
> – The Labour Party which is hell bent upon smashing up the UK
> by giving Scotland a separate parliament and devolution in Wales,
> which plays straight into Brussels' hands [how?];
> – OR CHRISTOPHER GILL.'

There was no mention of the Conservative Party, or of John Major . . . More sinister was the circulation at the same meeting of a leaflet printed by the Campaign for an Independent Britain (CIB). It adver-tised an open meeting to be held at Bridgnorth on the evening of 15 April, and read as follows:

> As an organisation which is not affiliate (*sic*) to any Political Party;
> we have invited all candidates for the forthcoming election to the
> Westminster parliament to hear their views on the most neglected
> topic of this election, BRITAIN AND THE EUROPEAN
> UNION. REMEMBER – nearly all Law for Britain is made now
> by the European Commission, then controlled and implemented at
> the behest of the European Court. The Westminster Parliament
> will soon be reduced to the status of little more than a County
> Council – and – YOU WILL PAY FOR THE DOUBTFUL
> PRIVILEGE. Come and hear what your Prospective Member of
> Parliament has to say about it.

At the back of one leaflet, Gill listed his achievements, most of them modest in the extreme. What he left out was his management of John Redwood's campaign to take the leadership of the party from John Major, the period when the party whip was withdrawn from him, and his long record of hostility towards Britain's European role. Had I felt strong enough to attend his adoption, I would, in the immortal words of the reporter from the *News of the World*, have 'made my excuses and left'.

What we shall await with some trepidation is the publication of the election addresses of the 'bastards' – those Cabinet ministers described as such by John Major in a post-interview aside subsequently made public. What will Michael Portillo put in his election address, or Michael Howard, the judges' friend, in his? Peter Lilley is a Eurosceptic, while Malcolm Rifkind, the Foreign Secretary, is anyway very unlikely to hold his Scottish seat. However disloyal any of these men were, Major would be unable to sack them in the middle of the campaign.

Just when the Tories seem to have had some successes, in particular in highlighting Labour's attitude to the trades unions and Blair's equivocation on privatisation, Europe emerges as the bottom layer of the sandwich which, paired with the top half of sleaze, will give Conservative Central Office acute indigestion. More than anything else the voter dislikes a divided party. The electorate might not consider Europe to be very important, but they do like a certain harmony of view. Why else did Labour lose three elections running in the 1980s, split as it was over collective security and unilateral nuclear disarmament? Major will be made to appear foolish, and not in command of his ship. This may be attributed in part to his lack of leadership, which has permitted the least attractive section of the Tory party to assume a reactionary stance, and in part, perhaps, to the inevitable consequences of the passage of time.

The dissident Conservatives are particularly fond of two emotive words: 'identity' and 'sovereignty'. Let us examine both briefly. Even were we to join a United States of Europe, fifty years from now, the identity of the component parts of the union would remain. Wales has been linked to England since 1536; yet no one who goes to Cardiff Arms Park to see England play Wales at rugby could be in doubt about the strength of Welsh 'identity'. And sovereignty is a commodity

like any other. It can be relinquished (as in British membership of
NATO) or shared (as it would be in a common currency to which
our partners would have to make a similar contribution). In a world
dominated by the dollar, the mark, the yen, to say nothing of the
currencies of China and the Pacific Rim, sterling on its own would
be vulnerable to every speculator in New York or Hong Kong. Has
the Tory party finally lost its marbles? I fear so.

21 April

Throughout the election campaign, John Major has been defending
the national interest. Not against wicked and ambitious foreigners,
but against those within his own party who see a common currency
as the end of independent statehood. Consider what he said at his
famous press conference when he talked of 'bound hands': 'I will
negotiate in the interests of the country as a whole, not in the convenient party political interests of the Conservative Party.' It is hard
to recall a previous Tory leader, whether Disraeli, Salisbury, Balfour
or Churchill, who has acknowledged with such candour that the interests of the Conservative Party and the nation are readily distinguish-
able. Not even Harold Macmillan or Ted Heath, who certainly drew
such a distinction in private, ever dared to do so publicly.

Now, at the start of the penultimate week of the campaign, defeat
stares John Major in the face. What will be its consequences for him
and his party?

The most obvious one, after eighteen years in power, will be the
search for scapegoats. John Major will be blamed by the rump of the
Conservative Party for what they will claim to be his weak leadership.
But that is a complaint that Tories have been making throughout his
premiership. Ken Clarke will be the second scapegoat, while Heseltine's many enemies will include him in what will become a general
condemnation.

Major will announce that there will be an election for the party
leadership in November, and that he will not be a candidate. Once
the dust of that contest has settled, he will take himself off to the red
benches of the House of Lords.

The left will be represented by the Chancellor, who would be
unfairly blamed by 'the fools' (we are never short of fools). Unlikely

to be appointed shadow Chancellor in May, he will not be able to garner enough votes to win the day in November. His position within a right-wing, Eurosceptic Tory party will rapidly become untenable. He could cross the floor, form a variant of the Fourth Party, or retire from politics altogether.

The right will suffer from what someone more charitable than I would call an *embarras de richesse*: the oily Howard, the scheming Portillo, the sly Redwood and the wet Lilley. Stephen, who has been Dorrelling away recently shifting his stance, will vanish without trace. But Redwood has his fair share of enemies, even on the right, and Lilley has not got the balls for the job. The two contenders will be Howard and Portillo, and some arrangement will have to be reached between them if the vote of the right-wing majority is not to be hopelessly split, permitting Clarke to come in through the middle. The parliamentary party, consisting of those who took Paul Sykes's shilling, will revert to type, adopting a nationalist/populist attitude and a stance of bitter opposition to whatever emerges from the Amsterdam summit. I am glad I shall no longer be on the Tory back benches.

The principal casualty of the Tory party's defeat at the 1997 election will be Michael Heseltine, who has played a relatively small part in the Tories' election campaign so far. It does appear that he was responsible for sketching out the rough of the fatuous advertisement (later withdrawn) showing a tiny Blair sitting on Chancellor Kohl's knee. He should have known that so jejune an image would not only anger the party's 'Europeans', who look to Michael for support – to say nothing of the Chancellor of Germany – but also open up the Tory party to ripostes such as cartoons featuring a tiny John Major sitting on John Redwood's knee. For the Prime Minister has dominated the news, but certainly not his party. Even Norma Major feels compelled to complain publicly about the lack of support among Tories for her embattled husband. This in-fighting among Conservatives is seen by most newspapers as confirmation of the inevitability not only of their defeat on 1 May, but of the break-up of the party when in opposition.

The European view within the party has been espoused by Kenneth Clarke, who, as one would expect, has fought his corner savagely, confident in the knowledge that John Major cannot afford to lose his Chancellor. But why this silence from Michael Heseltine, the Deputy Prime Minister? Has he not the reputation of being the party's heavyweight? The explanation lies in Michael's character, which has been dissected both by myself in my book *Heseltine* and by Michael Crick in his biography. Michael is at his happiest turning his fire upon the enemy, that is, upon the Labour and Liberal parties. This extraordinarily long, six-week campaign has been bogged down in sleaze (on which he has no view) and Europe (over which he has remained silent, disinclined to exacerbate divisions within his own party). The old knockabout in which Michael excelled, particularly in his party conference speeches, has been almost entirely absent.

Michael Crick's biography of Heseltine will not be read by its subject: he has told me as much. Nor was Michael prepared to be interviewed by Crick. Heseltine strives to be his own best-kept secret. Crick has done his homework, and has interviewed everyone who has ever had anything to do with Michael – except, that is, for me. He is content to 'lift' many of my better stories. But then, what else could I expect? I was at preparatory school, Shrewsbury and Oxford with Michael; he was my best man; I was his when he married Anne Williams in 1962. Until he got his sidekick Lindsay Masters to sack me as editor of *Town* in 1967, I was his best friend. As far as I know Crick has never met him. He has borrowed from a variety of sources besides mine, and has leant on the dull memoirs of Thatcherite ministers, many of whom were third-rate and all of whom were jealous of Heseltine.

What, then, is the answer to the riddle of the Sphinx? Is there one? One thing is not hard to discern. Michael was born with an overweening ambition to succeed, to become, in fact, Prime Minister. Of that he has no reason to be ashamed. There is nothing wrong in having ambition, for ambition is the engine of the public good. He is also ruthless, especially with his personal relationships, as many past friends will testify. His failure to capture the party leadership has been largely due to his contempt for his friends and allies. He does not cultivate people, nor does he reward them for their loyalty (save, perhaps, for my knighthood). In 1990 his two lieutenants, Michael Mates and Keith Hampson, were left out in the cold. After a Conservative defeat on 1 May there will be barely a handful of Tories prepared to vote for him in a November 1997 leadership poll. He has formidable horsepower. While addicted to publicity, he tries nonetheless to protect his privacy. Of his close friends, only the writer and broadcaster

Anthony Howard (who lives in Ludlow) has lasted the course. But Tony has never presented a challenge to him. Michael Heseltine is a cold fish, and as Crick correctly observes, a slow starter but a quick finisher. Pembroke College Oxford was too small a pond for so large a fish. He blossomed. The university was his stage: the presidency of the Union, his target; Downing Street, the ultimate objective.

I am sad he will not achieve his ambition; had he done so, I would be more optimistic about the Conservative government's chances at this election. Although loyal to Major, Heseltine is the consummate politician, probably the best platform speaker in politics, possessed of flair and the ability to give leadership at a time when that elusive quality has been much in demand. If we lose the election, Michael will go to the Lords (he would not be able to stand the sheer awfulness of the rump of the Tory party), convinced at long last that his chances of leading the party are nil, and spend much of his time reforesting the country between Oxford and Northamptonshire. Michael is never happier than when there is mud on his boots.

I doubt if anyone will ever do Michael Heseltine justice. Crick called my book 'witty, irreverent and affectionate'. But it is ten years old. Crick has picked up most of the pieces (he is very good on Michael's brief service in the 'Foreign Legion', as the Welsh Guards are known in the army), save for Michael's partner Clive Labovitch's observation that 'Michael is the only gentile my Jewish friends are chary of doing business with.' Should that be Michael's epitaph? Crick's book consists of something old, something new, something borrowed and something blue. But he has not discovered the man behind the mask, possibly because there is no one there. And of one thing we can be sure, Michael will never put pen to paper himself.

22 April

From the point of view of the Conservative Party in particular, the election will be won or lost 'on the knocker'. I have long depended upon Tory ladies for my parliamentary livelihood. In 1957, when at the age of twenty-six I was selected as the Tory candidate for the then Labour marginal of Rochester and Chatham (Arthur Bottomley's majority was 2,000), the ladies of the local association plumped for me. I was inarticulate and inexperienced, but good-looking. My rival

bore the unhappy name of Raper, and, after his rejection, never surfaced again.

In 1969, when the Aldershot Tories chose me to succeed Sir Eric
Errington as their candidate, I had been an MP for five years, had
worked for Michael Heseltine – and was still good-looking. I had
been to Shrewsbury, the Sorbonne and Oxford, where I had acquired
a certain gloss; not, it is true, sufficient to justify comparison with
Alan Clark (then an unknown historian and one-time trooper in the
Household Cavalry), but gloss enough to please the audience of
middle-aged, middle-class women. I was top in every stage of the
contest.

I was then thirty-eight, married to a pretty wife, and seemed to
have all the qualities needed to satisfy a largely undemanding set of
selectors. It was only later, when I gained a certain notoriety for being
less than enthusiastic about Margaret Thatcher, that I lost the support
of some, at least, of 'the ladies'. But, even so, their disapproval was
nothing when compared to that of the men.

In recent years the party has witnessed what has been called 'the
flight of the men'; a haemorrhage of husbands who were less than
eager to carry the burden of endless meetings at inconvenient times,
to say nothing of stuffing propaganda into envelopes and then
delivering them down rainswept and chilly streets. It was hard to find
a man to stand for the Council. It was difficult to tell which was
worse: canvassing in the mean streets of Aldershot, or struggling to
find voters' houses scattered in the rural areas of the constituency by
the light of a torch. And, anyway, the husbands were responding to
Margaret's cry of *enrichessez-vous*, pinched unknowingly from Guizot,
Louis Philippe's chief minister. Towards the end of my stint in Aldershot all the constituency officers were women.

Politically, the 'ladies', as they were invariably called ('women' being
in English usage deemed a shade derogatory), were remarkably undemanding. They had a fierce loyalty to the Conservative Party, a loyalty
which was easily transferable from one leader to another. Some were
even loyal to their Member, to whom the more old-fashioned were
happy to leave the business of 'politics' – an activity of which they
secretly disapproved. What was vitally important was good manners.
This meant a general courtesy, the habit of turning up on time, and
an obvious generosity when it came to buying raffle tickets, which

the candidate/Member was then usually obliged to draw. Usually the first prize was a 'funny' bottle with a tree growing up the middle, an incautious foreign purchase on the part of someone or other. I always made a habit of buying the wine for the top table at our frequent association dinners and branch suppers.

The branch suppers became renowned for the quality of the food, which was essential, given that the quality of the speaker (John Patten comes to mind) frequently left much to be desired. The food was cooked by the ladies themselves and they were, without exception, much better than the firms of caterers we were obliged to employ for our principal dinners. It was the MP's task to give the vote of thanks at the end of what were often tedious proceedings. In the twenty-seven years I represented Aldershot and North Hampshire we entertained almost every prominent Conservative politician of note, save for Mrs Thatcher. I refused to invite her; had I done so I doubt very much that she would have come. This some of the ladies felt to be a shame, especially after the successful conclusion of the Falklands War, but I stuck to my guns.

Keith Joseph lectured my women as if they were graduate students. Eyes became glassy and the applause was tinged with relief. Willie Whitelaw was jovial and flattering to me. What he said would not have gone down at a dinner at All Souls, but he had the knack of telling them what they wanted to hear. John Major came down before he was ever thought of as a future leader. He said I was 'a good egg' – a back-handed compliment as he dined at the height of Edwina Currie's salmonella-in-eggs controversy. He was charming, but it was not only Michael Heseltine who was surprised when 'dear John' emerged as Margaret's successor in 1990.

John Patten spoke to a supper club meeting on the day Britain was forced to leave the ERM. He arrived late, spoke badly and made no reference whatsoever to the crisis. Not only did he arrive when the guests were eating their first course, he then insisted on going round the hall shaking everyone by the hand. He could have been running for office. As the hour was late, I asked him to make his speech brief, but he took not the slightest notice. In my vote of thanks I pretended he was Chris Patten, and explained just how difficult it was to travel the 12,000 miles from Hong Kong and arrive in darkest Hampshire on time.

Enoch Powell spoke at an association dinner and by an act of intellectual levitation lost the attention of his audience within five minutes. We were all a little bewildered, but were, as ever, polite. We presented Ted Heath with a bottle of 1970 claret (the year of his premiership but not a good vintage); as he was unpopular with the party activists because of his dislike of Margaret, he seemed pleased by the gift. He spoke about Europe (in those days there were no such things as Eurosceptics). Cecil Parkinson spoke, escorted by his beady wife (it was after the Sarah Keays *affaire*), and John Biffen came down to Aldershot at a time when Angus Maude had publicly stated that no Cabinet minister would do so, as I had written an anonymous article attacking Thatcherism in the *Observer*.

At general elections, the agent's room would be packed. The agent herself – mostly, though not invariably, it was a woman – would be on the telephone to Central Office reading the contents of some Labour leaflet that had been circulating in Aldershot's army town while a table-full of the ladies addressed envelopes and stuffed them with election addresses, ready for delivery by another band of the faithful that night. Another lady from Fleet, usually a colonel's widow, would have been put in charge of 'mutual help', in which more good ladies from Camberley (who had finished canvassing their own sandy streets) would come to Aldershot that evening, called upon to tackle the roughest area of that unlovely town.

Tory ladies have suffered badly at the hands of the cartoonists, especially at party conference time when they are depicted as having all the charm of Giles's Grandma but wearing somewhat smarter hats. They would be baying for blood, and it was the custom at Tory party conferences when we were in government, which was most of the time, for some hapless minister to be thrown into the crowd as a blood sacrifice. It happened to John Moore. But taken individually, they were usually as nice as pie. They rarely discussed politics, considering it bad manners to hector 'the Member' – which was just as well, because I shared few, if any, of their gut views. My principal enemy was a Mrs Maureen Cooper, a feisty, working-class woman who was for a time the chairman of the association. When she let it be known that it was her ambition to get rid of me, she was, in her turn, quickly got rid of. It was simply not done to bring 'politics' so close to home.

I must have been inside more houses than the Man from the Pru. Canvassing always ended with a cup of coffee, or, if one was in the far-flung villages, a gin and tonic. A plate of biscuits would be passed round, and tales of old contests recounted. In Hartley Wintney the houses had all the signs of 'old money' and the china was Worcester, or if not Worcester, Minton. Those who had served abroad with the army had Indian brass-topped tables, and very occasionally a Kangxi *famille verte* plate hanging on the wall: a treasure picked up after the war in Hong Kong when refugees from China had no money, only ceramics to sell. In Aldershot, where the money was 'new', I would be shown a husband's medals; in Farnborough, home of the air show, aviation memorabilia.

Tory women are the foot soldiers of every election campaign. If they are not putting pen to paper, they are tramping the streets looking for votes. On election day all thirty committee rooms are manned by ward members, always ready with a cup of tea or milky coffee to accompany their inevitable forecast of victory. This time I imagine they smelt defeat. A Tory campaign that began with sleaze and continued with the revolt of the Eurosceptics, and the jockeying for position among those prominent members of the parliamentary party who saw a Labour victory on the cards, must have had the effect of lowering the morale of the faithful. But it did not keep them off the streets.

23 April

This morning I had a reply from a friend who is defending his Labour seat in South Wales. I had written to him – along with a couple of Tories – wishing him luck and office were Labour to win the election. I will quote from his letter: 'The sun's gone in and Europe's come out on the doorsteps. I am now wading through newly manifested swamps of anti-German vitriol and choruses of "Now don't let those bloody Krauts take us over ..." Anti-French sentiment is not far behind, like the smell of fried onions.'

How ironic it would be were the Tories to snatch victory from the jaws of defeat because of Jacques Santer's ill-timed intervention. What he said was unexceptional, but the timing was stupid. I gather he did not consult either of our two Commissioners, who would, surely, have advised caution. Santer's remarks came as music to the ears of the Eurosceptic majority of voters, to the awful Bill Cash, and to the latent nationalism on which a beleaguered John Major immediately began to play for all it was worth. And Tony Blair, terrified of being outflanked, was not very far behind.

Today's *Sun* contained an article by Blair that included the following passage: 'On the day we remember the legend that St George slayed the dragon to protect England [he didn't actually; he was in Cyprus at the time], some will argue there is another dragon to be slain: Europe.' Note the weasel words 'some will argue'. The piece taken as a whole could have been written by some of the least attractive figures in British politics: by either of the Normans, Tebbit and Lamont; by Bill Cash, the biggest bore in the House of Commons; by Michael Portillo when 'off the record'; or by the ghastly John Redwood. Blair clearly feels that the campaign could be slipping away from him and that he, too, must play the jingoist card.

Is Europe all threat? I have never thought so. And yet Tory back-benchers, many of them handpicked by Dame Angela Rumbold (herself a lobbyist in the past), have abandoned the European ideal so carefully cultivated by Macmillan and Heath in favour of a spiteful nationalism. It is the price, in historical terms, that we are paying for the quite extraordinary conversion that former premiers and many other Tories such as Peter Kirk, Iain Macleod, Douglas Hurd, Geoffrey Howe and Sir Alec Douglas-Home brought about among Tories in the pre-Thatcher years. Even Margaret signed the Single European Act, although she now wishes she had not and blames Howe and Lawson for taking her up the garden path.

John Major always felt that the only way he could manage a divided party was by nods and winks. To the pro-Europeans he repeated that he wished to be 'at the heart of Europe'; to Mrs Gorman he probably stressed that British identity and sovereignty were 'safe in my hands'. For as long as Douglas Hurd was at the Foreign Office all was well. His replacement by a glib Scots lawyer who has his eye on the main chance served to tip the balance in favour of the antis. Had it not been for the presence of Ken Clarke and Michael Heseltine, no doubt 'dear John' would have come off the fence weeks ago.

John Major cannot escape the charge of trying to be all things to all men. Perhaps that is what party management means? It was certainly

Harold Wilson's trademark. In the Labour Party it was the Social Democrats to be that kept the blue banner flying, in particular the eloquence of Roy Jenkins. Harold Macmillan knew that the only way he could take the bulk of his party with him over Europe was to remind it of Dean Acheson's dictum that Britain had lost an empire but not yet found a role. That role was to be Europe. But de Gaulle's veto delayed our entry until 1973, and diluted the power of the argument deployed by Macmillan that Britain was joining Europe in order to lead it. He wished to place Britain at the forefront of what he described as the most exciting political development of his lifetime. Today, so great has been our loss of national confidence, and so dramatic the change for the worse in the Tory party, that we can see only the disadvantages, not the advantages, of participation in the new Europe.

The antis in both the main parties argue that Europe, or further European integration, will reduce the power of the Westminster Parliament; some have even said to the status of a county council. And yet all the parties have conceded a referendum before taking a decision whether or not to join a common currency. Is Westminster not important enough to decide whether the pound becomes an ecu? Apparently, it is not. Referenda are a cheat upon the public. Everything usually depends on how the question is put. The nationalist card having been played in this election, even were a future Cabinet and Parliament to decide in favour of a single currency it might well prove impossible to get agreement to it in such a referendum. Britain is a parliamentary democracy. Referenda have been the weapon of dictators from Napoleon III to Hitler. How typical it was of Harold Wilson to call one in 1976 as a device whereby the divisions within his own party might be papered over. He let the genie out of the bottle. Now, poor leadership of both the main parties means that we will probably not be able to participate fully in a grouping that takes 57 per cent of our exports and provides 55 per cent of our imports and was directly responsible for 30 per cent of our inward investment last year (more than Japan, and creating 32,000 new jobs). What ever the bigots might claim, British business is solid in its support for Europe.

Of whom are we frightened? It is not really the Germans and the French. We are frightened by Conrad Black, a Canadian adventurer who owns the *Telegraph*, and by Rupert Murdoch, who changes his nationality as often as he changes his shirt. Are we really scared of Goldsmith, the Anglo-French billionaire whose participation in our election was nothing but an ego trip by a man with money to burn? Or of Paul Sykes, a Yorkshire 'tyke' with a desire to see his name in the papers? And what of the Johnson clan, Boris, Frank and Paul? Boris is a Eurosceptic Tory candidate for whom the *Telegraph* has provided a convenient platform; Frank edits the pro-Thatcher weekly, the *Spectator*; and Paul Johnson, who has been round the political compass twice, is the *Mail*'s hired gun. These people do not deserve the influence they peddle.

After the Eurosceptic Tory candidate Alan Duncan had written a piece in mid-April in the *Telegraph* attacking the common currency, I rang the paper and spoke to its features editor, Paul Goodman. I asked whether I could reply. He refused. I asked him then whether his paper believed in balance. His reply was that in March it had carried a piece by the German foreign minister, Klaus Kinkel. Some balance!

It is clear that Jacques Santer should have kept his mouth shut. No sooner had he made his speech defending Europe against a campaign of deliberate misinformation than he was cast by both the main parties in the role of his predecessor Jacques Delors, the man we loved to hate. If the dramatic narrowing in the gap between Labour and Conservative shown in the *Guardian*'s ICM survey today (and contradicted by Gallup) is accurate, Conservative Central Office can thank Jacques Santer for it: the man chosen by John Major to succeed Delors.

Today one of the broadsheets printed a picture in colour of Ted Heath and Douglas Hurd canvassing in a supermarket in Ted's constituency. Ted has never feared to speak his mind. How sad that neither Douglas Hurd nor Michael Heseltine succeeded Margaret Thatcher in 1990. But the Tory party always plays safe. They 'invented' John Major against whom nothing was known, and promptly elected him. Major has many virtues, and was infinitely to be preferred to Mrs Thatcher. Yet he has lacked vision. Without vision, the people perish.

24 April

The candidate will find that of all the days of an unprecedented six-week election campaign, polling day is the most traumatic. I have written the following account because it does not differ very much from the ordeal of all candidates, of whatever party.

As Tory candidate for Aldershot I would be picked up early in the day by my minder, who would have on his knee a clip-board to which was fixed the day's itinerary, calculated with military precision. There were twenty or more committee rooms to be visited before being taken home, exhausted, at around six to bathe, rest, eat a small supper and wait until eleven o'clock when I would drive myself to the count.

These visits would begin in the far-flung villages of Rotherwick and Mattingley, where we would be greeted by generals and their ladies with cups of proper coffee. After fifteen minutes in which we relived the campaign, and to cries of 'good luck', we would move across the constituency to Eversley, a smart village where generals were equally thick on the ground. More coffee; more chat. Slowly during the morning we would visit the committee rooms of Yateley, a fast-growing dormitory where many Wates houses would flaunt a yellow Liberal bill. Being of a neurotic disposition, I would be cast by this sight into temporary feelings of gloom. Surely Aldershot, a Tory seat ever since its inception in the 1890s, would not go Liberal now?

Lunch would be at the house of Mrs Esther Chappell, widow of a submariner, and a good friend. She had been a Wren officer during the war, and ran her ward (Darby Green) with charm and efficiency. There we would be joined by the chairman of the association and her minder. Dr Monique Simmons is a scientist working at Kew, highly intelligent with an international reputation in her field, and a very untypical Tory chairman. Her car would have set out in an anti-clockwise direction early that morning, beginning in those parts of Aldershot that returned Labour councillors. We came together for lunch, and then departed on our separate ways. I was headed for Farnborough; she for Yateley and the smarter villages. We would meet again later that day at the count.

I found as I grew older, and especially in 1992 when I could not walk without the help of crutches, that the continual getting in and

out of motor cars was very exhausting. By the afternoon all I wanted
to do was to go home to Farnham to rest. But it was not to be. We
drove through the middle-class streets of Farnborough where, happily,
there was a good showing of blue bills. At each committee room we
would glance at the figures returned by those unfortunates whose job
it was to tell, that is to stand, beribboned, outside the polling stations
ticking off the votes of known supporters. 'How's it going?' was my
inevitable question. The answer was usually 'very well'.

Although the association, like many others, had done a lot of canvassing it had failed to cover the entire constituency. We simply lacked
the numbers to do so. So the reports we received contained a good
deal of guesswork. Milky coffee gave way to sergeants' tea (which I
hate) and plates of Marie biscuits. We talked of old times and older
victories. Reluctantly, I was driven to my feet by my indefatigable
minder, and the car, which I drove, turned south, past the army town
(soldiers do not vote; officers do) into Aldershot town itself. We would
generally end up at the house of Mrs Joan King, the president of the
association, a lovely woman who had once run a baker's shop. There
we would find an old-fashioned spread: Victoria sponge and currant
buns, washed down with Earl Grey. Dizzy with fatigue, I would then
drive the two miles or so to Farnham to bathe, eat and worry.

I would take care to arrive at the count quite late. The poll having
closed at ten o'clock, it would be midnight before the boxes of votes
would have been opened and distributed among several tables, manned
in the main by bank clerks, supervised by members of the three candidates' teams. At midnight the count began, with the votes assembled
into bundles of 500 and placed in a trough with three 'corridors'.
Early on the Tory, Labour and Liberal piles would remain level; then,
at about two o'clock, the blue pile would begin remorselessly to forge
ahead, until the result was no longer in doubt. This sight banished
all fatigue. Victory was in the bag. Even so, it was not until four that
the returning officer would gather the three candidates on to the
platform and solemnly read out the number of votes cast in alphabeti-
cal order. My victory was announced to a mingling of cheers and
boos, and then the three candidates would take it in turn to make a
little speech thanking everyone for a hard night's work; I promised
to do my best for every voter regardless of his or her allegiance. The
Liberals were, in my experience, almost always bad losers. Not so the

Labour candidate, who invariably came third. I imagine the Liberals had convinced themselves of victory and were bitter in defeat.

The campaign, three weeks or more of fatigue and boredom, was thankfully over. I drove home happily, pleased that the initials MP could once again be affixed to my name.

I have written in my autobiography *A Bag of Boiled Sweets* of my arrival at the Commons in October 1959, the victor of Rochester and Chatham. I drove into New Palace Yard in my new Ford Prefect, wearing my Burton's suit, purchased for all of £10. The Tory MPs were very different from what they have now become. They were usually called Charlie, often related to one another and had enjoyed what was euphemistically called 'a good war'. In the 1980s they were all called Norman; Mrs Thatcher had done her worst.

In 1959 the salary was £1,750 a year with no expenses. I had to pay for my secretary and my postage out of my own pocket. There were no rooms allocated to MPs; all we were given was a locker in the corridor, big enough for two files and a pair of football boots. We were introduced to our area whip (a wartime brigadier) and left to get on with it. The old things advised one not to hurry to make one's maiden speech: 'Take your time,' they said. 'Sit in the Chamber and listen. Get the feel of the place.'

In 1992 I fought the election a sick man. But in 1987 I achieved a certain fame by appearing every Saturday morning on *Today* in the company of Charles Kennedy and Austin Mitchell, our brief being to make fun of the election. This we most certainly did, and 'Critch, Mitch and Titch' became for a time quite famous. What pleased people was not simply the humour, but the realisation that three candidates drawn from different parties could be such friends. The public imagines that we are always at each other's throats.

After the 1987 election I decided to take a leaf out of Nye Bevan's book. In November 1959, already afflicted with cancer, Bevan made his last major speech in the Commons in the debate on the Queen's Speech. Looking up at the Tory benches, packed to the rafters with the victors of the recent election, Nye warned that the prospect before us was one of 'hours and hours of infinite boredom'. I made a similar speech, warning the smug ranks of the newly elected of the tedium that awaited them. I had my tongue in my cheek, but many of my constituents were not amused; why, they asked, should they have worked so hard to return me only for me to say how boring Parliament was? The moral is, if you have a sense of humour, curb it. In politics one can only too easily be misunderstood.

What advice would I give now to the newly elected? First, keep on the right side of the whips, who hate unpredictability. Don't sneak off home early; your vote will be missed and it will be a black mark against you. Remember when you speak in the Chamber (which is not as well attended as it once was) that there is always a whip on duty with his own clip-board on which he write comments on your performance. 'Most unhelpful' will not get you far. Be careful when your write for the newspapers. This was once, in my early days, frowned upon; today, it is an accepted practice – but never forget that the whips can read quite well.

Get yourself on a select committee and play a part. Election as an officer of one of the many party committees can help towards eventual promotion. Take care not to disregard 'Walder's Law' which states that the first three MPs to speak at the weekly meeting of the 1922 Committee are mad. Congratulate ministers on the quality of their speeches. Most important of all, if you are invited to become a whip, accept. The Tory whips' office has changed out of all recognition. Once it was run by former adjutants of good regiments who had no political ambitions: people like Martin Redmayne and Michael Hughes Young. Today, only the brightest are recruited. They serve their time doing a fascinating and highly political job. It must be hard to be bored as a whip; it is all too easy to become bored to death on the back benches. Three years in the whips' office will lead to junior office, the first major step on the ladder of promotion.

On the other hand, you might be invited to become a PPS, a parliamentary private secretary to a minister. In my early days there were only three: the Prime Minister's, the Chancellor's and the Foreign Minister's. Today every pipsqueak of a junior minister is entitled to a PPS – someone who will refresh his drinks, and listen out for praise or blame in the tea room. The catch is that parliamentary private secretaries are now regarded as part of the payroll vote, an extension of the government, and are not permitted to kick over the traces. This development is a whips' trick, and the wiser of the newly elected will politely decline the 'honour'. Be your own man – but within reason.

Today, the salary is £43,000 with as much again in expenses to enable one to employ several secretaries and research assistants. There is a London allowance of some £10,000 for those who are obliged to run two homes, and a generous motor car allowance, although the fees office has not yet gone so far as to make money available to purchase a new car. Most Tory MPs, at least, drive second-hand Rover 827s. For those who wished to cut corners there were always lobbyists like Ian Greer ready and willing to put you on their payroll; but the Greers are already a thing of the past.

All the indications are that MPs' expenses will be more carefully scrutinised by the fees office as a result of Scott and Downey. It was rumoured of Scots Labour MPs that four of them would travel to London in one car, each of the four then putting in for a considerable sum of money in recompense. No check was made. MPs were put on their honour not to fiddle their expenses; not all of them have played the game according to the rules.

25 April

The Tories have waged a bad campaign. It grieves me to say so, but after five weeks, I can only suggest that John Major deserves to win, and the Conservatives to lose.

John has suffered from two insuperable difficulties. First, although he has been Prime Minister for the past five years, he is shouldering the blame for the past eighteen. He is a victim of that most powerful of political emotions: 'It is time for a change.' The second difficulty is that he has shown that he is unable to control his party, and the evidence of its factionalism has prompted the electorate to ask, if Major cannot control his party, how can he govern?

The Eurosceptics have done what they always wanted to do: they have defeated John Major. Time has eaten into the Tory party, and, as a result, it has become rotten to the core. Starting with the two Angelas, Browning and Rumbold, and bribed by a certain Paul Sykes, 200 or so of the party's candidates broke ranks, disregarding government policy over the common currency. Why Dame Angela Rumbold, who looks as if she were a Derby winner who has come last past the post, should ever have been made a vice-chairman of the party in charge of candidates, defeats me. She has done nothing but harm, picking candidates who shared her obscurantist views, and who will make up the bulk of the rump of the Tory party. How predictable that she should have 'rocked the boat' in the foolish way she did. Let down by the two Angelas and all those who disregarded the party's manifesto over Europe, and by the coded opposition of Hague, Redwood and Portillo, Major was not given a chance. He was left fighting bravely with the support of Michael Heseltine and Ken Clarke – whom I hereby nominate as 'man of the match'.

Major was also poorly served by Conservative Central Office. Tory party publicity was lamentable, its tactics juvenile (recall the out-of-work actor dressed in the costume of a chicken), and the campaign itself bedevilled by sleaze at the beginnning and by personal abuse at the end. I do not blame Mawhinney, who was the organ-grinder's monkey. The real mistake was to rely upon Tim Bell, Peter Gummer and the Saatchi brothers, who imagine that fighting elections is no different from selling soap. Central Office must now be returned into the hands of the professionals.

The campaign began with the 'devil's eyes' on a thousand posters, demonising Tony Blair – a wheeze presumably set up by the Saatchis, which had the effect of irritating many Tories, who saw it as too silly for words, and, what was worse, was deemed incredible by the general public. Whatever one thinks of Blair, he is no demon. He is Bambi.

This nonsense was followed by the poster (soon withdrawn) of a tiny Blair seated on Chancellor Kohl's knee. This idea may have originally been Michael Heseltine's; the Saatchis, however, had their doubts. It was immediately ridiculed. Cartoonists drew pictures of a tiny John Major sitting on a huge John Redwood's knee (which was much more to the point), and the Tory party stood accused not only of personalising the campaign but of making a subliminal pitch for anti-German feeling. The impression given was one of panic and despair.

No sooner had Chancellor Kohl been cast as the new Bismarck, if not Hitler, of the Eurosceptics, than Jacques Santer, John Major's choice as President of the European Commission, was goaded into making a speech which, though perfectly sensible in content, was ill-judged in its timing and had the inevitable effect of making the two main parties strive to see which of them could play the nationalist card the more successfully. Labour adopted and then put down an overweight bulldog. Major, who had previously pleaded that he his hands be left free in any future negotiation, moved in the direction of the Eurosceptics.

Finally – at least at the time of writing – there was the exchange of insults between the Tories ('you're a liar') and Labour over Labour's charge that the Conservatives would do away with the state old-age pension by privatising it, and extend VAT to food. The first charge was clearly wrong, although the Conservatives had muddied the waters with their pension reform proposals; the second had a modicum of validity as the Major government had already extended VAT to fuel. The effect of the spat was to turn off an electorate already heartily sick of a campaign that had gone on for twice as long as is usual.

In the middle of the penultimate week a *Guardian* poll gave short-lived encouragement to the Tories, but within a day three other polls had reconfirmed Labour's decisive lead. It seemed that all 'New' Labour had to do, given its large lead in the polls, was to avoid error and concentrate on sending Blair to play the role of the young Jack Kennedy. Only Paddy Ashdown, his eyes screwed up against the glare of the television cameras, generally spoke sense. But to no effect.

Who has come out well from the Tory campaign? Certainly not Stephen Dorrell, who seems too young to be cast in the role of hatchet man. Heseltine has been excellent on the radio and television, but much of the time has been curiously invisible. Ken Clarke has been the most successful Tory campaigner, bluff, quick-witted, and talking sound sense. His reference to 'paranoia' was a hat that fitted the Eurosceptics. John Major has played 'the nice bloke', but the impression given on the telly has been that of a solitary campaigner doing his level best to pull a rabbit out of his hat.

The principal Eurosceptics have, to be fair, taken care to bite their tongues. Portillo, with his eye firmly fixed on the main chance, has played a muted role. Redwood has continued to campaign on his own behalf; Howard, so far, has stuck to crime. But the two Angelas have already done the damage. As we go into the last weekend of the election campaign I can only forecast a Labour majority of around 100 seats. What, in heaven's name, will happen to the Conservative Party if I am correct in my forecast, I shudder to think.

27 April

Yesterday we drove from Ludlow to Eccleshall, a small town in Staffordshire, to have lunch with friends. We drove from Ludlow to Bridgnorth through some of the most beautiful countryside in south Shropshire – but three sets of posters spoilt the journey for me. The Ludlow roads were covered with posters urging the voter to support Gill, a committed Eurosceptic who fought his campaign without even making mention of the subject. When we left Gill country, the bills called upon the ignorant voter to plump for Peter Bruinvels, the Conservative Party's Pocket Hercules (he is under five feet). He made a fool of himself in the parliament before last by volunteering to become the public hangman: it was quickly pointed out by his colleagues that if his request were granted he would need two chairs to stand on. He, too, is an extreme right-winger and Eurosceptic. But worse was to come. In Eccleshall the blue bills showed a bespectacled Bill Cash, the arch-Eurosceptic of them all. The fact that they are all likely to hold their seats casts me into deep depression. I am reminded that in Aldershot, the seat which I had represented since 1970, I was succeeded as candidate by Gerald Howarth, Margaret's last PPS (after her defenestration): a former member of the Monday Club and as right-wing as it is possible for a 'respectable' Tory to be. His choice to fight the seat was one in the eye for me.

John Major has put up with more than enough from a fragmented and divided party. He will surely give notice before the election is long over that the party will hold a leadership election in November, but that he will not be a candidate. This would give the Tory opposition time to consider at some leisure whom it should now choose in his place. It would also permit the contenders to trip the light fantastic before the October seaside party conference, which will be packed to the rafters with vengeful party activists. Who will those contenders be? Michael Forsyth, Malcolm Rifkind and Ian Lang will have vanished into a Scottish limbo. Mrs Teresa Gorman ('Mother Teresa') will be obliged to turn her hand to architecture. But the three musketeers, Portillo, Howard and Redwood, will all have retained their seats, along with the two leading moderate Tory candidates, Michael Heseltine and Ken Clarke. Much will depend up the number of Tory MPs returned: the smaller the number (there were

201 in 1945), the greater the chances of a right-winger succeeding to the leadership.

John Major's first task will be to summon all the elected Tory MPs to some hotel ballroom where he will probably (and quite undeservedly) shoulder the blame for the party's defeat, attempt to raise the morale of his defeated army, and announce his intention not to stand in November. It will be his task in the meantime to choose his shadow Cabinet. I imagine he will keep Heseltine as his deputy and Clarke to shadow Gordon Brown. Portillo might be given the foreign affairs job, while Howard shadows Jack Straw, the new Home Secretary. He will have to pick a Chief Whip and will probably stick with Goodlad. What he will not do is give a job of any sort to John Redwood, long regarded by Major as the chief of the party's 'bastards'. Stephen Dorrell or Gillian Shephard might become the shadow Leader of the House. Betty Boothroyd, despite her fishwife tendencies, will be shooed back into the Speakership by the Labour majority.

The end of the Cold War put an end to bipartisanship in foreign affairs. The Tory party is bound to move to the right, to become more nationalistic and populist, and will attack the government's position at Amsterdam in June.

In 1945, a humiliated Churchill (an old Liberal Unionist, if truth be told) permitted Rab Butler and the party's research department to embark on a period of re-education which brought the Tories to accept the need for full employment and the recommendations of the Beveridge Report. He was aided by people like the young Ted Heath, Reginald Maudling and Cuthbert Alport, who, when they entered the House in 1950, found allies of the calibre of David Eccles, Captain Macmillan and Peter Thorneycroft. Can something similar happen again? I doubt it. History is reluctant to repeat itself.

Defeat is a purgative of sorts, but I fear that it will be the better elements in the Tory party who will be flushed down the tubes. It will not be very long before several, like Ted Heath and Hugh Dykes, will sit as Independent Conservatives, or even cross the floor of the House. John Major will have joined the bulk of the 'old' Tory party which events have promoted to the other place, where they will sit upon red benches and regret the passing of time.

29 April

It is not just the Major government that is fighting for its life in this election; it is the Tory party itself. John Major is a moderate Tory, described by one cynical newspaper as 'a clone of Edward Heath'. The Prime Minister has talked of 'One Nation', which has been for many years the slogan of the more progressive Conservative. With an impertinence that is breathtaking, Tony Blair has pinched the phrase and now also talks of One Nation. Both parties are clearly aiming their appeal at the centre ground of politics.

According to MORI, the Tories remain twenty-eight points behind 'New Labour'. It will take something of a miracle to close the gap, let alone overtake Blair and form a fifth Tory government. Were we for the moment to assume that a Tory defeat is inevitable, where would that catastrophe leave what remained of the party? I could only borrow the word used lately to such effect by Miss Anna Ford.

In 1945, after fifteen years of Tory or Tory-dominated governments, Labour won the election with an overall majority of 146. Against 393 Labour MPs, the Conservatives, led by that old Liberal Unionist, Winston Churchill, could field only field 213. Had it not been for party apparatchiks such as Iain Macleod, Michael Fraser and Enoch Powell, and senior MPs such as Rab Butler, Peter Thorneycroft, David Eccles and Harold Macmillan, the Conservative Party might well have reverted to being the party of Neville Chamberlain: narrowly nationalistic, hostile to the wartime Beveridge reforms, bored by European unity and cheerfully unreconstructed. Would we be as unlucky were the results of 1945 to be repeated in 1997? I fear so.

Members of a defeated Tory party, able to muster some 200 MPs, would be at each others' throats. Life would not be worth living in the 1922 Committee. The party's defeat would be blamed on Disraelian Toryism ('there are two nations . . .'), which would be jettisoned in favour of a revived Thatcherism, encouraged by the Lady herself, whose tune from the wings would be 'I told you so.' John Major would be blamed personally by the majority of the survivors, and would, in all likelihood, give notice of his withdrawal from the Commons, leaving the scene open for an autumn leadership campaign. The campaign against him would be opened by Michael Portillo,

Peter Lilley, Michael Howard and John Redwood – the 'bastards' who combined between 1992 and 1997 to make the Prime Minister's life a misery.

The Eurosceptics would come into their own. Our front bench would be packed by people like Bill Cash. Teresa Gorman would be appointed shadow minister for women. Sir Teddy Taylor would re-emerge from obscurity to speak for his native Scotland. Christopher Gill, the Shropshire meat pie manufacturer, would be made shadow agriculture minister, and John Townend would replace Sir Marcus 'Compo' Fox as chairman of the 1922 Committee. Sir Edward Heath, the Father of the House, a lone voice, would be howled down by the massed ranks of the newly elected.

Sixty-two Tory MPs are not standing at the election. Not all are in safe seats, but those of their replacements who are returned would be largely Thatcherite in tone and allegiance. The balance of the party would have shifted dramatically to the right, with all the political consequences that would bring in its wake. The party would eventually become the anti-Europe party: no longer Eurosceptic, but determined to take Britain out of Europe. Such a U-turn would drive the few remaining Tory moderates to cross the floor, either to a reduced Liberal Democratic party or, *à la* Howarth, to Labour itself. The more romantic might consider setting up a Fourth Party with echoes of Lord Randolph Churchill.

Had I been fit enough to stand (and been able to persuade either Aldershot or North Hampshire to adopt me), I would have sat most unhappily on the opposition benches. But all is not yet lost. Victory could be snatched from the jaws of defeat, or the result might be a Labour win with a narrow majority – in which case my analysis would not stand. But eighteen years is too long in what purports to be a parliamentary democracy, and when tossing sleepless in the small hours of the morning, I can see the inevitability of a decisive Labour victory. If so, God help the Tory party I once knew and, at times, loved.

30 April

The night before Waterloo.

It is a sobering thought that the outcome of the battle of Waterloo could have been very different in the era of public opinion polls and the Dimbleby brothers. By late afternoon of 18 June 1815, His Grace the Duke of Wellington might well have been persuaded to throw in the ducal towel. He would have been shown opinion polls demonstrating that 85 per cent of British soldiers (five being interviewed) were suffering from combat exhaustion and had lost faith in his leadership; the Dimblebys would have ridiculed and sneered their way through his campaign plan, and made disparaging comparisons with the brilliance of Napoleon. Fortunately, none of these factors was present to upset the equilibrium of Old Nosey, and the rest . . . well, the rest is history . . . our British history.

Let the Iron Duke's spirit inspire us.

Good luck!

PART III

After the Deluge

MORRISON HALCROW

On Wednesday 30 April, the eve of polling day, the hands of Big Ben got stuck at eleven minutes past noon and time at Westminster stood still for all of half an hour. Maybe Big Ben was trying to warn the Tories that for them the millennium was about to come early.

On the eve of the great New Labour victory there was an even more interesting portent on the stock market. The FTSE 100 index reached a record high. The markets, as we are always being told, like political certainty. And City people, who enjoy seeing a persuasive graph, had been watching the opinion polls which, for weeks now, had been recording a remarkably steady performance predicting a Labour win on a serious scale. The Conservative Party increasingly gave the impression of being out of touch with the City. The people who hold the world's purse strings had been observing the party posturings of the 1990s over British sovereignty, but with detached interest. What mattered were the realities of power. In the City they know that at the end of the day sovereignty is determined not by political correctness at Westminster but by the inexorable forces at work in the global economy.

The actual result of the election, when it came on the Friday morning, momentarily disconcerted some in the City when they saw the scale of the Labour victory and remembered the Labour landslide of 1945 that swept away the Churchill government. But only momentarily. Within hours the post-Major City had marked prices up even higher.

*

The consistency of those near-horizontal lines on their charts had done a power of good during the campaign to the frazzled nerves of the political pollsters. The industry had not had a good election in

1992. This time it still overestimated the Labour share of the vote, but only by a couple of points over the actual figure of 45 per cent; and it only slightly underestimated the Conservative share (31 per cent). Pollsters had worked hard over five years to refine their skills.

So far so good. The public hadn't lied to the interviewers. The shock that unnerved the Conservative Party in the small hours of Friday 2 May wasn't that the predictions for share of vote were wrong, but that, thanks to the first-past-the-post system, these shares were being reflected in a monstrous Labour majority in the House. That was not the pollsters' fault. It was the fault, if fault it be, of generations of politicians who preferred the prospect of unfettered power to the mathematical fairness of proportional representation.

Political pollsters are one of the most respectable of modern election-related professions. The straight horizontal lines on the graphs were less comforting to the newer and more wayward profession of spin-doctoring. The Conservative spin doctors had laboured in vain during the long six-week period which John Major had chosen for the election campaign. There had been no significant narrowing of the gap as polling day approached. No late surge of Tory support as canny voters determined to save themselves from the wild men of Old Labour who were going to emerge from the shadows once New Labour got elected. No last-minute panic about the prospect of being crunched under the European jackboot. No great moments of truth among the focus groups brought together to journey along the road to Damascus. The more we looked at the figures of the 1997 election, the more it seemed that that the voters had simply written John off months ago and paid not a blind bit of notice to the campaign – which meant, among other things, that the party had squandered a lot of money pointlessly on an expensive and sometimes embarrassing advertising campaign, thus ensuring that it would enter opposition under a massive financial handicap.

If this was the case, of course, it also meant that the Labour Party too had squandered resources in pushing on an open door. All the state-of-the-art presentational talent contributed by the gurus of the advertising and PR world, all that intellectual voltage assembled at the 'media centre' in Millbank, all the data-based speech-writing skills, all the computer boffinry applied to 'instant rebuttal' of points raised by the other side's speech-writing, all the sophisticated security applied by the Blair team to prevent the loony left from breaking loose from their kennels – had it all been unnecessary? The arm-twisters and the men in suits and mobile phones keeping the candidates 'on message' could have spent those six weeks down the pub every night and nobody would have noticed the difference.

On the other hand – as speech-writers used to make politicians say, back in the days before such prissy qualifying phrases were banned from party leaders' speeches – Peter Mandelson could fairly point out that the campaign which really mattered had been going on, not for six weeks, but for six years and longer. New Labour had spun its way to a famous victory.

The group who really emerged as blundering amateurs in the 1997 election were not the spin doctors but many of the Conservative Party's loyal door-knockers, the people supposed to know what is happening out in the streets. Salt of the earth, the party's canvassers. But less salty, evidently, than they used to be.

When party workers knock on doors, they know not to accept responses at face value. They know that British voters are polite people who don't, or not often, tell a candidate's representatives to go and stuff something other than envelopes. Good agents and their helpers develop skills which enable them to classify degrees of politeness on the doorstep and which make it possible for helpful and informative messages to be passed up through the hierarchy to Central Office.

Good campaign teams also know, of course, that when they come to add up the figures they don't have to be completely frank with any passing journalist who asks them how things are going on the doorstep. In such circumstances economy with the truth is only to be expected. The awful fact in the '97 election was that the Tory campaign teams not only told white lies to the press but deceived themselves. Many of them really seemed to believe what they were saying when they expressed public puzzlement at the figures being pumped out by Gallup and MORI. We don't understand all those opinion polls, they would say. Here in Old Tescofield, it's not like that at all. We're getting very positive reactions on the doorsteps, very positive indeed.

They deceived themselves for six weeks, and passed the deception up the line. Maybe it didn't matter. Even if they had been more astute, it would have been too late for anyone at Central Office to do much about the state of the party; but the party might have been saved the humiliation of ending up as only a rump of an opposition in the Commons. Certainly the colleagues would have been better prepared psychologically for the shock of election night. Yet even then, at one o'clock in the morning, some of the loyalists were still at it, still deceiving themselves. Against a background of emptied ballot boxes in town halls and leisure centres around the country, they were still desperately feeding pathetic messages to the media. No, no, they would say during the count, as news of the carnage of the early results spilled out from the television screen; no, these extraordinary trends you're hearing about from some other constituencies don't seem to apply here in Old Tescofield – we've been watching the votes pile up on the tables and we assure you . . .

One of the lessons for the elections of the twenty-first century must be that real people, with real doorsteps, matter more than focus groups. How on earth, to look at the scene of the Tories' greatest humiliation, could the party in Scotland have failed to warn Central Office that the official anti-devolution line was seen on Scottish doorsteps as an impertinent irrelevance? The party was left with no Scottish MPs at all. They would have done better under PR.

The faithful volunteers were still the salt of the earth, but in 1997 at least some of them did not enhance their reputation for political shrewdness. This did not bode well for the now frequently discussed idea of reforming the process of electing the party leader to involve constituency parties.

The people who came out of the six-week campaign looking most professional were the voters themselves. They didn't 'sleepwalk' into the election, as John Major, in one of his less felicitous election-eve predictions, had rashly accused them of doing. Seldom had a British electorate taken so much trouble over their votes. Millions of them took the view that this wasn't an 'either/or' two-horse race, even if this meant backing some pretty rum horses. Nearly a million of them voted for Goldsmith's Referendum Party or the UK Independence Party. A massive number of Conservative voters stayed at home – and many seemed to regard this as a positive thing to do, not an opt-out. Others crossed to the Liberal Democrats, as disgruntled Tories have traditionally done for years.

Overall, the voting figures were down, and this led to a potentially dangerous piece of folklore taking shape in the Tory party: namely, that the defeat could be wholly explained by Tory abstentions, and that it would be relatively simple to woo the abstainers back next time. But Tory abstentions were not the whole story by any means. For one thing, not all the abstentions were Tory: there were a lot of traditional Labour voters who didn't like Blair. For another, there was reasonably convincing evidence that perhaps as many as a million Tories went all the way and voted Labour. And if the British people were turning Eurosceptic, which was another essential part of the folklore, they chose a funny way of showing it. There was plenty of anecdotal evidence of downright anti-Europeanism expressed to canvassers on the doorsteps. But the expression of opinion that mattered – the actual election – showed almost twice as many people voting for the two parties, Labour and the Liberal Democrats, whom the sceptics accused of being soft on Europe.

On the fringes of Torydom in Birmingham Edgbaston there was a whispering campaign urging 'Don't vote for a Kraut'. The whisperers woke up to find that the German-raised Gisela Stuart had won that once safe Tory seat of Edgbaston for Labour. Other fringe electioneering, like queer-bashing, didn't do the party much good either. Nor did the strategy of patronising the white-suited Martin Bell as a hopeless idealist who didn't really understand the facts of political life. Martin Bell's victory over Neil Hamilton carried a lesson that the Tories would ignore at their peril.

The 1997 electorate was not somnolent: quite the reverse, it was alert and sophisticated. Tactical voting, hitherto a phrase in the psephology textbooks, became a reality for the ordinary voter, something to be talked of in the queue at the supermarket checkout. It was the extent of tactical voting that proved to be the real killer for Major. The Liberal Democrats actually attracted fewer votes than at the previous election (5.2 million against 6 million in 1992), but they doubled their number of seats in the House. Many Labour candidates, who found to their surprise on 2 May that they had an appointment to turn up at Westminster a few days later to take their oath, owed their success to the fact that staunch Liberals had voted for them, and some of them had been speeded on their way by staunch Conservatives.

Even more surprised, cruelly surprised, were scores of Tories standing in what had been regarded, just days earlier, as safe seats. An

unhappy twist was added to the truism about a week being a long
time in politics. The trauma would take years to heal. After eighteen
years in office, any party finds it hard even to contemplate being
anything but the party of government. And it was a double trauma
for the Eurosceptics, who had discovered, during the last six of those
eighteen years, that a minority of the parliamentary party could hold
their colleagues to ransom. Through the Major years, as the Commons
majority dwindled, an anti-Europe early day motion tabled by the
awkward squad could twist ministerial knickers beyond repair. In a
House with an overwhelming majority the sceptics now had to adjust
to a situation where, if anyone put down an anti-Maastricht motion,
the government whips probably wouldn't even bother to read it.

The Conservatives of 1997 did not even have the consolation available to their predecessors ninety years earlier who were heard to
remark urbanely, after a Liberal landslide victory paved the way for
radical reform under Asquith and Lloyd George, that it didn't really
matter which party was in office, so long as the Tories remained in
power. The establishment no longer ran the country in 1997. (Margaret Thatcher had seen to that.) The Tories had quarrelled with the
business establishment, the financial establishment, the educational
establishment. Certainly the Church of England was no longer the
Tory party at prayer. Even the House of Lords was no longer a
reliable ally.

It would take a long time to face up to the implications of being
out of office – possibly, probably, for ten years rather than five. It
was all very well to say the party had to keep its eye on the far horizon,
to focus on basic principles and not just the nitty-gritty of short-term
opposition. The world of the far horizon was one that many Conservatives, in the days after electoral disaster, couldn't bring themselves to
contemplate. How far would the goalposts have moved by the year
2005? By then, 'Europe' might be something the Tory right had to
live with, not a bogeyman with which to frighten the voters. And –
who could tell? – the whole profession of politics might have been
transformed under a Cromwellian Blairite regime that forbade politicians to earn a bit on the side. To say nothing of political parties
being forbidden to accept gifts from strange foreigners.

The election punished John Major far more harshly than he
deserved. Perhaps the electorate felt like one of those judges who

decide at an early stage in a trial that the defendant is clearly guilty and get increasingly irritated as he insists on spinning out his defence instead of saying 'It's a fair cop, guv' and pleading extenuating circumstances. Would the Conservative Party have fared better, and retained more of its seats, if it had said 'It's a fair cop' a year earlier, in 1996? Or if John Major hadn't chosen to spin out the campaign for six weeks? The second of May 1997 brought a special kind of trauma for John. On his first afternoon of freedom from office, when he went off to watch a cricket match while Tony Blair was appointing his Cabinet, he had to face up to the disagreeable fact which emerged from the details of the result: namely, that there had been a lot of citizens prepared to go to some trouble, many of them changing the voting pattern of a lifetime, to get rid of him. Or at least to see the back of his fractured party.

*

The Conservatives settled down to electing a new leader and rebuilding their party with all the enthusiasm of a bankrupt told by his bank manager to pull himself together, when the only thing that would really cheer him up would be to hear that all his creditors have dropped dead. They didn't feel like pulling themselves together and facing up to long years of opposition. In their heart they still desperately wanted to believe their own election campaign propaganda about how fast a victorious Labour Party would buckle under the strains of office. Within the month, they had warned the electorate, the callow young Blair would be tied in knots by those wily Europeans. Not to mention how Labour's woodwork was riddled with nasty things ready to crawl out if the voters were mad enough to vote for Blair.

In the event, the callow young Blair astonished even his friends. Some were secretly ashamed to admit that the sense of relief during the first days of the Blair administration was palpable. They were reminded of the classic scene in the film *Genevieve* where the incomparable Kay Kendall, to the alarm of her equally inebriated companions, staggers up to the musicians' rostrum and announces that she is going to play the trumpet . . . then – 'By God, she *can* play the trumpet,' they say. How could they ever have doubted?

Labour swept into office with trumpets playing and colours flying. The *chutzpah* was shameless. Neil Kinnock once boasted that the first thing he would do as Prime Minister would be to tear down the gates the IRA had forced Margaret Thatcher to put up at the entrance to Downing Street. Tony Blair made the gesture, but without compromising his safety, by ordering the gates open – only for an hour or so, but it was an important hour: the hour when he drove back from the Palace with the Queen's commission to form a government. There were the ordinary people of Britain, thronging Downing Street to welcome him. He and Cherie got out of their car and walked through the crowd to the door of No. 10. Scarcely a representative crowd, maybe, who had arrived conveniently equipped with little Union flags to wave; it was a vision bite to match the soundbites of the election campaign. And first impressions do matter. A few days later, an appropriate soundbite was worked into the Queen's Speech. Her government, she said, 'intends to govern for the benefit of the whole nation'. The Prime Minister reminded the successful Labour candidates, even before they had gone to the Commons to sign on as MPs, that it was the people who put them there and the people who could throw them out again. 'We are the servants of the people,' he declaimed.

It was easy to be cynical. We all know that those who sign their letters 'Your obedient servant' tend to be pretty arrogant people. As it was, the Conservatives were too shattered even to sneer. The Blair team knew, too, that what disarms cynicism is not words but action. After a couple of years of a government that behaved like an opposition, the public now had ministers who at least went through the motions of moving and shaking things. They arrived in Whitehall like a busy crew of removal men who know they are to be paid by results.

The buzz phrase had been that the Blair team would 'hit the ground running'. They had prepared their war book, setting out what had to be done in the first day, and the first week. They hit the Bank of England running. With the ink of the returning officers' signatures scarcely dry on the election results, Gordon Brown was in a huddle with officials at the Treasury, and the City was astonished, a few days later, when he announced the potentially revolutionary change giving the Bank of England independence to manage interest rates – a coup comparable with Mrs Thatcher's equally unheralded decision back in 1979 to abolish exchange controls and throw the country open to a whole new dimension of world competition. The House not yet being in session, Gordon Brown chose to make his announcement from a podium labelled 'HM Treasury', looking like a presbyterian version of an Arab potentate announcing a new Middle East peace initiative into a microphone bearing a Hyatt Hotels logo. It emerged that the Treasury apparently did not possess a suitable podium and the New Labour Chancellor himself had to advise his officials how to procure one.

A couple of weeks later Chancellor Brown hit again, hiving off the Bank of England's responsibilities for policing lesser banks. This time the Governor was seriously distressed. Overall, however, both these reforms in Threadneedle Street had widespread support among the politically correct and the great and the good, at least in theory. But the great and the good had mostly taken the view that one shouldn't rush such things, as St Augustine said when praying for the gift of chastity. New Labour were making it clear that they wanted their chastity now – and they wanted it sexy.

The new education secretary hit the educational establishment running by confronting the country's headmasters at their annual conference with the revolutionary notion that they were expected to achieve tangible results in their schools. Meanwhile the new Foreign Secretary hit the Foreign Office running with an event, set amid the High Victorian decor of Gilbert Scott's Whitehall palazzo, which would have puzzled Lord Curzon but was instantly recognisable by any modern marketing director: it was a state-of-the-art product launch, complete with multi-media thingies strung from the painted ceilings. Here it was announced that Britain's diplomacy would now be based on a mission statement – like the business plans of image-conscious tycoons and pizza parlour chains. Some of the stiffer elements in the Foreign Office were said to be more upset by the new Secretary of State's instruction to add the *Racing Post* to his daily papers.

Such was the whirr of legs as the government hit the ground, indeed, that some of its less nimble members, weeks later, still had difficulty in remembering at question time which side of the despatch box they were sitting on. The new health secretary, Frank Dobson, would engagingly tell the House, as he had done in opposition, that the defects of the health service were 'all the government's fault'. But Frank – unrepentantly hirsute among smoothly turned out young colleagues who took as much care over their hair styles as over their choice of cufflinks – was widely looked on indulgently as the Cabinet's token Old Labourer, not to be taken very seriously. Tony, understandably, had been unable to make up his mind what to do with the health service yet. He would hit the ground on that in due course.

Mission statement aside, there was a new dawn for diplomacy as New Labour's foreign affairs team found themselves notably more welcome in Europe than their predecessors. After the previous eighteen years, it could scarcely have been otherwise. The first substantive contribution by the new government to the European debate was a prime ministerial speech telling EU socialists that his Tory predecessor might have been wrongheaded about a lot of things but was right when he said that Europe was in danger of pricing itself out of world markets with its cosy old labour practices. In France (where a largely unreconstructed Socialist Party had just swept aside a right-wing government and its austerity programme) the word *Blairisme* was invented to describe something that the French ought to be looking for.

As for Anglo-American relations, the 'unique relationship', as it was now to be called, was fortified at a cosy dinner given by Tony and Cherie for Bill and Hillary at the Pont de la Tour in Terence Conranland at Islington-by-the-River. After the Bollinger 1989 the Prime Minister was reported to have chosen roast leg of rabbit and to have drunk a beer. Meanwhile various American spin doctors sold articles to the British press about how much the Blair style owed to the skill with which the Clinton administration had hit the Washington ground running. Other commentators wrote less kind articles pointing out that the President had shortly thereafter tripped up and found himself exposed in a variety of awkward postures.

*

New Labour hit the ground cunning as well as running. There were crafty undertones to the devolution of power to the Bank of England. Now the Bank, not the Chancellor, could be blamed when mortgage rates went up. Nothing to do with me, guv. The decision also sent out a robust message to Old Labour. New Labour were effectively reversing what had been Labour's very first exercise in nationalisation, under the post-war Attlee government. And boosting the status of the central bank could also be interpreted, by those who chose to do so, as a short but definitive step towards a single currency – but one cautious enough not to frighten the horses.

A whole clutch of chaste initiatives were unveiled in the first weeks. New Labour hit the gun lobby running. They also hit those who trade in land mines. They announced an independent food standards authority to avert further health scandals. The Lord Chancellor, old head of chambers to Blair – both Blairs – after playing a heavyweight role behind the scenes in the election campaign, promised legal reforms to cut the delay and expense of civil justice. The heavyweight John Prescott, as environment supremo, banged the table at a confrontation with the water companies over their leaky pipes. It was all good politics, and difficult for the Conservatives to oppose convincingly, even if they had been in a fit state to do so. Difficult, too, for the Treasury to complain that such things represented a return to the spendthrift ways of Old Labour.

There were plans for greater transparency to be imposed on contributions to political parties. Given the prominence of sleaze in their last couple of years in government, the Tories had difficulty in drumming up great moral outrage over that. They could and did quibble at the Prime Minister's unilateral decision to change the format of his Commons question time. Typical of the arrogance of this new regime, they said. Initial reaction to the new-style once-a-week PM's question time from Westminster *aficionados* was that the exchanges across the despatch box became more boring and less childish. An end of one part of parliamentary civilisation as we knew it, then – but the Tories were under no illusions that this was an issue that would have the masses marching to protest in Trafalgar Square.

Certainly a revolution of a kind was happening during those first few weeks of the Blair regime; but – and here was the cunning again– it was mostly revolution on the cheap, at least in the short run. In political terms it had a more substantial effect than mere trumpet-blowing. The first post-election Gallup poll showed, in the words of the *Telegraph*'s psephologist Anthony King, that 'Labour's honeymoon is so far proving the most passionate in history'. No fewer than 64 per cent of voters reckoned the government's performance in its first month had been good or excellent, and even more said enthusiastically that the Blair team had performed better than they had expected. Overwhelmingly the voters believed they had proved 'honest and trustworthy', and the most extraordinary figure was that 82 per cent felt satisfied with Tony Blair as Prime Minister.

As the Gallup records, going back over half a century, show, this is by no means the voters' typical reaction, one month on, to a government they have just elected. The Blair satisfaction factor of 82 per cent compared with 66 per cent for Clem Attlee after his Labour landslide, with only 55 per cent when he came back to power in 1951 – and with just 41 per cent satisfied with Margaret Thatcher a month after her victory in 1979.

Under the blue skies of the brilliant early summer of 1997, events seemed to conspire to turn the knife in the Conservatives' wounds. The Gallup figures were a reminder that Margaret had gone on to spectacular success after being notably unpopular to start with – but then, she was being compared with Michael Foot's Labour Party. Older Conservatives tried to console themselves by remembering 1964, when Harold Wilson – in his time, like Tony Blair, the youngest prime minister this century – swept into Downing Street promising the 'white heat' of radical change after the electorate had turned its back on a long-entrenched Tory government which had run into trouble. Harold, like Tony, knew all about spin-doctoring – 'the best news editor in the business', they had called him in Fleet Street. And in a couple of years, the Tories of 1997 could say, whistling to keep their spirits up, the Wilson regime looked distinctly dodgy and the white heat was no more than a muddy pink lukewarm memory.

Maybe the same would happen to the Blair magic; but even the most sanguine Tories in 1997 knew there were massive differences between Wilson's victory (with a majority that could be counted on the fingers of one hand) and the Blairite landslide – and it wasn't just a matter of arithmetic. Wilson had the impossible task of presiding over a country still grievously debilitated by the 'English disease' – which he had no chance of curing because the Labour Party was very much part of the cause of that disease. By 1997, the patient was well on the way to recovery, thanks largely (even more gall for the Tories) to the Conservative reforms of the 1980s. Meanwhile the Labour Party itself had been dragged into the twentieth century – with substantial help from the Thatcher assault on trade union powers in the 1980s. The Tories had shot their own foxes. Margaret, they realised ruefully, had dealt Tony Blair some of his strongest cards.

*

Put bluntly, the main reason the electorate got rid of the Major government was simply that they looked as if they couldn't run a whelk stall. Conservatives have never believed they could win elections on doctrine. Their electoral secret weapon throughout the twentieth century was that millions of ordinary people, albeit with a sigh, would say: 'At least they seem to be able to manage things better than the other lot.' In 1997, the party manifestly couldn't manage its relations with Europe, couldn't stop the food industry from poisoning us, couldn't maintain even a facade of rectitude in public life, and certainly couldn't manage itself. As the Gallup figures showed, the electorate's instinct was that on 1 May they had got themselves a government which manifestly, despite Labour having been out of office all those years, knew what it was doing. Running a country, according to one joke current among the New Labour team, is like riding a bicycle or making love. You can read books about it, but you don't know what it's like until you actually try it. Westminster was now swarming with bright young people scarcely old enough to do either when Labour was last in power. But they seemed to show an aptitude for it.

*

The chunkiest bit of the of the fledgling Blair government's pro-gramme was devolution. Not the most propitious battleground for testing the Tories' skills in opposition: the Blair government had a mandate for devolution for Scotland and Wales, no question. Voters may never read party manifestos, but Scottish and Welsh assemblies had been there all right, and all the party leaders had gone on about devolution, and broader issues of constitutional reform, in some detail during the election campaign. It had been, so to speak, a fair fight and Labour had won it. They had won it all the more convincingly because the election had transformed Scotland and Wales into Tory-free zones (to use a fashionable Celtic fringe phrase of 1997). The voters in those countries were clearly trying to tell the Conservatives something.

The Tory party, as if it didn't have enough internal problems to cope with at the start of the new parliament, thus found itself faced, when the devolution plans came up in the Commons, with the kind of challenge familiar to counsel at the Old Bailey defending an old lag who has unwisely made a damning confession in the police interview room. Able advocates, however, relish challenges, and the party put forward one of their ablest silks to open the anti-devolution attack: Michael Howard.

Devolving power to Edinburgh and Cardiff was indeed a lawyer's delight – and that was even before anyone got down to the arcane mysteries of the West Lothian Question which had been embarrassing the Labour Party for quarter of a century. If you have a Scottish parliament doing most of the law-making for Scotland, why should Scotland's solid core of Labour MPs be allowed to retain their considerable power in Parliament at Westminster as well?

But that was for later. The simple first step, the Labour whips thought, would be to get through the promised legislation to authorise a referendum in each country to find out whether people there wanted devolution. At least, that seemed to be the simple bit, before the amendments flowed in – some of them quite frivolous amendments, the whips declared sternly. They decided to limit the debate by using the guillotine. Governments always do this in these circumstances. Oppositions are always outraged. Michael Howard explained why the guillotining of this preliminary stage of the devolution debate was a wholly unprecedented assault on the democratic processes, an outrage against the rights of Parliament on the scale of King Charles arriving to arrest the Five Members. Its enormity, he said, was not remotely to be compared with the guillotine as used by the government of which Michael had been a member. The House listened, fascinated.

There were various ironies in all this. The last serious dispute over guillotining has occurred in relation to the Maastricht legislation. The complaints on that occasion had come from the Eurosceptics, with whom Michael, as a minister, had a certain sympathy. Arguably, the issues at stake then were substantive changes to the constitutional relationship between the UK and Europe, not to the preliminaries to constitutional change, as in the current proposals for referendums. (This, incidentally, was the form of the word now apparently to be accepted as the preferred plural: another sign of the decline of civilisation as we knew it.) Yet another irony was that Eurosceptical constitutional purists never made it clear why, if they were so keen on referendums in relation to Europe (and sometimes for Northern Ireland), they were so reluctant to give them to the Welsh and the Scots.

Logic, however, was not the driving force on the Conservative benches in the early days of the new government. What they wanted was not logic but a gutsy issue that would show up flaws in the shining armour of Blair's champions. The new Tory opposition sensed that they might just be on to something in the way the devolution legislation was being hurried along. The word 'arrogance' was much used. They probably had a point. Admiration there was, unquestionably, out there among ordinary voters for the sheer speed of the Blair government's administrative gymnastics. But it was mixed with streetwisdom which says that any organisation which does that much, that quickly, is probably run by people who may not be altogether, well, nice people. They may even be downright ruthless people. Many ordinary voters *were* worried that the Blair team were cutting corners.

The historically minded, as they stepped back to look at the new government, often dragged out the words of poor old Hartley Shawcross: 'We are the masters at the moment – and not only at the moment, but for a very long time to come,' he had told the Tories after the Labour landslide of 1945. Handily abbreviated as 'We are the masters now,' it had gone down as a classic slogan of political bombast. Like all such slogans, it had probably been intended to mean something a bit more subtle. Sir Hartley Floorcross, as the wags called him, soon to leave Labour and move significantly to the right, was not noted for his modesty, but it is charitable to assume that he wasn't simply uttering a tribal war cry. He was reminding the Tories of 1945, brutally, of a democratic fact of life that Tories were constitutionally slow to acknowledge: namely, the party that gets the most seats is entitled to rule the country. It can only cause grief when anti-government forces try to ignore the rules. Left-wing parties can be guilty too – as the miners, and some Labour councils, were during the Thatcher years when they acted as if they still had a god-given right to their privileges.

New brooms are entitled to sweep clean. New masters are entitled to give orders. Nobody ever said that the defeated have to enjoy it. Nor does it say anywhere that they have to like the people wielding the new brooms.

*

The New Labour success at the polls may have been historically inevitable, but the smooth efficiency of the operation depended significantly on the fairly small group of young people who had come to symbolise what the Blairite revolution was all about. They had been Tony's praetorian guard when he got shot of Clause Four, and when he emasculated the unions. They hadn't actually used physical pressure, but they had made sure that the rough soldiery of the Labour Party shaved and pressed their trousers before they went on parade and didn't talk in a way which would betray complete economic illiteracy. Operating out of the Millbank bunker, they had held together the election campaign itself. Now these same people, pausing only for a brisk swig of champagne at the victory party, had moved round the corner from Millbank to Whitehall.

It was easy to get things out of proportion. Political advisers in Whitehall are not new. Prime ministers have always liked to have a 'kitchen cabinet' of some kind. Harold Wilson took Marcia Williams with him to Downing Street – and there were famous demarcation problems between her and the civil servants. The Major government latterly had some forty 'special advisers' – 'policy wonks', experts in presentation, coordinators, back-room fixers – all political appointees but on the Civil Service payroll. The Blair administration put the figure up to about sixty, an important but not really revolutionary numerical increase. The incomers had a higher profile, though. The media had decided that these young men (and rather fewer young women than was right in the age of positive discrimination) were good copy as a cohesive class. Like the Sloane Rangers of the 1980s, they could be listed on the gossip pages with convoluted diagrams showing how they were interrelated by ancestry, marriage or cohabitation. Young David Miliband, an important figure in the No. 10 Policy Unit, was the son of the Marxist historian Ralph Miliband, once a name to conjure with in the academic hinterland of Old Labour. His brother Ed was brought in to advise Gordon Brown at the Treasury.

The gossipy diagrams had to criss-cross not just Old Labour and New but Thatcherism too. Tony Blair's 'chief of staff' in Downing Street (as he had been in the leader of the opposition's office) was Jonathan Powell, the curly-headed young brother of Charles, now Sir Charles, who had wielded such influence in Downing Street under Margaret. One of the brightest of young journalists ever to emerge from the *Financial Times* stable, Ed Balls, now the Chancellor's adviser, was in private life the partner of Yvette Cooper (former economics correspondent of the *Independent*), who had worked for the Clinton presidential campaign and was now the newly elected Labour Member for Pontefract and Castleford. And so on.

What was new and, some thought, sinister was not the numbers and the evident brainpower of these young people but the fact that, once they were installed in their cubbyholes around Whitehall, they worked as a team or, if you prefer, hunted in a pack. Coordinating the pack, of course, in Whitehall as at Millbank, was Peter Mandelson, now elevated to the post of – somebody had had a good laugh over this – minister without portfolio. As organiser extraordinary of the 1997 general election campaign, Mandelson had been accused of using his network like a team of Jesuits going round to warn of the awful penalties faced by those who fall away from the pure doctrine. Jesuitical zeal is never universally popular, even among the faithful. It raises questions of strained loyalties, of a faith within the faith. But it worked in securing a remarkable degree of consistency of doctrine in the Labour camp during the campaign.

The same techniques were now applied in Whitehall. Mandelson presided over daily prayer meetings of the team to take an overview of – more accurately, to enable the Prime Minister to keep his eye on – how far the pure doctrine was being applied across the whole government machine. Was the minister for so-and-so briefing a lobby correspondent? Mandelson had to know, lest the wrong message went out. (It had been decreed early on that briefings shouldn't be done over lunch. Lunches would in themselves send out the wrong message.) What was the minister going to say? When would he/she say it? Announcements had to be timed to achieve maximum impact. (Frank Dobson got into trouble for announcing a ban on tobacco advertising on the day that John Prescott wanted to keep the headlines to himself for his environmentally friendly water policy.)

The various strands of the Mandelson machinery all had precedents. Downing Street has always tried to stop ministers saying embarrassing things. The new regime would have had little to teach Bernard Ingham about the timing and style of announcements. Mandelson himself claimed, in a letter to *The Times*, that the machinery had always been there. The difference was that it was now 'thankfully, more effective and decisive'. However, the new arrangements were seized on by the Tories as proof that New Labour was Old Stalinism. John Major railed at the 'politicisation of the Civil Service'. It didn't actually delight Labour MPs either. It was one thing to submit to a central disciplinary machine to stop things going wrong during an election campaign. The prospect of central control for the whole of a five-year parliament was something else.

Nor was Peter Mandelson the only coordinator at work. A special role had been reserved for the Prime Minister's old friend and mentor and now Lord Chancellor, the burly Lord Irvine, another representative of the Scottish ascendancy in New Labour. Irvine it was who had licked the young Tony Blair into shape when he was a bright young barrister in Irvine's chambers (although not as bright as another young barrister there called Cherie Booth). During the election campaign his profile might not have so high as Mandelson's, but he had been a vital part of the power base at Millbank. Now the Prime Minister gave him the role of pulling together and setting priorities within the New Labour programme.

Events would determine the fate of the ship of state under Blair. But the Prime Minister, in the summer of 1997, looked like a captain who had taken every possible precaution to batten down everything that could be battened to withstand storms. A Captain Bligh, perhaps.

Disquiet over the arrival of the apparatchiks was voiced, fairly early on, by no less a figure than the Cabinet Secretary, Sir Robin Butler. The occasion was the idea that Jonathan Powell's role in No. 10 should be formalised by appointing him, and not a career civil servant, to the post of principal private secretary to the Prime Minister. Sir Robin let it be known that he was 'seriously unrelaxed' about this. This was real Sir Humphrey stuff: urbane, witty, with a horseshoe concealed in the boxing glove. As a piece of Whitehall phrasemaking it ranked with Sir Robert Armstrong's 'economical with the truth' and the prize phrase from the Scott inquiry about 'presentational problems'.

The announcement that a mandarin is 'seriously unrelaxed' means that he intends to fight to the death, draw lines in the sand and mutter about constitutional proprieties. It also means that compromises can be reached. A compromise was reached. Powell continued as chief of staff. The Civil Service would produce a private secretary, but his role would be restricted. He would be responsible, it was explained, for matters like relations with Buckingham Palace.

It was all straight out of *Yes, Prime Minister*. But behind the particular wrangle was a major structural issue which politicians of all parties knew they were going to have to face up to. They knew that some of the most intractable of issues, like dragging the welfare state into the twenty-first century, probably couldn't be tackled without real change in the departmental structure. Margaret Thatcher had toyed with, but rejected, the idea of a powerful machine in Downing Street to drive her reforms through. She had her own ways of putting lead in the political pencil. John Major had belatedly tried to use Michael Heseltine to give a political dimension to the coordination of policy which the mandarins liked to keep in their own hands.

In 1997, Britain wanted change. That much was clear from the election result. They wanted change of a kind that perhaps couldn't be provided within the structure of the traditional party system, or the traditional Civil Service system as it was laid bare by Scott. The Blair assault on the decision-making processes may have been arrogant and clumsy. But he was on to something. As he settled into the business of being a powerful head of government in the summer of 1997, the new, untried, Tory opposition watched in awe. What was happening in Whitehall was as good a measure as any of the size of the mountain they had to climb.

PART IV

Steering the Ship of Fools
The Tory Leadership Contest
2 May–20 June 1997

JULIAN CRITCHLEY

William Coutts has got the flu,
And Billy Higgins would never do,
And Guy de Vere is far too young,
and wasn't D'Alton's father hung?
And as for Alexander Byng! . . .
I think I know the kind of thing,
A churchman, cleanly, noble born,
Come, let us say Godolphin Horne?
But hardly had he said a word,
When murmurs of dissent were heard,
The King of Iceland's Eldest Son,
Said, 'thank you, I am taking none!'
The aged Duchess of Athlone
Remarked in her sub-acid tone,
'I doubt if He is what we need!'
With which the Bishops all agreed;
And even Lady Mary Flood
(So kind, and Oh so really good)
Said 'No'. He wouldn't do at all,
He'd make us feel a lot too small . . .

From *Cautionary Tales* by Hilaire Belloc

2 May

Not since the days of the Duke of Wellington in the 1830s has the Conservative Party suffered so severe a defeat. Now the defeated Tories will begin what must surely be a long and bitter post-mortem. They must also decide upon a new leader.

John Major is the principal casualty: always under-rated, and his achievements – the 1992 election result and the restoration of the economy – largely disregarded. The Thatcherite wing held him in contempt, and he never really emerged from the shadow of the 'Queen over the Water'. Ironically, he was at his best defending Europe and the common currency, but then spoilt the effect by giving the other point of view. He had fought the good fight and deserved better of his party. Who was it who once said that there is no such thing as gratitude in politics?

The Conservative Eurosceptics, who did badly at the polls, will blame first Ken Clarke, then Michael Heseltine, and finally John Major for the party's defeat. The Tory moderates will blame the 200-odd Conservative candidates who disregarded the party's manifesto over Europe. They will not forgive Angela Browning and Angela Rumbold (who not undeservedly lost her seat), who were the first to raise the tattered banner of Euroscepticism and disown party policy, or those of John Major's Cabinet colleagues who, by nods and winks, helped to sink the ship.

There is little doubt that the Conservative campaign was badly managed. Defeatism was rife within the party from the outset. Even the most loyal of Conservatives realised that John Major suffered from two insuperable handicaps. First, he had to carry the can for eighteen years of Conservative government, despite the fact that he had been in power for only five of them. As Prime Minister he had had the roughest of rides. Described initially by Margaret Thatcher as 'pure gold', John inherited the Lawson recession, the Gulf War, and the need to raise taxes. The 'honeymoon' between Margaret and John lasted barely a fortnight. 'Dear John' soon became Margaret's enemy and the target of hostility from the Thatcherite wing of the party (who had deceived themselves by voting for him in 1990) as well as continual sniping from Margaret herself. It did not go unnoticed that Denis Thatcher's estimate of Major's chances of election victory was 'nil'– a point of view uttered from the safety of Hong Kong in the last week of the campaign.

Secondly, the party was split from top to bottom over Europe, a division of opinion that could not be long disguised. In view of this, it was foolish beyond belief for the Tory strategists to focus upon Europe and not upon the booming economy. Rattled by the extent of the Eurosceptic revolt within the ranks of his candidates, Major disregarded his Chancellor's advice and played the 'Eurosceptic card'. He did not take the trick.

The secret defeatists included those who stood to gain most from John Major's defeat. The guilty men included Michael Portillo (who,

ironically, lost his seat), Michael Howard, who has long seen himself as
a future party leader, and John Redwood, who contested the leadership
unsuccessfully two years ago. They went through the motions of campaigning for victory, but they knew that only defeat, which would
bring about John Major's withdrawal sooner or later, would suit their
book. They were the 'men of Vichy'.

John Major swiftly announced his resignation as Tory leader.
Clearly he did not want to preside over the rump of a defeated party,
the majority of whose survivors blamed him for its humiliation. He
did not, however, immediately make it clear when the election for his
successor would be held. July? November? In the intervening period
Major will surely appoint a shadow Cabinet which will include all the
contenders – save for Redwood, whom he hates with a healthy passion.

It is the 1922 Committee of back-benchers that runs a Conservative
leadership election, and as its chairman Sir Marcus Fox ('Foxy' to his
enemies) has just lost his seat, the first task before the party will be
to elect a new chairman of the '22. This will probably be Sir Geoffrey
Johnson Smith, an existing vice-chairman who survived in Sussex.
Major's own first task will be to appoint a Chief Whip. I think Goodlad
will be replaced by Sir Norman Fowler.

The party should not act precipitately in choosing its new leader.
Delay would give it time to recover its balance, and, one hopes, its
wits, after so severe a defeat. It could also mean that the party conference due to be held in Brighton in early October would provide 7,000
defeated party activists with the pleasure of observing the antics of
the competing candidates. An election in mid-November would give
adequate time for left and right to sort themselves out, and for each
side to field the candidate of its choice. The disadvantage of waiting
until November would be the ushering in of a lengthy period of party
strife. But the public will be less interested in this than in Blair's first
'One Hundred Days', the Queen's Speech, the first New Labour
budget, the inevitable rise in interest rates, and just how well or
badly the Prime Minister fares at the Amsterdam intergovernmental
conference in June.

John Major laboured under a third handicap, too, namely the hostility of the Murdoch press and the equivocal attitude taken up by
Conrad Black's *Telegraph*. Both Murdoch and Black saw Major as
weak and indecisive. He was rubbished by their corps of columnists

and ridiculed by their cartoonists. Blowhards like Boris Johnson accurately reflected *Telegraph* editor Charles Moore's brand of 'Conservatism'. Murdoch has long been an enemy of British institutions, from the monarchy downwards. Profit is all. He saw the way the wind was blowing. The decision, taken nominally by the editor of the *Sun*, to encourage Essex man to vote Labour must have played a part in Labour's victory. This was followed by a change of heart, towards the end of the six-week campaign, by the editor of the *News of the World*, a working-class institution in which the sins of the great and small, and in particular of clergymen, have long been paraded before a huge, if barely literate, readership. Its leaders had, in the past, always been Tory, but probably went largely unread. The paper did, however, give a platform to Tories like Norman Tebbit. *The Times*, once the 'journal of record', came out in favour of Eurosceptics of whatever party, ranging from lunatic right-wingers like Tony 'Blazer' Marlow in the Tory party to the dotty veteran Tony Benn in Old Labour. This curious endorsement worked (or should have) in favour of mavericks like Sir James Goldsmith who, despite his billions, lost his deposit in Putney. Perhaps he will stand for election in Mexico?

Thus two rich men and a handful of bar-room pundits first split the Tory party and then brought about its defeat. Why does not Britain follow the French example and permit only its nationals to own newspapers and television stations?

Europe was the 'Aunt Sally' of the campaign. Brussels was unfairly blamed for the beef crisis, the shrinking stocks of fish and the proposal for a single currency. Murdoch and Black cheerfully played the jingoist card, threatening the British people with loss of both sovereignty and identity. Their organs made much use of the meaningless bogey word 'federal'. They lied in their teeth, distorting the objectives of Europe and making villains out of its leaders. The broadsheets frequently compared Chancellor Kohl to Bismarck, safe in the knowledge that their readers knew little or nothing about the Second Reich. For 'Bismarck' read 'Hitler', although nobody was crass enough to make a direct comparison. Our right-wing and largely foreign-owned press stoked the fires of latent anti-German feeling in order to bolster the electoral chances of Eurosceptics, regardless of party. In consequence, Tony Blair became Prime Minister. They could only have been believed by a nation in decline, a Britain that has lost its self-confidence. Can Tony Blair restore it? If so, some advantage will be gained from his landslide victory.

Schadenfreude lurks below the surface of many a Tory. Looking down the list of defeated Conservative MPs today – some 123 lost their seats – I cannot fail, in all honesty, to rejoice at some departures while regretting some others. For example, I was not sad to learn of the defeat of Norman Lamont at Harrogate. He took advantage of the despatch of a perfectly adequate sitting MP, Robert Banks, only to fall a surprise victim to the Liberal Democrats. I do regret the defeat of Robert Atkins, a 'cheerful chappie' who once travelled the canals of England in the company of a younger John Major. And the absence of Hugh Dykes, a leading pro-European, whose talents were never recognised by an unheeding whips' office, will surely be lamented.

Nick Budgen is a character. He is pretty tight-fisted and a passionate Eurosceptic; he also tried to play the race card in Wolverhampton. But he is clever and amusing and will be missed. No doubt he will spend his enforced leisure riding to hounds and writing wittily for the newspapers.

David Evans, the Luton Bugle, has at last run out of wind. I shed no tears for Michael Forsyth, an able right-winger, or for Sir Marcus Fox. Martin Bell might well have done Neil Hamilton a favour. Better to be defeated than run the risk of expulsion from the Commons. I cannot help but admire his wife's loyalty and pluck.

Jim Lester, a brave Tory moderate, will be a loss, which is more than can be said for the eccentric, blazer-wearing Tony Marlow, long thought of as a secret major in the Freikorps. I am sorry that the Tory party has lost both its Mitchells, father (Sir David, who retired) and son (Andrew, whose promising career has been interrupted by defeat). Sir Donald Thompson, a charming black-pudding manufacturer, will also be missed. David Shaw of Dover is a thug, who should be able to carve out a career for himself in the security business. As a former MP for Rochester I was interested to learn of the passing of Dame Peggy Fenner, who, after my defeat by Mrs Anne Kerr in 1966, inherited my old seat (now Medway). Jonathan Aitken, a rich and elegant right-winger who has always showed political courage, will be sorely missed. I could go on.

The defeat of the Major government could be as significant a political event as Robert Peel's repeal of the Corn Laws, or Balfour's defeat in the 1906 election. Eighteen years of Tory government could be followed by as many years in opposition. What alarms me is the absence of clever people like Rab Butler, the young Iain Macleod and Ted Heath in the Research Department, and Tory MPs of the quality of Macmillan, Eccles and Thorneycroft, who, after the defeat of the Churchill government in 1945, persuaded the Conservative Party to play in tune with the times. We accepted Beveridge and the need for full employment. What we have today is the promise of discordancy. Were Howard to become Tory leader, some Conservatives would cross the floor of the House, taking refuge among the Liberal Democrats. A Howard-led party would swiftly come to resemble a continental nationalist party, left stranded by the mainstream of contemporary politics. Such a Conservative Party could well be eventually replaced by the Liberal Democrats. What we have seen in 1997 is the end of the postwar Conservative Party, if not of the Tory party itself . . .

3 May

Out of the many statistics to be extracted from the 1997 general election, I think the most significant is the turnout of 71 per cent. In 1992, it was 77 per cent. A six-point drop can be explained in part by disillusioned Tories sitting on their hands (as I did in Ludlow, being unwilling to vote for Chris Gill). The disillusioned appear to be Tories unhappy with the Eurosceptic attitude adopted by the Conservative government and leadership. This can be demonstrated by the votes garnered by Goldsmith's Referendum Party and the UK Independence Party, who must have taken what would otherwise have been Tory votes. But that still leaves the uncomfortable fact that 29 per cent of the electorate did not bother to vote for anyone.

The second most significant statistic is that Labour was elected on 45 per cent of the vote and yet gained the party's largest ever majority. The Tories, of course, stayed in government for eighteen years on no more than 44 per cent of the vote. Is there not an argument for re-examining the case for proportional representation – all the more so because Blair once promised Ashdown a referendum on the subject? A 1997 election under PR would have given a very different result: a small Labour majority, balanced by the combined strengths of the Tory and Liberal parties.

It is the size of its majority that poses the real danger to the Blair government. Behind the Labour front bench will sit a motley army of inexperienced, single-issue MPs, many of whom will be of low grade. The trade union element has been reinforced, and one cannot but wonder how many of 'New' Labour's back-benchers are really 'Old' Labour. Time will tell. We heard nothing during the election of Benn, Banks and Livingstone.

The enthusiasm with which the other European Union governments have welcomed Blair's victory demonstrates how thoroughly John Major's Conservative Party dissipated the goodwill we once enjoyed among our European partners. It blamed Europe for not accepting British beef, ignoring the fact that both the United States and Canada banned our beef exports long before Brussels did. Major's threat of non-cooperation, forced upon him in part by his own weakness and in greater part by his hostile back-benchers, achieved nothing save the irritation, even enmity, of our partners. No wonder Messrs Kohl, Santer and Chirac have said 'good riddance'.

The *Guardian* published a chart showing the prejudices of the newly elected Tory MPs. They divided the Members into three arbitrary categories: pro-Europe, party loyalist and sceptic. The chart showed 20 per cent pro-European Tories, plus 3 per cent pro-European 'loyalists': a total of 23 per cent. On the other side of the equation there were 17 per cent 'agnostic loyalists', 27 per cent 'sceptic loyalists', and 31.5 per cent sceptics. If all the 'agnostic loyalists' are added to the pro-Europeans the total equals 40 per cent. Add the sceptic loyalists to the sceptics and the figure is 58.5 per cent: an 18.5 per cent majority for the sceptics. This is the field on which the Tory leadership campaign must be fought.

5 May

Who will be the contenders for the leadership of the Tory party in opposition? First, the Minnows, who include Stephen Dorrell and William Hague. Stephen Dorrell, who at forty-six is older than he looks, seems to have spoilt his chances during the election campaign. A left-winger, he tried to move to the right, thus losing old friends without, as yet, winning any new ones, while his views on Scottish devolution earned him a rebuke from John Major. He is articulate and clever, and a nice bloke; but I fear the role he will play in a summer election for the party leadership will be to take votes away from Ken Clarke.

William Hague, once the 'boy wonder' of the party, seemed for ever on the verge of making mischief. Hague is now thirty-six, and we have known, ever since he obliged Mrs Thatcher to get to her feet after a rabble-rousing party conference speech he gave at the age of sixteen, that he has the gift of the gab. But does he stand for anything, save a nebulous right-wingery? He does not look the part of national leader. His boyish, if balding, appearance marks him out as a juvenile who had not the time during the Major government to establish himself as a political figure of the first rank. In the election he could come through the middle, but many would not welcome such a prospect.

Both must surely wait their turn, which, given the size of the Labour majority, could work to their advantage; for it will take at least two general elections for the Tories to regain power.

Among the Sharks, Michael Portillo, a Great White indeed, lies stranded on the beach. His defeat was not unwelcome. Portillo, who, as Secretary of State for Defence, once confused NATO with the European Union, and claimed, when he thought he would not be reported, that continental children 'bought' their exam results, brought disgrace upon himself. Yet he fought a careful election campaign, his head well beneath the parapet. And he might once have been the favourite to succeed John Major. However, it will be a year or two before the Tories begin to win by-elections, by which time the party will have, for better or worse, a new leader.

John Redwood is the Eurosceptics' John the Baptist and the party's Michael Foot (but without either the eloquence or the charm). His head seems destined to end up on a platter. Delay on the part of John Major and his own personal unpopularity, even among elements of the right, will work against him. He gives a sinister impression, especially on television (where Clarke comes over as an 'honest bloke'), and his unremitting hostility towards John Major has made him many enemies, not only on the moderate, One Nation wing of the party. He is certainly clever – too clever by half, in fact – and articulate with it; but he is a schemer lacking political good manners. Long may he remain to dine in the College of All Souls.

Peter Lilley came across surprisingly well when I watched him on television over the May Bank Holiday. He clearly has intelligence and a certain fluency. But his reputation is that of a slightly 'wet' (not in the Thatcher-era political sense) young man of extreme right-wing views. Cast at party conferences as 'the enemy of the single mother', there has been, in the past, something cheap about him. The Portillo vote will fancy him, but I do not see him as the Blair of the Tory party. Even so, he remains a serious challenger, unlike the Wokingham Warlock.

Michael Howard narrowly held Folkestone. He has not yet received Lady Thatcher's endorsement (which Portillo secretly did), and gives rise to more hostility than any of the other candidates, save for Redwood. What are we to make of him? A Welsh Jew who first made his name in the Bow Group, Howard married a sixties model whose face appeared for many years on every pack of Lux toilet soap. Now aged fifty-six, he is a pleasant enough fellow who claims he was loyal to John Major throughout the election; but he is also a clever lawyer – a very different kind of Welsh lawyer from, say, Geoffrey Howe – and a man who would not hesitate to stoop to conquer. As Home Secretary he was not the judges' friend; his so-called reforms seemed to them a series of attempts to usurp the function of the judiciary. He was unenlightened in his dealings with the prison population, and was rebuked by Judge Tumim, Her Majesty's Chief Inspector of Prisons, for his reactionary views and actions. Howard made crime his own, and, taking over at the Home Office in the wake of a liberal like Douglas Hurd, he seemed unnecessarily severe. It seemed at times that it was his ambition to fill the prisons to overflowing, rather than to reduce their numbers. Nor did he succeed in building an adequate number of new prisons. Howard was at his most effective at Tory party conferences where his strong line on crime went down well with the party activists.

He was a good performer in the House, but his oily manner and curiously accented voice do not come over well on television, and he had a poor election campaign, deliberately kept off the box and prevented from raising the immigration issue. He is the champion of the authoritarian, populist right and will benefit from Michael Portillo's defeat at the polls. While not as sinister as John Redwood, he will find it difficult to place himself between Redwood and the juvenile lead, William Hague. The 'dream ticket' might have carried the day for Howard, but on his own, he may not be a match for Kenneth Clarke.

And what of the Tory moderates? A foreign observer of the Tory party's leadership election might wonder at the shortage of left-wing candidates. The contest seems monopolised by the right: Howard, Hague, Lilley and Redwood. (Gillian Shephard has wisely dropped out: a pleasant and able woman, and not too right-wing, she must have realised that, following Margaret's reign, it would be a long time before we chose another woman leader.) Three people might have represented One Nation Toryism: Chris Patten, Michael Heseltine and Ken Clarke. Stephen Dorrell is, as I have noted, not yet first-division material.

Chris Patten is the forgotten man; some would say the party's lost leader. His defeat in Bath while party chairman in 1992 was a double blow to the Conservative Party. He was, like the young Gladstone, 'the rising hope of the stern unbending Tories', often spoken of as a future leader of a party comfortable in office. Major sent him swiftly to be the last Governor of Hong Kong, where he performed admirably enough given the inevitability of the Chinese takeover in June 1997. How can he be brought from Hong Kong back to Westminster? After the Conservative defeat, he announced that he would not be a candidate for the leadership. This was hardly surprising as it would have been impossible to find him a Tory seat in time for a June vote. An elderly Tory MP might have persuaded to relinquish his seat for the greater good of the party, but, even were this opening to be contrived, given the rugged independence of local Tory party associations Patten might fall at the last hurdle. And anyway, he could not relaunch his political career in time. Nor could the sacrificial victim be rewarded, save possibly in Major's dissolution honours. But Patten will be back, and has a major part to play, particularly were a Howard-led Tory party to split under the pressure of events.

Michael Heseltine, the biggest beast in the Tory jungle, has said he will not be a candidate. He fought the good fight, but his efforts on behalf of the party seem to have served to ruin his health. In any case, he would be seventy-five before he could become Prime Minister, assuming it takes two elections for the Tories to replace Labour. He will surely retire to the Lords. Always a 'big man', and the most charis-matic of Tories, he might have been able to garner some votes from the right of the Tory party, but it is useless to speculate. The man who, as an Oxford undergraduate in 1953, plotted his route on the back of an envelope in Long John's Restaurant fell at the last fence.

That leaves the former Chancellor, Kenneth Clarke, whose hat was first in the ring, to carry the banner. He will be the candidate of the old, postwar Tory party in direct line of succession from Churchill via Macmillan and Heath – and even Margaret. Were I still a Tory MP, Clarke would certainly get my vote. As Chancellor, he was responsible for reviving the economy without increasing inflation – a trick pulled off in the past only by Roy Jenkins. In the election, he fought to win. He bribed nobody, and was fearless in telling the truth, brave enough to stand out against the tide of chauvinism that engulfed the Conservative Party. More important than his views on Europe is his all-round political ability. Clarke has personal qualities which his rivals lack, and has shown himself capable of holding down the highest offices in the land. In an ideal world, he would make by far the best Conservative leader of the opposition. A politician with the appeal of a 'good bloke', never reluctant to permit himself to be photographed in public bars, a pint in one hand and a pie in the other, he is a formidable debater, a bruiser, capable of taking on the Labour government's front bench and winning. Macmillan's dictum was that the first task was to establish dominance in the House, then over the party, and, what will follow is growing support within the country. Of the rivals, I can see only Ken Clarke achieving this progression. But the nature of the newly elected Tory party has cast him as de Gaulle to Michael Howard's Pétain.

Clarke has said that he would not be in favour of a 'fudged entry' into a common currency (would anyone else in Europe be in favour of doing so?) and that he would permit his MPs a free vote on European issues. This is a cunning move. It would enable the party to remain more or less united, while moving gradually to a common position once the Blair government's attitude to further integration became clear.

Clarke is the only one of the Tory candidates capable of restoring Conservative morale in the House of Commons. He is not as obsequious as Howard, as sinister as Redwood, or as untried as William Hague. For the better sort of Tory – and sadly, most of them seem to have either retired from the Commons or taken refuge in the Lords – Clarke is their man.

Messrs Redwood, Howard and Lilley will offer tempting alternatives to boring old Majorism: populism, extreme Euroscepticism,

pledges of sweeping tax cuts and the minimalist state. They will offer
to wrap themselves in the Union flag. The final will surely be fought
out between Kenneth Clarke and Michael Howard, with Howard
needing to persuade fewer MPs to change sides in order to win than
Clarke.

The Tories will also have to decide upon a Chief Whip. Norman
Fowler would make a good Chief Whip, and has the authority of long
service. But there are other MPs who fancy him as the next chairman
of the 1922 Committee, although the obvious choice there appears
to be Geoffrey Johnson Smith, the vice-chairman and the sole survivor
of the pre-election executive committee.

6 May

One by one the contenders for the Tory party leadership have written
their manifestos, which they have happily sold to the broadsheets. It
might be fun to examine these examples of special pleading, one by
one.

Let us begin with Peter Lilley, a right-winger of deceptively youthful appearance who has drawn most attention to himself by his
speeches at a series of Tory party conferences. In today's *Daily Telegraph*, under the heading 'Reunite, Rebuild and Renew', he writes:
'Churchill always advised Conservatives to "trust the people".' He
will not be alone in dragging Churchill's name into his prospectus.
Churchill was both loved and hated by the Conservatives. He was, in
fact, a Liberal Unionist, and his wife Clementine voted Liberal all
her life; but WSC has become a Tory totem, despite the fact that he
was almost de-selected in Epping in April 1939 for his opposition to
Chamberlain. Anyway, 'trust the people' does not mean very much.

Lilley continues: 'We have to recognise and respond to the message
the people have sent us. And it was a message of rejection for us
rather than approval for Labour. After all, Labour received fewer
votes than we did in 1992. But that means that the collapse in our
support was all the more serious.' So far, so good. Two comments
are surely worth making: the percentage voting dropped from 77 per
cent to 71 per cent; and the swing towards Labour averaged over 10
per cent, which does suggest a degree of approval.

The candidate goes on: 'The ERM fiasco [I do not remember Lilley speaking out against entry or, indeed, resigning after we quit], the recession [caused in the main by the Lawson-induced boom designed to win the 1987 election] and the tax increases which resulted all contributed to that collapse.' But, he says, 'those policy issues were compounded by deeper causes – division at Westminster [in which he played an active part, being one of John Major's so-called 'bastards'], decay of our grass roots organisation and our local government base [true, but the phenomenon is largely self-correcting] and degradation of our image [by which I assume he means sleaze; true again, although we suffered more from press ridicule than from a general moral disapproval: when it comes to matters of morality, the public puts journalists on a par with politicians].'

'Unity', he proclaims, 'is paramount. A party at odds with itself cannot be at one with the nation.' What can one say to that, save 'Gentlemen will please adjust their dress before leaving'?

Nobody with any experience of politics expects politicians to give their opponents the benefit of the doubt, but the next paragraph is a bit breathtaking. 'Cracks are already appearing in Labour over Europe. During the election, Tony Blair hid his Eurofederalism behind a Eurosceptic mask.' Here the mind does begin to boggle. Whatever the word 'Eurofederalist' may mean, Blair is not one. And as for Eurosceptic masks, Lilley and the like-minded had no need of masks; they did not bother to hide their opposition to John Major's policies. 'Now, with breathtaking contempt for the electorate, Blair appears hell-bent on European integration . . .' According to Lilley's own assumptions 45 per cent of the electorate voted Labour and 20 per cent Liberal Democrat, both parties less Eurosceptic than the bulk of the Tories, so how come 'contempt'? The use of the word 'hell-bent' tells us that a Lilley-led Tory party would be an anti-European party. And the Tory party, lest we are allowed to forget the fact, is the party of Harold Macmillan and Ted Heath.

Much further on, Lilley seems to hint at the desirability of widening the franchise for the leadership election beyond the 165 survivors of the 1922 Committee, a wheeze once suggested, but hurriedly dropped in 1990, by Michael Heseltine. And in respect of 'yoof', Lilley 'intends to be accessible and responsive to their views'.

Perhaps the most interesting part of Lilley's prospectus – most of which borders on the unreadable – is the passage where he writes:

'After our crushing defeat in 1945, Rab Butler's renewal of Tory policy thinking paved the way for our return within six years. We need a similar renewal to restore our rapport with the British people.' I have already pointed out that Rab moved the party towards the centre, not to the right of dinosaurs like Sir Waldron Smithers. In which direction would Leader Lilley move the Tory party? Not to the centre, surely.

Lilley is intelligent and articulate; but he is not an impressive figure, and most certainly lacks Blair's 'glitz', if not the 'glibness' he ascribes to the new Prime Minister. Frankly, he does not look the part. Compared to the candidates of 1964, he has neither Reggie Maudling's brains and bonhomie nor Ted's razor-sharp mind and dogged determination. Compared to those of 1974, he has neither Margaret Thatcher's glamour nor Willie Whitelaw's 'bottom'; he would be a boy sent on a man's errand.

7 *May*

Thinking Tories, in the aftermath of a crushing defeat, when 'Middle England' deserted their party in droves, are worried lest the Conservative Party make the same mistake as did Labour, after Mrs Thatcher's first victory in 1979, when it chose a leader to appease its extremists – Michael Foot – rather than one – Dennis Healey – to appeal to the country at large. If it elects a Eurosceptic right-winger such as Howard, Lilley or, in particular, John Redwood, the Tory party might well fail to gain any advantage from the Blair government's eventual and inevitable unpopularity. Political honeymoons are notoriously short-lived.

As a consequence of Michael Foot's narrow victory over Dennis Healey (surely the best Prime Minister Britain never had), the Labour Party split, giving birth to the Social Democrats. The same could happen to the Tories, for there are not a few Tory MPs – including one who said as much when we took lunch together on the Sunday after polling day – who would quit the party were it to fall into the hands of, say, 'the urban fox', as John Redwood is known within John Major's extended family.

While Peter Lilley offered his prospectus to the nation in the columns of Conrad Black's *Telegraph* yesterday, John Redwood did as much in Murdoch's *Times*. Let us examine carefully what it was John Redwood had to say.

The piece was headed 'I can't defend the past; I can unite the party'. I would not have expected him to defend the past, but I find it very hard to believe that he, among the plethora of candidates on offer, could reunite the Tory party. The split over Europe could be terminal.

Beneath a photograph of a shirt-sleeved Redwood looking pensive, the subs had written on his behalf: 'In sadness at the size of our defeat, in humility at the verdict of the people, but with optimism for the future, I put myself forward for the leadership.'

Redwood began by saying that it was not a time for recrimination. 'We all feel a sense of loss. It is like being at the bedside when a well loved relative has been badly hurt. It doesn't help to hurl insults or to abuse the doctors.' Could 'the relative' have been at the kerb while Redwood was driving dangerously? Is this a plea in mitigation? I'm not sure the 165-strong 'jury' will take so forgiving a view. It was, after all, John Redwood who took advantage of his party's turmoil to stand against the then Prime Minister, and in the middle of a parliament. Are Tory memories that short?

Later on, Redwood touches on *les événements de* 1995. He writes: 'I wanted the government to apologise for this mistake [entering and then leaving the ERM. Did Redwood resign at the time?], and to keep VAT down as was promised in the 1992 election. I was unsuccessful in making my case within government. So in 1995, when John Major resigned [the party leadership, but, in effect, the premiership], I made the difficult decision to give up my Cabinet job.' He continues blithely: 'I tried to shock the government into a change of tone, style and policy. I hoped it would generate the change we needed to have a chance of winning the general election.'

These are weasel words.

Mr Redwood, who suffers from an image problem (is he quite right in the head?), chose the Goring Hotel in which to put forward his somewhat tenuous claim to the leadership of the Tory party. How very unfortunate! When asked at his press conference when he would reveal the names of his backers, Redwood archly replied: 'We will be doing the dance of the seven veils. It is so much more exciting that way.' I have a feeling that Redwood will remain overdressed.

Were Redwood to be picked as the next leader of the Tory party,

I would not eat my hat, but I would be certain that any number of Tory MPs would abandon ship, perhaps in order to found a fourth party (British Christian Democrats?), or even, if the worst came to the worst, to join up with Paddy Ashdown's band of forty-six Liberal Democrat MPs.

8 May

Michael Howard's campaign got off to a bad start. William Hague, having spent an evening with Howard in which the two forged a 'dream ticket' (their words, not mine) and sealed their bond in champagne, went home and slept on it. The next morning, as Howard held a press conference which he expected his running-mate to attend, Hague announced that the deal was off. Champagne was no match, it seemed, to a telephone answering machine crammed full of messages of support. Howard was left making the best of a bad job, while the boy wonder was left looking particularly foolish.

Today Howard published what amounted to his manifesto in an article in the *Daily Telegraph*, the newspaper that was once, before Black took it over, the house journal of the Conservative Party.

Under the heading 'I have beaten Blair before – and can beat him again', Howard promises that he would lead a reunited and revitalised Conservative Party 'from the front'. Why do candidates talk in Great War terms as if they were junior officers ready to go over the top armed with nothing but a walking stick? There is much to be said for leading from behind – especially if living in a comfortable château. Harold Macmillan fought bravely as a Grenadier in the Kaiser's War, but as Prime Minister he was never prepared to 'lead from the front'.

Howard's first point is a perfectly reasonable one. Alluding to the wipe-out of Tories in Wales and Scotland, he states that the Conservative Party must never become an English party. In Wales the Tories were always 'the English party' (Welsh conservatives voted Liberal), but that was not the case in Scotland. However, unionism without a Scottish assembly no longer seems a practical proposition. His second point about the need for strong leadership is largely rhubarb, but his third is more interesting. He embarks on it by saying 'we must take the fight back to Labour' and referring to the new government's 'twin plans for devolution and European integration'. (Do Labour plans for further

European integration go much beyond signing the Social Chapter? We can only wait and see.) He then goes on to say: 'We must throw ourselves wholeheartedly into the referendums [sic] on devolution and press for a referendum on the outcome of the Amsterdam Summit.'

The Tory party is a parliamentary party, and one which has always been suspicious of referenda, the device of dictators from Napoleon III to Adolf Hitler. A referendum after Amsterdam would need the approval of the House of Commons. How can Howard, who as Conservative leader would be able to muster only 165 votes, expect to carry the day? It is pure hot air.

Howard then makes a promise he might well find difficult to fulfil. He undertakes to visit every Conservative association in the country during the next parliament. This would prove a dreary pilgrimage, speaking to small numbers of the over-sixties (unless our new leader and policies can make a rapid and dramatic appeal to the young) in shabby rooms decorated by glossy, polychrome pictures of Margaret Thatcher in her prime.

Howard then boasts about his record on crime as Home Secretary. He claims a 10 per cent decrease in crime, but offers no details and makes no mention of the increase in crimes of violence. He describes his policies as 'creative and imaginative' and admits that they attracted a good deal of hostility from vested interest groups (the judges?) and the left-wing press. Warming to his theme, he proclaims: 'I have held true to my convictions when consensus offered the easier path. I have won through and shown that it is possible to build a new consensus on Conservative terms.' He continues: 'As we fight a long war of attrition against Labour's plans to regulate our economy [freedom to the Bank of England to fix interest rates?], mangle our constitution and erode our nationhood . . .' To speak of the erosion of nationhood is another way of giving voice to the Eurosceptic case according to which both our identity and our sovereignty are threatened by 'faceless bureaucrats' in Brussels.

He then goes on to appeal for unity within the Tory party without offering any suggestions as how that unity could be brought about. He boasts yet again, this time that 'as a loyal member of the last government' he argued his case vigorously within it. He plainly did not get his way. 'Our first task will be to expose the Treaty of Amsterdam, as negotiated by Labour, for what it is: a significant net diminution of our right to govern ourselves.' As, at the time of writing, the Amsterdam summit is a month off, I am not sure how he can attack concessions to Brussels which have not yet been made. But the impression he seeks to give is clearly that of a committed right-winger, determined to defend what he sees as British interests.

9 May

The *Telegraph* has told us that two of 'the most colourful characters of the Thatcher era are backing Peter Lilley's leadership bid by giving him lessons on how to improve his public image'. These two are Lord Archer and Sir Timothy Bell.

Jeffrey Archer is a windbag with a unique capacity to jump from one camp to another, as he demonstrated with both Lady Thatcher and John Major. And anyone who has read Michael Crick's biography of the great novelist will learn just what a fantasist Archer is. Now he has come out in favour of extending the franchise for the leadership election to unspecified party activists; surely, if there is a case for a larger electorate, former Tory MPs now in the Lords could be added to the 165 sitting MPs?

Sir Tim Bell is a spin doctor. He advised Norman Lamont to wear a different pair of spectacles, but that did not save his 'safe' Harrogate seat. Bell was one of Margaret's more assiduous courtiers and was probably responsible for the colour of her hair, her sexy voice and her expensive dentistry. Is Lilley now to become a brighter blond and wear horn-rimmed spectacles? Bell is not only good at getting puffs into papers but even more skilled at keeping news out of the papers. With friends like Bell and Archer, who needs enemies?

The same edition of the *Telegraph* carries a column telling us who's backing whom. Peter Lilley, who seems to have drawn heavily upon Portillo's former supporters, now appears as a member of yet another 'dream ticket', namely an alliance with Gillian Shephard. His other backers include David 'two brains' Willetts, the dandy Eric Forth, Lady Thatcher's former political secretary John Whittingdale, and the Eurosceptic Bernard Jenkin, as well as Piers Merchant (French kissing in the *Sun*), Ann Widdecombe, and Gerald Howarth, the victor of Aldershot. The *Telegraph* writer describes the above liquorice allsorts as 'the most glittering array of supporters'.

Michael Howard's campaign is being run by Sir Michael Spicer, another committed Eurosceptic. Howard has the support of Virginia Bottomley, David Maclean, David Davis, Liam Fox, Oliver Heald and Francis Maude. More significantly, he has the support of Lord Hanson. His campaign is being run from Jonathan Aitken's house. Aitken was, sadly, a casualty of the election.

William Hague is being masterminded by James Arbuthnot, while Alan Duncan is in charge of his press relations. Also on board are James Clappison, Nigel Evans, Jonathan Sayeed, Julie Kirkbride, Nick Hawkins and Roger Gale.

Stephen Dorrell's leading backers include David Faber and Peter Luff, who are pro-Europeans, with the help of Graham Mather, the MEP.

John Redwood is supported by the extremely right-wing Iain Duncan Smith, who is expected to be his campaign manager. His other declared supporters include Andrew Hunter, the Basingstoke school teacher; the two Julians, Brazier and Lewis; Charles Wardle; and David Heathcoat-Amory, who resigned from the Major government over Europe.

Kenneth Clarke – who in a rational world should win the contest; but the Tories, shell-shocked to a man, are far from rational – has taken up his quarters in the offices of the Tory Reform Group. John Gummer will probably be his campaign manager, while David Curry and Ian Taylor are among his early supporters.

10 May

Having gained only 31 per cent of the votes cast on 1 May, the Tories face a long and uphill struggle if they are to win back power in less than two elections. Some of the contenders for the party leadership, John Redwood in particular, have compared the position today with that in 1945, when the Tories took just six years, albeit two elections, to regain power. This is wishful thinking. There are dramatic differences between the Attlee years and the prospects for Britain over the next decade.

The Attlee government achieved a social revolution but at the cost of a depressed, cold and very hungry population. Bread and potatoes were rationed, and shortages of basic foodstuffs and consumer goods were worse than at the height of Hitler's war. No one who lived through it, as I did, will have forgotten the pain of the Shinwell Winter of 1946–7. In retrospect, one marvels at the docility of the British working class, whose standard of living remained at prewar levels until the end of the Tory fifties. In the 1959 general election, the Conservative slogan 'Britain is better under the Tories – Don't let Labour ruin it' sent the Tories back for a further five years of power. The transformation was devoutly to be wished.

Tony Blair might well have to wrestle with his over-large majority, but he will not have to ration clothes and potatoes – or fight the Cold War. Redwood is an optimist: for six read ten years of Labour rule.

12 May

What should we make of Stephen Dorrell? I remember him as a Tory whip in the late eighties and early nineties, sitting silently in the tea room, listening to the gossip. His reputation was that of 'a nice young man'; good looking in a conventional way, and definitely a Man of the Left. His promotion to office was well deserved, and he became a controversial health minister who enjoyed more than the average media exposure. But, even before the election was called (although it had long been signalled), Dorrell had made, in private, two decisions: that he would be a candidate for office in the event of a Tory defeat; and that in order to give himself a chance he would move gingerly, but obviously, to the right.

This shift did not do much for the sense of some of his comments. His claim (echoed by John Redwood) after the election had been lost that Labour had proved from day one that it had no idea how to negotiate with Europe caused hilarity in the Foreign and Common-wealth Office. *Punch* quoted one senior diplomat as saying:

The new Labour Government will certainly need its hand holding on many issues, but if Robin Cook went into negotiations in Brussels dressed as a clown, refusing to speak any language other than Swahili and ended the day by urinating in the German Chancellor's coffee, his negotiating stance would still be seen as an improvement over his predecessors. Tory ministers had become so terrified by their Eurosceptics at home that they had simply stopped negotiating. It did immense harm to the British national interest. One day the

21

story will be told of how much the Eurosceptics lost this country in terms of hard cash and influence. For Tories now to try to preach to Labour about how to negotiate with Brussels would be a bit like Myra Hindley setting up a seminar in child care.

To that diplomat I say 'Amen'.

Now, like all the contenders, Dorrell has published his manifesto: not in *The Times* or *Telegraph* but in the *Sunday Express*, a newspaper that is not what it once was. Under a suspiciously youthful photograph, a sub has extracted the words: 'Labour has raised expectations to unattainable levels. Public disappointment is inevitable.' After the necessary rhubarb, Dorrell asserts that Blair has five years and no more to repay the trust placed in him in 1997. He is thus a five-year and not a ten-year man. Given the volatility of the electorate, it could be five years; given the sound economic situation that Blair has inherited (according to Dorrell), it might well be ten.

He goes on: 'The task for the Conservatives over the next five years is simply put – it is to rebuild the Conservative coalition so that those former voters feel the party once again speaks for them.' This statement shows that Dorrell is still a moderate, who believes the Tory party to be a broad church. In that he is to be preferred to Hague, Redwood and Howard who are all, to a greater or lesser extent, ideologues.

It is when Dorrell comes to Europe – the great divisive force within the party – that his words become more interesting. 'And we must show where Britain's interests lie in Europe. Britain is in the European Union because our economic interests are closely tied up with those of our neighbours [trite, but true], and because we share wider political interests with them.' Then, watching his back, he says: 'The European Union is not, and should not become, a Federation.'

There are relatively few 'federalists' in Europe, and most of them are to be found in the Netherlands, Luxembourg and Belgium. What Dorrell has ducked is the desire on the part of Germany and France 'to share wider political interests'. What are they? They are the extension of majority voting so that more states might join; the formation of a common defence policy (why not a British contribution to the Franco-German brigade?); and moves towards a common foreign policy which would give Europe a voice in a world dominated by the United States, Japan, China and, eventually, Russia. Such progress does not amount to a United States of Europe, although a common currency might give that impression.

The purpose of the common currency project is to create an international currency based on sound money, sound public finances and the kind of structural reform brought about in the UK in the past decade and a half. With all fourteen members of the Union contributing a large share of their gold and currency reserves, the euro is designed to withstand the kind of speculation against sterling, for instance, that drove Britain out of the ERM and made one speculator rich beyond the dreams of avarice. But did anyone during the election say as much? No Tory, save possibly Ken Clarke, had the guts to tell it as it is.

Dorrell, who approached the truth about the European Union only to back away from it, finishes his manifesto on a sensible note. He writes: 'Finally and probably most important, we must demolish the glib pretensions of the millenarians who have their own reasons for wanting to write off the Tory party. In the end, the single argument which did most harm to the Conservative cause was the simplest – it was time for a change. Indeed, it would have been extraordinary if the party had won a fifth consecutive term. No party has ever done that in our history.'

The sense that it was time for a change was a frustrating argument for canvassers. It seemed to avoid the questions which voters were being asked. But, in retrospect, it was encouraging to remember the force the argument had. It demonstrates the weakness of Mr Blair's underlying appeal. And it is one argument that cannot be used against us next time.

14 May

The Tory party, having lost two million votes on 1 May, is in a state of shock. With 165 MPs, none of them in Scotland or Wales, it is in no fit state to elect a successor to John Major. But this is the task facing it in the next month. How are the candidates shaping up?

For some unknown reason the bookies have William Hague, the 36-year-old *Wunderkind*, as the favourite. The man whose running mate he was to have been, before deciding to go it alone, appears to be in decline. Left standing at the church by his Hague, with whom the night before he had cemented their alliance with champagne,

Michael Howard is now under fire from two of his former Home Office ministers: Ann Widdecombe (a sassy lady known to her enemies as 'Doris Karloff'), who has spoken out against Howard's conduct in dismissing Derek Lewis as head of the prison service in 1995; and Charles Wardle, who has said that he will raise the delicate matter of the Al Fayeds' citizenship.

Miss Widdecombe has been incensed by a piece in the Daily Mail in which she is accused of accepting flowers, chocolates and *diners intimes* from Derek Lewis. Miss Widdecombe is what the Americans call 'homely', and, at the age of forty-three, a devout and newly converted Roman Catholic, seems unlikely to have embarked on an affair with the former prisons chief. Miss Widdecombe has accused the Howard camp of hitting below the belt (which could be true), but it is more likely that the Mail was simply out to make mischief. Mr Lewis admits that they dined together, but only months after his sacking: as for the flowers, that symbol of infatuation, Miss Widdecombe admits only to having sent flowers to Mrs Lewis after her husband's sacking. If it were not so sad, it would be funny.

The cartoonists have had a field day, showing an enraged Miss Widdecombe driving a stake into the heart of Michael Howard. (She described him as having 'a dark side' and being 'a man of the night'.) The dispute centres on the fact that Miss Widdecombe, as prisons minister, took a liberal view over prison conditions and reform, and claims to have visited every one of HM prisons. Mr Howard took the opposite view, and had, according to Miss Widdecombe at least, never set foot in a prison in the United Kingdom. The hard-line Secretary of State met the softer Minister of State, and much hilarity has been caused in consequence of their clash.

Stephen Dorrell has launched a counter-attack against Hague, stressing both the former Welsh secretary's comparative youth and his own far greater experience. Dorrell should ideally be combining with Ken Clarke to make a 'dream ticket' for the centre of the Tory party. It could well come to that.

It is rumoured that the ghastly Bill Cash, the arch-Eurosceptic, is about to throw his hat in the ring. He would be the joke candidate who, if he were to get more than one vote, would presumably rob John Redwood of one of his small number. Cash is believed to be 'putting down a marker', but for what, it is difficult to say.

Ken Clarke is certainly the public's favourite to succeed. He has the talent and the experience to make a formidable leader of the opposition. One can only hope that the parliamentary party has the sense to realise it. Sadly, the bulk of the 165 survivors in the Commons tend to the right of the party, consisting, by and large, of undistinguished back-benchers and inexperienced newcomers.

I understand Ken Clarke has now written a two-page letter to all Tory MPs, warning them of the dangers inherent in moving the party to extremes, as the Labour Party did in 1983 when it picked Michael Foot as its leader rather than Dennis Healey. He has also warned his colleagues that, under right-wing leadership, the party would marginalise itself both at home and in Europe. Clarke's views on both domestic politics and Britain in Europe are sensible and his letter, unlike the anodyne attempts at electioneering by his rivals, at least goes right to the heart of the debate. In it he puts himself forward as the man who could defeat Blair in 2002 in a presidential-style election. In response to those who argue that he is too pro-European to be Tory leader, he says that while unity is essential it is not an end in itself to be secured at the expense of wider public appeal and electoral success. He adds: 'I believe firmly that if the Conservative Party is perceived to swing further to the ideological right and also to become hard-line nationalist and anti-European, it will make itself unelectable.' Such policies, he says in another part of the letter, 'would drive us to the fringe both at home and in European politics. It is not just that the prudent politician knows that he should never say "never", nor that the public favour keeping the options open. Most of the business and financial community of this country would reject such a dogmatic and isolationist position and reject our party if we espoused it.'

With what I believe to be unassailable logic, he continues: 'The British people did not vote for Blair because they thought the Conservatives were not sufficiently right-wing or Eurosceptic. When Blair betrays their trust, many of the moderate voters who have left us could turn to the Liberal Democrats if they believe the Conservatives have migrated to the hard right of politics.'

The implication of this, of course, is that the Tories might well compound their massive defeat by some foolishness in which someone entirely unsuitable is elected party leader. I suppose, if the worst came to the worst, we could hold yet another leadership election, but that would only hold the party up to ridicule. Clarke versus Blair would give the Tories hope of returning to office in 2002. Hague versus Blair would keep us out of power indefinitely.

16 May

Some Tories, who now regret the substitution of the old 'magic circle' through which leaders used to 'emerge' (the whole party both within and outside Westminster having been consulted) by elections for the leadership (thanks to the late Humphry Berkeley), are desperately seeking to widen the franchise before someone unsuitable is elected.

I wrote a letter to the *Telegraph* suggesting that it would be wise to include in the electorate former Tory MPs now sitting in the Lords; I ought to have included Tory MEPs. Others would extend the vote to members of the National Union or even to the officers of Conservative constituency associations. The 1922 Committee, which runs the leadership election, can do as it wishes; but any change in the rules would be likely to be opposed bitterly by those candidates who see themselves losing out by it. Were ex-MPs in the Lords to be brought in, for example, Clarke would win the contest with ease; and the Eurosceptics would oppose bitterly the inclusion of Tory MEPs, who have always been independent of the party as a whole.

But first the 1922 Committee must reconstitute itself. Next Wednesday the 165 survivors of the Massacre of the First of May will meet to elect a new chairman of the '22, the committee of all Tory Members when the party is in opposition; of back-benchers only when the party is in government. For most of my time in the Commons, the '22 was the parliament of the skimmed milk, the cleverer MPs having been elevated to political office. Its most recent chairman, Sir Marcus 'Compo' Fox ('Foxy' to his enemies) lost Shipley to the Labour Party. This was not a serious blow as Fox, loquacious to the point of indiscretion, was never regarded as being up to the job: his executive committee and fellow officers were careful not to let him loose upon the airwaves as he was almost always bound to open his mouth and put his Yorkshire foot in it. But who will succeed him?

One possibility is Sir Geoffrey Johnson Smith, a minister under Ted Heath and a vice chairman in the last parliament; but he will not start favourite. Archie Hamilton (Question: 'Where is Archie?' Answer: 'Anywhere in the Palace except the library') is another, but although large in stature he is not thought to be very clever. Although how a Tory can tell is something of a mystery. Alan Clark, anxious to keep in the public eye, tossed his hat into the ring only to withdraw it. Several of the greybeards have approached 'Nice Norman', that is, Sir Norman Fowler, once chairman of the party and a former Cabinet minister, but he seems to have refused the offer. ('Nice' Norman should not be confused with 'Little Norm' Lamont, who lost Harrogate, and 'Big Norm' Tebbit, who has been put out to grass in the Lords.)

The favourite must be John MacGregor, a Tory of Scots descent who sits for a seat in the east of England. MacGregor, who it is said tends to wear kilts to which he is not entitled, is a small man with brains, whose Cabinet career seemed nevertheless to have run into the sands. He has the necessary authority to preside over a party deep in shock – and a committee which now faces the urgent task of laying down the rules that will determine the new leader.

21 May

William Hague, the Tory contender who has most closely associated himself with widening the franchise to include party activists, has attacked John Major. As the elections for the '22 were taking place, Hague called for a fresh start under a clear lead. The *Wunderkind* continued: 'A fresh start means reuniting the party behind a clear position. One of the lessons of the past few years is that it is easier to unite the party behind a clear position than a constantly shifting fudge.' He then hurried on to claim that he did not intend to criticise any individual. What humbug. Many of the more senior Tories were reported in *The Times* as considering Hague's speech to be rather naïve: 'it showed up his lack of experience and might cost him votes'.

22 May

The fact that both Chris Gill (Redwood's chief of staff in 1995) and Nicholas Winterton (often top of the annual 'shits list' compiled by the Tory whips' office) have been elected to the new executive of the

1922 Committee must be making Sir Cranley Onslow turn in his grave. No clearer indication could have been given as to the flavour and quality of the 165 Tory MPs who survived the May holocaust. Five years ago neither of them would have seen the light of day.

The new chairman is Archie Hamilton, a six foot six inch ex-Coldstreamer who belongs to the traditional, that is, non-ideological right wing of the party. John MacGregor got the most votes, but the fancy electoral system of the transferable vote meant that Hamilton pipped him to the post. It is somewhat ironic that at a time when the Tory party in the House is less impressive than it has ever been, a traditional Tory who would have felt very much at home in 1959 should have been wafted in to lead the '22. Not a man of huge intelligence, Archie is nevertheless as straight as a die, and as conventional as Sir Hugh Monro Lucas Tooth, of blessed memory.

There are, however, some encouraging signs for Ken Clarke: several centre-left candidates were among those elected to the eighteen-strong executive committee, including Ray Whitney, Michael Mates and David Madel. The right can claim Michael Spicer (who is running Michael Howard's leadership campaign), John Townend (the leader of the '92 Club of obscurantist right-wingers, so called after the number of Sir Patrick Wall's flat in Pimlico), Gill, Marion Roe and Nicholas Winterton.

It has been said that too frequent an attendance at the '22 would give one what religious people call Doubts; certainly one should not forget Walder's Law, which states that the first three people to speak at a meeting of the 1922 Committee are mad. However, ship of fools though it may be, it does wield power. The officers and committee have automatic access to the Prime Minister/leader of the opposition and their view as to the behaviour of any minister/shadow minister can be a matter of political life or death. It was, after all, the granite-faced executive of the '22 that forced David Mellor out of office.

Although it is perhaps too early to tell, Hamilton will probably come out against an extension of the electorate for the leadership, despite the existence of a large number of former Tory Members now sitting in 'the other place', and the ambitions of Sir Robin Hodgson, the ex-MP who now presides over the National Union. There are even some – like Jeffrey Archer, who has become a master of the radio soundbite – to advocate one man, one vote. God help us!

Today I had a reply from Michael Heseltine in response to my note conveying my good wishes. He wrote that he was certainly 'for Ken', but had yet to make his views public. I hope that when he does he can carry sufficient weight. With the first ballot for the leadership only a couple of weeks away, Clarke remains the favourite of the public at large, and his performance against Gordon Brown in the debate on the Queen's Speech can only have won him praise. He is clearly the best parliamentary performer the Tories have to offer, and the nicely balanced executive of the '22 suggests that he might well come first in the opening ballot. But that is not to say that he will emerge as the eventual winner. Will Heseltine's (and perhaps Major's) support make any difference to his chances?

As for the others' prospects at this stage, Michael Howard seems to have been holed below the waterline by Ann Widdecombe, who won their exchange on points. His loss of support will undoubtedly translate into gains for Lilley – whose calm intelligence has come across well on his television appearances, although he still seems to lack charisma. I do not see him dominating the Chamber and getting the better of Tony Blair. Redwood does not seem to have made any progress; indeed, he seems to have been cast in the role of villain of the piece.

I suggest that Redwood will be the first to be eliminated, followed by Howard, and then Hague. Clarke will get more votes than anyone else, but the second preferences of those who vote for Redwood, Howard and Hague will go, in the main, not to him but to Lilley. Thus Lilley, elected by 164 Tory MPs with no Scots or Welsh among them and on a narrow franchise, will complete the rout of what was once the most successful political party in the world. But we should wait and see.

23 May

Willie Whitelaw has come out in favour of Ken. Writing in the *Telegraph*, he calls upon the party to end its theological disputes, and points out that it did not move significantly to the right after the defeats of 1945 and 1966. He makes no mention of 1974–5 when, had he entered the contest against Ted Heath before Margaret Thatcher did so, he would most likely have won the leadership and thereby prevented the shift to the right the party experienced with her at the helm.

After the Lord Mayor's show comes the dustcart. William Hague, the first to attack John Major's leadership openly, has now been followed by John Redwood. There is an hilarious photograph in today's *Times* of his head appearing above what appears to be an enormous dustbin, designed by a communications agency hired by his wife, Gail. Behind his head, and partly obscured by it, is the slogan 'To lead – to win'. The Tory party torch burns brightly to his left. There is a touch of infantile fascism about the whole thing.

Redwood says that it was the drift over Europe and the neglect of small businesses and traditional Tory concerns such as the erosion of the countryside which led to a sharp fall in party membership. 'Some', he says, 'have quietly slipped away from the Conservatives, others have joined and worked for the Eurosceptic parties that formed our flank. Towards the end of the last government many party activists left the theatre. By the time the curtain came down we were playing to an empty house.' The implication we are invited to draw from this analogy is that had we been sensible enough to vote for him and not for John Major, we would have been playing to full houses, even after eighteen years.

Stephen Dorrell, once tipped by Major as a future leader of the party, has come out in support for the ex-premier: 'History will be very kind to John Major ... Conservatives should be proud of our record ... I am proud to have been a member of the government during that time.'

There has been much debate within the party about whether or not the leadership election should have been postponed for several months, giving the party time to recover from its humiliation. Alan Clark has said as much, but few take the great diarist as seriously as he would like to be taken. Nevertheless, he has a point. John Major should have announced, on the morrow of defeat, that he would remain as leader until, say, November, thus giving the party some breathing space. But, dismayed by the size of the defeat he had suffered, and sick of the disloyalty which had contributed so much towards it, he threw in the towel too hastily.

There has been equally lively debate about who should constitute the electorate for this precipitate poll. The Dirty (Half) Dozen – that is, Clarke, Dorrell, Howard, Lilley, Redwood and Hague – are keeping quiet on this point (though Stephen Dorrell did break the silence, if only to tell listeners to Today that any reform should follow on what presumably would be his victory). Norman Fowler has suggested including the chairmen of each and every Conservative constituency association; my own suggestion has been to include all former Tory MPs who are now in the Lords – which would have the benefit of ensuring victory for Kenneth Clarke.

William Rees-Mogg addressed this problem in his weekly article in *The Times*, a newspaper of which he was once a distinguished editor. Rees-Mogg has an engaging eccentricity, but also, usually, something interesting to say. He suggested that the reason for the speed of John Major's resignation was that he believed the Tory party would move swiftly to elect his deputy to the leadership; but Michael Heseltine's attack of angina and subsequent operation caused his withdrawal from any leadership race. I do not believe Michael would have been elected anyway; the rump is far too right-wing.

Rees-Mogg has no time for the Dirty Dozen: Clarke because he is in favour of the euro; Hague because he is too young and 'Majorish' (whatever that might mean); Peter Lilley because he lacks charisma; Stephen Dorrell because he lacks the charisma of Peter Lilley; Michael Howard because Tories believe everything Ann Widdecombe has to say about him; and John Redwood, the Cassandra of the party, because he is unelectable. Rees-Mogg points out that there were only four candidates of leadership stature: Clarke (then why not support him?); Portillo, who was rejected by the electors of Enfield; Michael Heseltine, who has been eliminated by illness; and Chris Patten, who is stuck in Hong Kong for another six weeks.

The piece flirts with the old idea of the magic circle; but the idea is not consummated. Clearly, it is out of the question. As is often the case with Rees-Mogg, a good article trails away to an indecisive end. He believes the electorate should be widened and concludes magisterially by writing 'trust the People', the Churchillian dictum which might have served us in the past. If Rees-Mogg were not blinded by his anti-European prejudice, he would have picked Ken Clarke as leader – he, at least, is of prime ministerial calibre.

Now the eighteen newly elected officers and executive of the 1922 Committee have announced that there will be no change to the electorate and that the first ballot will be held on 10 June. If no candidate achieves an overall majority on 10 June (as is very likely to be the outcome), there will be a second ballot a week later. If there is still no outright majority, the two top candidates will hold a run-off two days later, on 19 June.

The '22 executive did acknowledge the need for eventual reform, and this contest will no doubt be the last to be fought with MPs as the sole arbiters. Dr Mawhinney, the chairman of the party (but for how much longer?) had striven for a change in the rules that would have permitted an unspecified number of party activists to take part. He was roundly snubbed for his pains.

The turmoil will continue at least until the party conference in October, with Lord Archer of Weston-Super-Mare acting as resident conductor. We should pause before moving to New Labour-type democracy, that is, one member one vote. We ought not to forget the plea of the Younger Pitt after Trafalgar: 'May the liberties of the people never be trampled in pieces by democracy.' I have spent thirty-one years as a Tory MP, a period during which most of the changes I have witnessed have been for the worse. Given that I was selected for Rochester and Chatham in 1957 and for Aldershot in 1969, I have spent a total of thirty-four years in close proximity with what Marxists were the first to call 'party activists' – the bakers of Victoria sponges, the drawers of raffles and the fillers of envelopes. All too often they are a tiresome bunch of the self-selected, generally unsophisticated and ill-educated, with as many prejudices as a dog has fleas. 'Let's get rid of them blacks' was the rallying cry of the Aldershot Conservative Club.

There are, of course, exceptions; some of my best friends have been my local party workers (on whom I was obliged to rely when there was an attempt to deselect me for having voted for Michael Heseltine in the 1990 contest). I remember Frank Bannister in Chatham and, in Aldershot, Dr Monique Simmonds, a woman of high intelligence and obvious probity. And there are many others among the brave women (so few men nowadays) who, in all weathers, risk the hazards of savage dogs and curmudgeonly voters in order to push leaflets that will not be read through other people's front doors. They deserve the MBE certainly; but not a vote in the election of the party leader and putative Prime Minister. One has only to be a spectator at a Conservative party conference – and I have lost count of how many of those seaside jamborees I have attended – to perceive quickly enough the low quality of the average representative. They are usually far to the right, easily roused by mob oratory, and like nothing more than to be fed tit-bits from the platform – as Michael Portillo and Peter Lilley were particularly skilled at doing, the latter with his attacks on single mothers and the former by eliding the EU and NATO in infelicitous tirades against 'Brussels'. Sensible Tories, like Heseltine and Clarke, usually attack our opponents, not ourselves. Given that a high proportion of the newly elected Tory Members have never heard of Arthur Balfour, it would perhaps be as well to remind the 1922 Committee of his famous dictum, namely that he would sooner take advice from his valet than from the Conservative party conference. Do we really want to give the vote to the Tartan-drinking Young Conservatives, or to the self-selected representatives of the so-called 'grass roots'? God forbid.

Surely the most sensible reform would be to permit former Tory MPs who have been elevated to the Lords a vote in picking the party leader? If we have to make concessions to *hoi polloi*, we should go no further than members of Robin Hodgson's National Union executive, who have at least proved themselves steady under political fire. Thus far, but no further.

24 May

I have often wondered who it is who writes leader columns in papers broad and narrow. Can they be young men with first-class honours just down from Teddy Hall? For example, in yesterday's *Telegraph* the anonymous writer offered (under the heading 'Six men and their mission') the following comments on Kenneth Clarke: 'Kenneth Clarke is the best known. What you see is what you get, and what you see is a brave, disorganised, lazy-minded, combative, humane and out of date man who cannot analyse anything but can attack anyone. His recent assertion that the question of Europe is "an obsession" which can be safely laid on one side for the next five years is a measure of his understanding of the Tory and the national predicament.'

This scribe continued in much the same vein, although with perhaps more kindness towards the other five contenders. When he came to William Hague, he asked rhetorically: 'Is Mr Hague John Major with a first-class degree from Oxford?' Poor John Major. The *Telegraph* has never forgiven him his Brixton background.

I shall confine myself here to his remarks about Clarke – who is definitely not the *Telegraph*'s candidate.

Why is Ken Clarke 'out of date'? No reason is offered, and the charge is ridiculous. The Tory party *has* been obsessed with Europe. (One of the blessings of the Blair regime has been the disappearance from the political scene of Mrs Gorman, Chris 'Pork Pie' Gill and Teddy Taylor. Nick Budgen is currently out of work.) The Tory Eurosceptics, and the newspapers that supported them, were responsible in large part for Major's defeat. And is Ken Clarke really 'disorganised'? I have heard no evidence to support so silly an assertion.

After reading this ill-considered screed, I was amused to see the poll published in today's *Telegraph*. Under a front-page heading 'Clarke only Tory with poll appeal', the paper was obliged to print the findings of its own survey showing that Clarke was the favourite candidate among both Tory supporters and the wider public. Clarke was the choice of 30 per cent of respondents, followed by Redwood with 10 per cent, Howard with 9 per cent, Lilley with 7 per cent, and Dorrell with 5 per cent. Putting a brave face on it, Robert Shrimsley and Anthony King called it 'a result which will profoundly depress Tory MPs before the June 10 contest'. What evidence have they for such an assertion? None. So much for the pundits, leader-writers and editors, all of whom are far too big for their boots.

I spoke to John Biffen, an old friend who is to take his seat in the Lords on 10 June (and the day after goes into the London Clinic for a kidney operation). He felt that the Tory party 'was all in pieces'. The plethora of candidates showed how poverty-stricken we are; where, asked John, is the young F. E. Smith? He thought he might have voted for Ken Clarke in the hope that he would survive for only one term, although he did not think Clarke as good a parliamentary performer as Howard. Biffen took the view that it would take at least two elections to get rid of Blair. As for the extension of the franchise, he viewed it with apprehension. 'It will be much harder to get rid of anyone if the constituencies are given a part to play,' and he gave Ted Heath in 1975 as an example. Nevertheless he felt that some extension was inevitable.

I then spoke to Keith Simpson, a former constituent who failed to get selected for Aldershot, but ended up as MP for Mid Norfolk – Richard Ryder's old seat. He told me that he was coming out for Ken Clarke and would make an announcement to that effect later in the week. He had consulted his fifty-strong executive and their support seemed to be divided equally between Clarke and Hague. Simpson's executive committee, which would appear to be of a much higher quality than, for instance, Aldershot's, was looking for the old-fashioned qualities of leadership, skill and good judgement. He felt that there was little or no antisemitic feeling with regard to Howard (who has enemies enough) but some anxieties about William Hague's private life, which have been hinted at by the gutter press. (A friend from Hartley Wintney, who had been to a Hague rally, came away saying that the star of the show had been his warm-up man, Steve Norris.)

Simpson talked of the forty-one newly elected MPs, citing examples such as James Arbuthnot, who inherited some of my green acres and is a Hague supporter. Julian Lewis is for Redwood and Shaun Woodward for Dorrell. Andrew Lansley is for Howard. Keith said that he had got the impression from conversation with John Major that the former Prime Minister was 'sick to death of the Tory party' and, although favouring Clarke, was worried lest his support prove to be counterproductive. The party had been kept together, thought Simpson, in its state of shell-shock, not so much by the Chief Whip, Alastair Goodlad (who appeared to be 'on auto-pilot') as by whips such as Andrew MacKay, Patrick McLoughlin and Richard Ottaway.

Simpson feared that the complexities of the voting system might lead to the election of someone whom nobody really wanted.

26 May

Clarke's campaign has been strengthened by the support of Sir Leon Brittan and of Sir Bryan Nicholson, a lifelong Conservative who has taken the trouble to write a letter to all Tory MPs pleading with them not to 'choose the Michael Foot option'. On the other hand, Clarke has been attacked by Lord Parkinson, once the Great Chamberlain of Queen Margaret's court, who told the *Telegraph*: 'He is too old . . . He has offended a broad swathe of the party by his cavalier attitude towards opponents and his attempt to hold the government to ransom over Europe.' Cecil Parkinson has been as disloyal to John Major as he was loyal to Margaret Thatcher. Clarke is in his mid-fifties, and could, even if it were to take two bites at the cherry, be in Downing Street by the time he reached his mid-sixties. As for his 'cavalier attitude', it would be seen to best advantage from the opposition front bench. Macmillan's dictum remains as true as ever: begin, said the old actor-manager, by dominating the House; then your party in the House; and then the country.

27 May

The *Telegraph* today carries two profiles: one of Peter and Gail Lilley, the other of John and Gail Redwood. Not to be outdone, *The Times* carries an op-ed piece by Redwood himself, entitled by some sympathetic sub 'Amsterdam is the end of Britain'. The piece is much as one would expect: a series of assertions unqualified by either the facts or the political realities. Let me quote directly from this diatribe. (Note the use of the conditional tense: the 'urban fox' is out to frighten us.) 'The new union would even have the right to take Britain's votes away in the Council of Ministers. At the moment we have the right to vote against proposals we do not like, and the right to veto the most important.' We are told that 'the union is founded "on the principles of liberty, democracy, respect for human rights and for fundamental freedoms and the rule of law"', and that these rights are reflected in the European Convention on Human Rights and Fundamental Freedoms: 'if other members think we are in breach of any of the rights or freedoms, we will lose our votes and our veto in the Council.' Here there is a clash between the idea of written constitutions prevalent among continental Europeans (and, given the recent history of Germany and Italy, who shall blame them?) and the British concept of an unwritten constitution. Britain has already been subject to adverse rulings of the European Court of Justice, but I see no real diminution of our sovereignty. These are proposals, no more, no less. Whether they are agreed to by the new British Foreign Secretary remains to be seen.

After reminding his readers, not unfairly, that for the benefit of *Sun* readers Tony Blair wrapped himself in the Union flag and adopted a bulldog, Redwood concludes: 'We have a need of a government which will explain all this honestly to the British people, and then

explain to our partners that we cannot sign up to a single word of the
Amsterdam Treaty. This is a Federal Treaty. It is the last main treaty
they need to take our country away. Sign this and we have no longer
a powerful British democracy capable of righting our wrongs and
representing our interests . . .'

Redwood is playing the nationalist card. He does not realise (or
does not admit) that no single nation today is 'independent' in any
meaningful sense. French nationalism has always been a potent force;
but France seems nevertheless to have realised that Franco-German
cooperation is to be preferred to *la gloire*. One French politician, asked
whether he feared a resurgent Germany after Kohl, said he did not,
because 'we French have the bomb and the Germans do not'. The
British have the world's third most powerful nuclear capability, after
the USA and Russia. This gives us a privileged position within the
European Union. More importantly, the nation-states of Europe, having endured a century which has been riven by two terrible 'civil
wars', are moving beyond petty nationalism towards a greater unity.
This could (to adopt the Redwood conditional) mean a reduction
in sovereignty in less important matters in order to gain additional
economic, political and military clout. The world does consist of giant
nations – the USA, Japan, China, the tigers of South-East Asia and
an unstable Russia – as well as a dangerously hostile Islam. A United
Europe must remain allied to the United States.

Redwood is a nineteenth-century candidate in a twenty-first-
century world. He is backed by Conservative 2000, an organisation
with a good deal of money, and is operating from their headquarters
in Wilfred Street. About a dozen MPs have declared their support
for him, and he is supposed to have another twenty-five 'sympathisers'.
He will probably win the wooden spoon.

The *Telegraph*'s profile is sympathetic. We are told that Redwood's
idea of an ideal evening is to stay at home with his wife and drink a
bottle of 'Thames Valley Vineyard White'. He may drive three
Jaguars, but his taste in wine seems frankly deplorable; or is it that,
as a patriot, he has spurned the wines of either France or Germany?

The profile of Lilley in the same paper is also sympathetic, but
concludes by saying: 'But on television or speaking to crowds, Mr
Lilley comes across as wooden. His supporters are doing everything
they can to improve his image. Lord Archer is giving him advice on

television appearances, and Mrs Lilley has taken her husband shopping for a new suit and a selection of shirts and ties.' It also appears that Jeffrey Archer 'will host' a cocktail party at his Thames-side apartment. With friends like Jeffrey . . .

I think Lilley has all the charisma of a privet hedge, but one never can tell what a Burton's suit and an Old Etonian tie bought at Waterloo station will do. He seems to have won over Patrick Cormack, who confesses that politically he is nearer to Clarke but believes that Lilley can unite the party. His principal supporters seem to be Gillian Shephard and David Willetts. I doubt very much whether Lilley will come top of the ballot, but he might well gain the bulk of second preference votes. Clever and sensitive though he is, I cannot see him dominating the Commons. Someone has uncharitably described Peter Lilley as suffering from a 'charisma bypass' – something that could not be said of Ken Clarke. Clarke has the wit and ability to rough up Blair, ridicule Prescott and drive that bearded gnome Robin Cook back to Edinburgh. He is clearly the best man to lead the Tory party and to restore its morale.

I once took Ken, when he was health secretary, to a fight between Herol Graham and Michael McCallum at the Albert Hall. We sat ringside, behind a battery of cameramen. With admirable *sangfroid* the minister sat eating a large fatty beef sandwich and smoking a Will's panatella. I told him to watch his image. 'Bugger my image,' he retorted. And the cameras were concentrated on the action.

30 May

The defeat of the Tories a month ago was, if anything, worse than the defeats of 1906 and 1945. Besides recovering from a state of nervous shock, there is much that the Conservatives must do to refurbish their appeal: appoint a new chairman (possibly Chris Patten or Michael Portillo), attempt to recruit more members on a national scale, modify the party conference and introduce greater party democracy, for a start. But that will not be enough. We lost not solely because two million Tories (including myself) sat on their hands, but because we had lost the confidence of the people. We were a divided party, weakly led, faced by a rejuvenated Labour Party, unrecognisable in style and content to the mass of the electorate.

Indeed, the greatest achievement of the eighteen years of Thatcher/ Major rule will probably be seen as the destruction of British socialism (however defined). What appeared during the 1980s to be an unelectable Labour Party took itself by the scruff of the neck and shook out nearly all its old policies. Whether John Smith would have done as well as Tony Blair – *gravitas versus levitas* – it is impossible to say; but I feel that the end result in the election would have been much the same. 'Oppositions do not win elections; governments defeat themselves.' This rule of thumb will surely continue to apply: the Tories will not begin to make real progress in the country as a whole until the Blair government, through either arrogance or inexperience, begins to make mistakes. But I suspect that Tony Blair's honeymoon will be of longer than usual duration.

The party must show that it has learned the lessons of defeat and not respond to past humiliation by moving to the extremes. It must also avoid taking premature positions when it has no control over the political landscape. Let New Labour wrestle with the common currency. The Tories would be foolish to say 'no' to it when any decision to take part will probably be taken by Labour. If monetary union succeeds, there will be no mileage in calling for withdrawal. If it fails, then the Tories could gain. When once asked what he most feared as Prime Minister, Harold Macmillan replied: 'Events, dear boy, events.' The Tory party has little choice now but to wait upon events. They will come soon enough.

This autumn should see the publication of a book by Anthony Seldon on *How Tory Governments Arise*. It should achieve a substantial sale. According to Peter Riddell – much the best *Times* journalist writing today – Seldon will list six factors, not all of which will come into play at the same time. They are: a revivified party organisation; a programme realigned with voter preferences; either a new or a reinvigorated party leader; a tired and divided government; a sea change in intellectual or popular opinion; and a record of demonstrable failure on the part of the government.

A new chairman could revitalise the party. A new advertising agency could do more for us than the Saatchi brothers. Party democracy must be improved; but this carries with it the risk of extremists climbing on board. The 'flight of the men' from membership of the constituency associations must somehow be stopped. In the 1980s, Tory women moved from cake-baking to running the local associations: in Aldershot from 1992 to 1997 all three of my party officers and the agent were women. There is also anecdotal evidence of a decline in the quality of people putting themselves forward either to stand for local government or to run the local Tory parties. The upper classes have long ago subsided into *Country Life*, and even county councils like Shropshire, once run by the gentry, have fallen into the hands of *hoi polloi*. The local Tory associations are increasingly run by the less well educated who, in their turn, thus assume the power of picking the parliamentary candidate. It is essential that the new leader of the party and its new chairman choose someone more able and less prejudiced than Dame Angela Rumbold to be in charge of the candidates' list. A member of the unrepresentative '92 Group (a right-wing club once led by the renegade Sir George Gardiner) and a poor minister of the Crown, she did her bit during the election campaign to draw attention to the divisions within the party. The swing of the pendulum will mean that the Tories will begin their comeback by taking local government seats. It is essential that the right people come forward as candidates. The Tories should come to terms with their defeat in Scotland and Wales by campaigning actively for seats in any new assembly. The same applies to the election for the new Mayor of London.

Riddell argues that with a declining party membership (below half a million, compared with 2.8 million in the early 1950s), recruitment would benefit from the gift of one member, one vote in the election of the leader. I have grave doubts about this. Let us increase our membership in both quantity and quality. The key for the Tories is to choose their new leader wisely, and that can only mean voting for Ken Clarke.

1 June

We lunched with Carole and Tony Howard at a pub overlooking the River Corve. As we ate our roast pork and crackling in the sun, Tony told me the story of someone suggesting to Jim Callaghan when he was Prime Minister that a job might be given to the philosopher and Labour (later Social Democrat) MP Bryan Magee. Callaghan was dismissive of the idea. 'He makes me feel as if I had just come down from the trees.'

Most of our conversation focused on the Tory leadership. Michael Heseltine came out this morning in favour of Ken Clarke, as he had said he would in his letter to me. Howard, though a lifelong Christian socialist, also thinks Clarke the best bet.

We agreed that the likely order of the contenders after the first ballot on Tuesday week is: Clarke, Hague, Lilley, Howard, Redwood, Dorrell. Were Ken Clarke to get over 50 per cent of the total vote, together with a margin of 15 per cent over his nearest challenger, he would have won. Margaret Thatcher failed to win on the first ballot in 1990 and withdrew, having fallen short of the required 15 per cent 'surcharge' by four votes. Clarke will win if he gets 83 and the nearest other candidate no more than 58.

I find it hard to believe that Clarke – or anyone else for that matter – can win on the first ballot. The contest is far more likely to go to a second ballot, a week later. This is actually a misnomer, for it is not really a second 'ballot' at all, but a second election, from which candidates can and will withdraw, as they did in 1990, or into which they may enter for the first time. (On this occasion withdrawals are more likely than additions.) In this round the 'surcharge' disappears and a vote of 50 per cent – 83 in this case – is sufficient for victory, however many candidates are standing. If no one obtains an absolute majority in the second round, the top two (Clarke, plus Hague or Lilley?) go on to a third ballot, in which a simple majority will suffice.

Michael Heseltine having come out publicly for Clarke, it is hardly surprising that Lady Thatcher has appealed to the right-wing candidates not to split the vote. Were Dorrell to withdraw, it seems that his votes would go to Clarke – but there would not be very many of them. If Redwood were to withdraw, the bulk of his votes would go to the man most likely to beat Clarke. Were Howard to withdraw, the same would apply – Hague would get most of his votes. The prospect for Clarke seems gloomy: just as John MacGregor got more votes than Archie Hamilton in the first ballot for the chairmanship of the 1922 Committee, but lost to him in the end, so Clarke could lead until the third ballot and then be overtaken by Hague or Lilley.

A party leader aged thirty-six, with Hague's alarming inexperience, would be the source of many problems for the Tory opposition. There are those who see him as a major political figure of the future, and they could be right; I see him as being far too young, chipper and brash to be elected leader of the opposition. Sooner or later he would be challenged, and the party would have to go through the whole rigmarole again.

3 June

Today's *Telegraph*, which prints John Major's speech arguing for a delay in the launch of the common currency, carries in its centre spread yet another manifesto, this time from the hand of William Hague. It is not hard to write such a piece, and some smart alec on your staff will take you through the first two drafts. Let us examine what the young Hague has to say on the basis of thirty-six years of life and a record in government that is at best mediocre.

'The Conservative Party will need a new sense of purpose and a heightened sense of ambition.' Rhubarb, rhubarb. '. . . At this moment we need humility but we also need ambition. Self-indulgence, remoteness, arrogance are out. Ambition for our party and our country is in.' So far, he has said nothing of the remotest significance. Since when has self-indulgence been party policy?

Now he begins to warm to what might become this theme. 'My first ambition is to see an election-winning machine [you bet; but how exactly?] that is driven by ideas [such as?] and manned by high calibre politicians [where do we find them?].' Surely by now any half-way ill-disposed reader will have turned to the sports pages. But we should show patience; someone has gone to a good deal of trouble to concoct this rubbish. 'Some people say our goal is to win back our traditional supporters. I say our ambition is to make it possible for people to vote Conservative when they have never done so.' Given that two million 'Tories' stayed at home on 1 May, I prefer the more modest alternative. 'To achieve this we need to make these the watchwords of our party: Fresh, Open, Clear.' This is pure copywriting. 'And being clear means knowing our role and purpose . . .' How to say nowt in 300 words.

Hague moves up a notch. 'It is our role to defend the best economic inheritance any government has handed on for generations [the credit for this goes to Clarke, not Hague] against the damage that the social chapter can do.' How does an opposition of 164 MPs 'defend' the economy against the government and its overwhelming mandate? By pieces such as these? He moves on to accuse New Labour of seeing defence as 'an easy target'. There is, so far, no evidence of this. 'It is our role to show a line can be drawn in the transfer of sovereignty to elsewhere, that we can be in Europe, yet not run by Europe, and that we will fight a government [back to our 164 brave boys] that will sell off our sovereignty for the sake of happy summit photo-calls.' Neater, perhaps; but the phrase 'we can be in Europe and yet not be run by Europe' is meaningless. The whole point of Europe is the sharing of sovereignty in pursuit of common goals. 'Labour has been clever enough to occupy our ground [the social chapter, I presume?]. But it has arrived there by focus groups [which, I take it, means single-issue politics], not by conviction.' Is not Tony Blair at least sincere in his New Model Army? He seems to me to be so, rather nauseatingly so.

I cannot plod through the whole two columns of verbiage in close detail. It is all much of a muchness. But I will extract one final quotation: 'The Conservative Party should stand for choice without privilege [John Major's classless society?], freedom without irresponsibility, patriotism without bigotry.' These somewhat sanctimonious aspirations could have been voiced by any leading Tory politician since the war. Iain Macleod would have expressed them better, as did Harold Macmillan. But, given that the Tory party is a pragmatic party, hot air has to be of the right temperature. We can only judge Hague by what we know of his achievements; am I being uncharitable to suggest that they do not yet add up to very much?

John Major's intervention is more interesting than Hague's vapourings. The ex-premier suggests that the introduction of the common currency should be postponed in order to prevent other countries from proceeding with a fudged version in eighteen months' time. As indications of this danger, Major points to the obvious: Chancellor Kohl's attempt at revaluing the German mark, and the surprise victory of the left in the French legislative elections. Interestingly, Major's message in advocating delay is echoed by Ken Clarke, the only pro-European candidate in the Tory leadership election. Clarke has said that it is now clear that the single currency cannot proceed on 'a safe and sustainable basis' on 1 January 1999. Michael Howard, meanwhile, has reaffirmed his opposition 'in principle as well as for practical reasons' to the abolition of the pound. John Major's contribution is an attempt to defuse a highly sensitive issue; ironically enough, the move away from the January 1999 deadline can only help Ken Clarke, who will not now be obliged to defend the ecu against the pound.

4 June

The *Telegraph* leader-writers are up to their old tricks. Terrified lest Ken Clarke be elected leader of the Conservative Party, one such scribe, under the heading 'Labour's Tory', embarks on a diatribe foolish even for that once great newspaper. Take that heading, for example. This assertion is bolstered in the body of the copy by the sentence: 'The same idea, and the same form of words, is going round the comparable tracks of the Labour Party.' What evidence is there for this remarkable assertion? Has Tony Blair come out for Ken Clarke? Clearly not.

The editorial begins thus: 'Wouldn't it be nice were Kenneth Clarke to be the next leader of the Tory party? That is the big idea going round those reaches of the Conservative Party so grand that they do not like the Conservative Party, the stratosphere where Douglas Hurd is at home, and the rest of us get altitude sickness . . .' It is significant that both Hurd and Heseltine, rivals in 1990, should have come out in support of Clarke. No doubt John Major will follow their example. Why, then, should they dislike the Conservative Party? Does Douglas Hurd hate Tories? If so, he has kept it a secret for a long time. Does Michael Heseltine hate Tories? I suppose the answer must be 'some of them', but surely not the generality. He has managed to work with the party successfully enough for many years.

This leader-writer is an ideologue; only ideologues talk of one Tory hating another. He is an unreconstructed Thatcherite, who takes the reader back to the 1981 budget, to which he claims Ken Clarke was opposed. That budget, claims the writer, 'laid the foundations for the prosperity of the eighties'. It did not: it was unnecessarily deflationary; the 1983 election was won because of the Falklands war. It was not until Nigel Lawson went over the top as Chancellor that the boom was created that characterised the 1980s – and with it the bust that was John Major's inheritance. Kenneth Clarke was the best Chancellor since Roy Jenkins. He curbed inflation and kept public spending under tight control. The Labour Party has never before entered into government with such an encouraging inheritance.

We are told that 'Mr Clarke never came to terms with Mrs Thatcher's leadership.' As much is true of many of us, who disliked her terrifying simplicities, her personal rudeness and her growing eccentricities. The Thatcherites have never forgiven Clarke for telling Mrs T that enough was enough. Peter Lilley did nothing to save her; only Michael Portillo raised a finger to help her, and Portillo, humiliated by the New Labour candidate in Enfield, is out of the game.

Let me continue, if only to reveal the shallowness of this editorial. 'How can a man who hates thinking assist re-thinking?' Is it only the ideologues who are capable of thought? And how does the writer know that Clarke hates thinking? The answer is, of course, that he cannot know it, but has been carried away, like a petty Gladstone, inebriated by the exuberance of his own verbosity. 'Mr Clarke regards the Eurosceptics in his party with serene contempt. They are lunatics, he thinks, and he wants to put straitjackets on them.' I must confess that last week at a meeting of the Malvern Literary Society I ran into a former Tory MP who thought Redwood to be 'mad'; and wasn't it the case that the same prominent Eurosceptics were described by John Major as 'bastards'? Yet the *Daily Telegraph* wants one of them to lead the Tory party backwards into the promised land.

5 June

I am sad that I will not be in the Commons for the leadership election. In 1975 I was persuaded to vote for Margaret Thatcher, a deed that I soon came to regret bitterly. In 1990 I nailed my colours to Michael Heseltine's mast, an act of friendship on my part that had both advantages and disadvantages. On the one hand I made a small fortune out of the media, appearing more often than ever before on the box for fat fees and, as Michael's (then) only biographer, winning handsome commissions to write pieces about 'the young Heseltine' for newspapers like the *Mail* and the *Express*. On the other hand, nobody – not even Michael – took me out to dine, invited me to the Savoy Grill for lunch, or even bothered to convert me to the side of one of the rival candidates. I was given my instructions by that pompous ass Peter Tapsell, an avid Heseltine supporter: 'Do not make jokes about Michael on television.'

Could that message have come from Heseltine himself, who does have the habit of leaving his dirty work to others? I have already mentioned that when I was sacked as editor of his glossy magazine *Town* in 1966, Michael got his sidekick, Lindsay Masters, to winkle me out; and when Michael Mates, who was Heseltine's *chef du cabinet* during the two rounds of the 1990 leadership election, asked his boss why he had received no reward for all his efforts on the new secretary of state's behalf, Heseltine is supposed to have replied: 'You know what I'm like, Michael.' Still, I owe my knighthood to Heseltine – or at least, I imagine I do.

Were I still the Tory MP for Aldershot I would, on this occasion, keep my mouth shut. I would not do what some MPs have been known to do, that is, to tell each of the candidates in turn that he has their undying support. I would not go public, for that would be to discourage the onset of hospitality. I would play possum. I would not tell a single colleague of my intentions. Keeping my cards close to my chest, in the tea room I would listen quietly to the blandishments of the candidates' chiefs of staff, recognising that every one of the principals, even John Redwood, had a point or two in his favour. Anyone who preferred to sleep with his wife rather than spend the night in Cardiff while Secretary of State for Wales must be a very unusual Tory MP.

It would not be long before Alan Clark would invite me to his club, along with some others, in order to twist my arm in favour of X or Y. As Alan (who is as rich as Croesus) believes that the only claret worth drinking costs over £100 a bottle, I would sip his Latour '85 with a quiet pleasure, while playing with a quail or two brought in from Fortnum and Mason. Once again I would murmur something charitable about the candidate of Alan's choice, at the same time congratulating him on his selection as candidate for Kensington – the only bright spot in the election. The Harknesses would come in for some ribald comment. I would love to have caught sight of the South African judge, his ravished wife and seduced daughter canvassing the streets of Kensington for New Labour. The poor judge must have had horns like an elk.

On entering the Members' Lobby shortly thereafter, I would very likely be handed a note from the journalist Simon Heffer, a ginger-haired right-winger and co-originator with myself of 'Essex man'.

'Have booked a table at Tante Claire. One or two of your friends will be there – and John Redwood, of course. 12.45 OK?' Now, Tante Claire is my favourite restaurant. Its pigs' trotters are a great delicacy. I would listen with good manners to the pleadings of my joint hosts, although Redwood's manners are not all they should be (he visited my constituency on more than one occasion in the last parliament without dropping me the customary letter of intent), marvelling at his saturnine charm and somewhat sinister views. Foreign-looking, had he been a Frenchman in the thirties he would probably have been a follower of Charles Maurras and a member of L'Action Française. Still I would give nothing away. I would smile when he attacked John Major's dithering, and cringe imperceptibly behind the vast menu when he spoke of putting the 'great' back into Great Britain. Of what institution was he a Fellow? The Zoological Society?

Ken Clarke would skilfully repay past hospitality, taking me to the Latchmore Baths in Battersea to see a fight between two promising middleweights. We would sit surrounded by large men in purple striped suits, each responsible for a Barbara Windsor lookalike. I suggest that as a Nottingham MP he should urge the local authority to erect a statue to Lawrence. 'TE or DH?' he replies.

An old friend – could it be Jeffrey Archer? – would tell me that 'the friends of William Hague' were invited to the Archer penthouse flat whence we could look down on the Palace of Westminster. 'I will be giving you all Krug and cottage pie.' (Why can't Archer use the word 'champagne' or even 'wine' like everyone else? He has a thing about labels.) My guarded remarks, the hints I would drop, the praise I would spread thinly on the boasting of both candidate and friend, would ensure that my glass was never left unfilled. Lord Parkinson, another of Hague's supporters, would bring the unofficial blessing of his Mistress. Hague, I would be assured, was 'one of us'. Hague himself would no doubt pace the spacious drawing room, asking each of the guests in turn for his views on the problems facing the Tory party. As we left, tipsy but unconvinced, a copy of our host's latest book, signed by the author, would be pressed into our hands.

The fact that someone caught sight of me taking a cup of coffee with Miss Ann Widdecombe, a sassy lady who had the good manners to write to me on the dissolution of Parliament wishing me well, might well put me at a disadvantage with the Michael Howard camp

– or at least prompt some interest from that quarter. Instead of an invitation to the Carlton for lunch (not a gastronomic experience) or to the Red Fort for dinner (much better), I would receive a note asking me to take tea with the former Home Secretary. Although Howard is not my favourite candidate, I would do him the courtesy of sipping a cup of Earl Grey and nibbling a Marie biscuit. Howard has a very pretty wife, the former model Sandra Paul, but I am not as susceptible as I once was. I would make my excuses and leave.

Tea with Howard, the Latchmore Baths with Clarke, Jeffrey Archer's penthouse on behalf of William Hague, Tante Claire as the guest of John Redwood – where would that leave the two remaining candidates, Stephen Dorrell and Peter Lilley? I was once fond of Dorrell, seeing in him the rising hope of the stern unbending left-wing Tories, but his shift to the right has done him a lot of harm and he will probably poll fewer votes than any of the others. In which case I would be only too pleased to dine with him at the Chinese restaurant within the Dorchester, where, over dim sum, prawns with black bean sauce and Czech-brewed beer, I would ask him his views on Chris Patten. Could he be the party's lost leader?

Taking advantage of an interview with the BBC's political correspondent I would let it drop that, although I have not finally made up my mind, I am inclining towards Peter Lilley. As if carried on the wings of Mercury, an invitation would arrive to a *diner intime* at Lilley's Westminster house. The candidate would be wearing his newly purchased suit, shirt and tie (chosen by his wife, Gail). Lilley is refreshingly frank: he confesses that he lacks charisma, without which no Tory can become leader in the age of the soundbite. Did I know a spin doctor whose services I could recommend? Would a Mr Peter Mandelson do, I wonder . . . ?

6 June

Today is nomination day for the five remaining candidates, Stephen Dorrell having dropped out and transferred his support to Kenneth Clarke. The former health secretary's campaign had become increasingly lacklustre; last Saturday he attracted only fifty to a meeting at the Manchester Hilton, which had been packed with 600 who had come to hear Hague the previous night, and on Monday evening only twenty-five to the St James's Court Hotel in London, where 150 had turned up to listen to Peter Lilley.

Clarke remains the most likely to come first in next Tuesday's poll, although it is doubtful whether he will reach the magic figure of 83 which will give him an outright victory. It remains to be seen how many of Dorrell's supporters will switch their allegiance to him. It is just as well that the party activists, however experienced, are excluded from this election, for most of them incline to the right and favour Hague, Howard or, to a lesser extent (because of his disloyalty) Redwood. Senior Tories, on the other hand, who have either retired (as I have) or moved to the Lords (as will John Biffen), would vote overwhelmingly in favour of Clarke. But as it is, the result rests with 164 MPs alone.

At a joint press conference with Dorrell, Clarke said: 'I do not agree that there are many MPs who think the leadership election is about policy towards the single currency. The leadership is about how to win office in five years' time on the basis of a superior body of ideas to that being put forward by the Labour Party and a clear vision of where this country needs to go.' In a pally exchange of compliments, Dorrell said of Clarke: 'Ken Clarke is the outstanding figure of contemporary British politics. He is, in fact, the unity candidate. He is the big hitter of this generation. He should be the next Conservative leader and the next Prime Minister of the United Kingdom.'

The *Times* leader-writer still clings to his doubts about Clarke, while admitting that the former Chancellor's stock seems to be rising. 'He is in the country clearly the most popular potential leader. His personality is bigger and more rumbustious than those of his rivals (*sic*). He is engagingly frank and has proved his combativeness in the Commons.' But 'disdain for the views of others is his most dangerous weakness'. Having compared Clarke with Dennis Healey, who lost the Labour leadership election to Michael Foot, the anonymous writer then expresses his fear that Clarke might well find himself to the left of Blair on many issues. Clarke 'defends the welfare state as if the design of 1948 could not be improved upon.' This cannot be the case, given the way, as health secretary, Clarke upset the doctors by the introduction of the internal market in the health service – now to be abolished by Labour. To accuse Clarke, as *The Times* does, of 'inflexibility' on Europe is to ignore his change of mind on the single currency and his refusal to enter it should the criteria be 'fudged'.

The Times describes Hague as 'a plausible Tony Blair', but on the basis of scant evidence, and John Redwood as a brave politician, principled enough to resign in 1995 and courageous enough since then to speak the truth to power. In fact there was little that was courageous about his machinations in 1995: by a programme of calculated disloyalty he compelled an embattled Prime Minister to lance the wound that Redwood, Howard, Portillo and others had kept festering within the government and party. Redwood then won 89 votes: far more than he is likely to garner next Tuesday at the first ballot. Nevertheless, despite its words of praise, *The Times* does not endorse his candidature this time round on the grounds that his colleagues do not discern within him the lineaments of a leader, and certainly do not detect the talents of a healer. The leader-writer is right on both counts; but he accords too much importance to the capacity to heal the party.

'Kenneth Clarke', he says, 'is another unlikely binder of the party's wounds.' Is the ability to heal really the most important quality needed in the new party leader? Surely not. What is needed is a robust debater, experienced in office, capable of rebuilding the party's morale in the House by a series of scintillating parliamentary performances. But *The Times*, clearly, does not think so. 'Mr Clarke's talents are obvious; his ability to map a path out of the mire for the Tory party is not.' What an example of magisterial claptrap.

The writer then goes on to discuss in flattering terms the talents and records of the two right-wingers, Howard and Lilley. Howard receives high praise for his stint at the Home Office (not widely shared by those at the sharp end), but his chances of leading the party are dismissed without any specific reason being given. Lilley does not possess the 'charisma' of Margaret Thatcher in her early days: 'He is not a grand master of the electronic media.' You can say that again: his performances are generally as wooden as a country oak table. But 'his instincts are the soundest and surest in the field. He is rigorously sceptical about the current European project but never narrowly strident.' He certainly has been at recent party conferences. 'He appreciates the complementary traditions within the Tory party and wants to make use of them all . . .' While not as virulently hostile as his counterpart on the *Telegraph*, the *Times* leader-writer still has to overcome his prejudices against the centre-left of the Tory party.

Around the country, too, the party is ruminating on the leadership. The Ludlow Tories met in the town last night to discuss the matter. Sixteen people were present, all members of the constituency party that readopted Chris Gill. The idea behind the meeting was to ascertain (on Gill's behalf) the feeling within the constituency. The sixteen voted as follows: Lilley 0, Howard 2, Redwood 3, Hague 5, Clarke 6. Gill, of course, will not take a scrap of notice; he is not mandated to vote for anyone save his own choice, which I assume to be Redwood.

Bill Cash, the arch-Eurosceptic who steamrollered his selection at Stone (Sir David Knox suddenly withdrew) has become quite remarkably unpopular in the west midlands. He did not turn up at the association's AGM, pleading a three-line whip. This could have been midweek on the Queen's Speech; it seems curious that the local party did not hold its AGM on a Friday, the one evening in the week when Members are free to visit their constituencies. It is not so much his views that have upset many of his constituents as his arrogance. I have, in my time, sat through a couple of Cash's speeches and have never been so bored in my life. He is lucky to be sustained by a charming wife and pretty daughter. A small fish in a small Westminster pond, he is now likely to sink into obscurity from which, in the past, he was drawn only by John Major's vulnerability. What was fun was to receive the information that the Stone Tories also favoured Clarke.

William Hill's odds on the contenders are at present: Redwood 33–1; Howard 16–1; Lilley 11–2; Hague 6–5; Clarke 5–6.

7 June

During a weekend in which the remnant of the Tory party tried to make up its collective mind about the leadership, the Bruges Society sent me a leaflet for a forthcoming publication called *Britain Held Hostage: The Common Euro-Dictatorship* by one Lindsay Jenkins (no relation of Roy). It bears a quotation from Lord Harris of High Cross, a Thatcher courtier: 'A persuasive case that United Europe was always a political wolf disguised in economic clothing.'

The body copy read: 'The how and why of the European Union explained and exposed. Discover which British and American friends in high places were planning one Europe even before the Second World War and how they took over American policy after the war.

They backed resistance leaders who had fought for a superstate like Nazi Europe but without Hitler.' It goes on to tell us that today Britain has a new constitution, the Treaty of Rome; British law is subservient to European law. 'Shortly Britain may be a province in a German Europe.' Proposals for one army and one police force are only the latest in a long line of 'small steps' leading to 'major consequences' for British voters. 'Soon the British will know they won the war but lost the peace.

That there are still intelligent people who can write and believe such tosh beggars belief. While I am prepared to admit that the speed of progress within Europe towards integration has left a section of public opinion behind, it is the far right, whether in Britain, France or Germany, that is most bitterly opposed to the New Europe. They are as unscrupulous as they are obscurantist. The sentence 'Shortly Britain may be a province in a German Europe' is a shameful appeal to anti-German sentiment which is still strong among the unsophisticated. Another sentence, 'They had backed a superstate like Nazi Europe but without Hitler', is a good example of conferring guilt by false association. The resistance leaders in France, the Netherlands and Belgium were too busy killing Germans to consider building a similar totalitarian superstate.

The anti-Hitler conspirators in Germany, men such as Beck, Gordeler and Von Stauffenberg, wanted to see a new Europe purged of fascism and free of communist domination. The European Movement began immediately after the war under the auspices of Schuman, an Alsatian Frenchman who had fought in the German army but had reverted to French nationality, de Gasperi of Italy, a country dragged unwillingly into war by Mussolini, and Chancellor Adenauer, whose aim it was to turn Germany away from conquest in the east towards European unity. German democracy has been a triumph for good sense and wise leadership.

That organisations like the Bruges Group, which consists of nationalists like Norman Tebbit – to name only one of its more respectable members – should have gained such a hold on the Conservative Party demonstrates a failure of leadership on the part of the forces of light. They would back Redwood or, if not him, Howard. They speak for one of the most unpleasant manifestations of contemporary British politics.

8 June

The *Independent on Sunday* carried a story claiming that the three right-wing candidates would meet privately to see how best one of them can stop Clarke and, if it comes to that, Hague ('the new Major'). Peter Lilley is, as I feared, emerging as the man most likely to beat Clarke. He expects to come third on Tuesday behind Clarke and Hague, and then, with Clarke falling short of the 83 votes he needs to win outright, to persuade Howard and Redwood to stand down, thus transferring their votes to Lilley on the second ballot a week later. However, Michael Howard is still making confident noises suggesting he will come second on Tuesday, and that Lilley and Redwood will then be obliged to fall out.

Hague, who so far has received more publicity than any of the other contenders, is the subject of a profile by Marianne Macdonald in the paper's magazine section. The article seems to concentrate on Hague's fiancée, and alludes in passing to the suspicion voiced by some in the past that Hague is a homosexual. In the same paper Hague comes out in favour of gay marriage: 'When they are not causing any harm to other people why should we object?', he asks. In order to maintain some sort of balance he comes down against abortion, however.

Redwood has won the support of John Townend, chairman of the right-wing '92 Club and one of the stupidest and least impressive Tory MPs on record. What a pity that he should have survived the May holocaust. Ninety per cent of the Tory right are as thick as two short planks; 10 per cent are clever men, such as David Davis.

Archie Norman, the Asda whiz-kid, is, so I am told by my spies, becoming increasingly bored with the House. He has been described as being like 'Albert Speer without the humour'. The trouble with businessmen in politics is that they swiftly find they cannot give orders; they are obliged to persuade – and soon get bored.

The atmosphere among the new intake is just as I would have expected: not one of them has had to pay for his own lunch or dinner for the past fortnight, so intensely have the rivals been canvassing. Damien Green and Shaun Woodward have declared their support for Ken Clarke, as have all seventeen Tory MEPs, including Graham Mather. Among the 'stars' of the new intake are Keith Simpson, Teresa May and Andrew Lansley, who was once political secretary to

Norman Tebbit and is known as 'the convenor' owing to his habit of getting the new intake together in order to take its temperature. Desmond Swain – a 'headbanger' – has come out for Howard.

My successor Gerald Howarth, who is voting for Lilley, spent part of his first speech as Member for Aldershot making references to his predecessor (I am sending for the *Hansard*) and the rest attacking Martin Bell and defending Neil Hamilton. He did not 'catch the ear of the House'. Bill Cash, I gather, is now regarded as old hat. He spoiled PM's questions (in which John Major had done well attacking Tony Blair) by asking a final question on Europe, thus bringing forth groans from his own side (and the chance for Blair to strike back at Major). He now rings up the media, only to be told that events have moved on and he is no longer of any interest. He is yesterday's man.

9 June

D–1. Today's papers show that the right has got its knickers in a twist. *The Times*' headline reads 'Tory right battles for chance to beat Clarke', while the *Telegraph* trumpets that Lady Thatcher has intervened in order to persuade the right to run one candidate against Clarke in the second round. The paper reports that 'the Lady' is disenchanted with Hague. Howard robustly refuses to be the one to give way: he sees a Clarke v. Howard final, while Redwood, basking in the support of *Sun* readers, says he will continue the fight. The *Telegraph* leader-writer repeats his efforts of last week and once again rehearses his arguments in favour of Peter Lilley. The *Times* leader-writers are presumably holding their fire until tomorrow.

The *Express* has declared itself for Michael Howard, and the *Financial Times* for Kenneth Clarke.

The *Express*, true to the Max Beaverbrook inheritance, declares that 'the new leader must unite the party on the one issue that split it, Europe. Given the dominant Tory sentiment, this must mean a clear policy of Euroscepticism and principled opposition to a single currency.' There is no evidence that Euroscepticism is the 'dominant Tory sentiment'. It was not so at the election; in fact, since the premiership of Harold Macmillan the Tory party has been the European party. I suspect that what the *Express* really wants is for Britain to leave the European Union, which, although close to what has come

to be called Euroscepticism, is not quite the same thing. As for the
common currency, that is now the responsibility of the government.
Were it to decide on entry in the second wave in the year 2000, the
result of a vote in favour in Parliament would be put to the country
in a referendum. The Tory party's view can only count for less and
less – a factor which works in favour of Ken Clarke.

The *Express* leader-writer talks of 'an ERM-induced recession', a
false attribution. The recession with which John Major had to wrestle
during his period of office was induced by the combination of Lawson
as Chancellor and Thatcher as Prime Minister. The writer, who appears
to be more ignorant than most of his sub-species, doubts whether Clarke
has the vision (to do what, exactly? He does not say) or the capacity for
strategic thinking (about what? Once again, we are not told). The paper
finally comes down in favour of Howard, despite the fact that he is perceived to be 'unattractively belligerent'. Little wonder the *Express* is but
a shadow of the newspaper it once was.

The *Financial Times* plainly employs a better class of leader-writer.
'The next election will be won and lost in the centre ground.' He
continues: 'Of the five candidates for the leadership, Mr William
Hague offers youth and a fresh start, while Mr Peter Lilley offers
intellectual edge. Publicly, at least, both have been prepared to temper
their Euroscepticism, a shift that Mr Michael Howard and Mr John
Redwood have been unwilling to make. Mr Kenneth Clarke, the
former Chancellor, has been alone, however, in confronting openly
the real lessons of defeat. He has the experience and the pugnacity
required to restore the party's spirits at Westminster and to capitalise
on the inevitable mistakes of Mr Blair's government. His powerful
political presence and natural charm give him a strong public profile
. . . The choice is between the indulgence of introspection and the
hard task of winning the next election. By electing Mr Clarke as leader
the party would send a powerful signal that it had opted for the second
course.'

Most unusually, yesterday's *Sunday Express*, once the paper in which
the late John Junor flourished his prejudices, gave Lady Thatcher a
stinging rebuke. Its leader began: 'Like old soldiers, old politicians
should face gracefully away. They have had their day on the battlefield
and in the Commons. Margaret Thatcher had a longer day than most.
As the first woman Prime Minister and holder of that office for eleven

years, she left behind a name to be remembered with respect and even affection. It is then sad indeed that, as the *Sunday Express* reveals, she should contemplate sullying her reputation.'

The suggestion is that if Kenneth Clarke, her former Cabinet colleague and ex-Chancellor of the Exchequer, were to be elected as the new party leader, she would form a group within the party to oppose and obstruct him. What could she possibly hope to achieve by such antics? 'Westminster and the party now belongs to a new generation.'

This rebuke for Lady Thatcher is well deserved. She has been a pain in the butt ever since her ejection in 1990. She must have exulted (privately) at John Major's defeat. She has been prompt to give Blair advice. On the assumption that Redwood comes last tomorrow, she will come out for either Howard or Lilley. She has never forgiven Clarke for his advice in 1990 that she should abandon the premiership on the not unreasonable grounds that she had become intolerable and that her poll tax was a certain vote-loser.

The *Mail on Sunday*, on the other hand, came out not for one candidate but for three – or, to be fair, for the one on the right of the party who polls the most votes tomorrow. Ken Clarke it describes as 'bluff and blowsy'; the writer fears that he will either win outright in the first ballot or, more likely, develop an unstoppable momentum that will carry him to victory in the second ballot. Clarke is then blamed for losing the Tories the election. The anonymous scribe borrows heavily from his *Telegraph* colleague in giving an opinion on Clarke's character: 'All too often Mr Clarke gives the impression of being indifferent to detail and averse to hard work and remarkably closed to new ideas.' He 'gives the impression'? Either he is bone idle or he is not. The *Mail on Sunday*'s leader-writer is worthy of his calling.

10 June

Last night's *Panorama* devoted itself to an over-dramatised and only partially accurate account of the decline and fall of the Tory government. It made no mention whatever of public disquiet with the lack of spending on education or the unabsorbed and unpopular reforms within the health service – which can be traced back directly to the Thatcher years. Instead, it showed John Major at bay, surrounded by 'bastards' both within and beyond his Cabinet, fighting a losing battle against disloyalty and deceit. The BBC paraded before the cameras as nasty a bunch of Tories as one could hope to find – the Kray Brothers of contemporary Conservatism. No wonder Major is reported as having said during the campaign, when someone as unimportant as John Horam (ex-Labour, ex-SDP and then a Tory junior minister) refused to follow the government's 'wait and see' line on a common currency, 'Sometimes I wonder why I bother.'

11 June

The result of the first ballot: Clarke 49 (less than he had hoped for); Hague 41 (more than he dared contemplate); Redwood 27 (more than he expected); Lilley 24; Howard 23.

On the same day, the unofficial ballots from the Tory associations and Tory peers gave Clarke a massive lead; and he got the votes of all seventeen Conservative MEPs.

Thus we are, at first sight, little better off. Today Lilley and Howard withdrew, saying they would back Hague. Much indignation in the Redwood camp, some of whose members spoke of broken undertakings.

At this stage one can only guess, but it seems likely to me that Clarke will come out of round two slightly ahead of Hague, who will be slightly further ahead of Redwood. The overwhelming majority of Redwood's votes will then go to Hague in the final round, which will give him the victory over Clarke. Be vague; ask for Hague. What fools we Tories are.

13 June

Who would be a *Telegraph* leader-writer? Having backed all the wrong horses (with bad arguments), today's piece was entitled 'Who is William Hague?'

I think we all have a right to know, as it is looking likely that he might, narrowly, come out on top in the third round. We know that in the past he has been a considerable teenage conference orator and an undistinguished Secretary of State for Wales; and that he is now thirty-six, balding and engaged to be married, having been a victim of the usual malicious gossip. I listened yesterday to Hague being cross-examined by John Humphrys on the wireless. Humphrys failed to ask the one question that would have really mattered, namely: 'Were Blair to take Britain into the common currency and the ecu prove a success, would you bring back the pound?' In the absence of that fast ball, Hague was able to keep his bat reasonably straight.

The *Telegraph*, which is clearly punch-drunk after what happened to Lilley and Howard in the first ballot, posed several questions. First it noted that 'Mr Hague said yesterday that he would fight the next general election on a pledge that "we would not abolish the pound", although he refuses to rule the move out for ever.' Back to John Humphrys' unasked question. The leader-writer continues: 'Does he also believe that the United Kingdom has already conceded too much power to the EU? If so, does he believe that no more power should be conceded, or that some should be regained? If so, again would he be prepared to renegotiate some parts of the Maastricht Treaty and the Treaty of Rome? As well as parts of the Treaty that Labour will sign in Amsterdam?'

These questions show how suspicious the *Telegraph* is of Hague. In order to win, Hague has to collect most, if not all, of Redwood's votes. The questions are unfair because they assume not only that Hague will beat Clarke, but that Hague's Tories will win the next general election – two imponderables. The leader-writer should be reminded that Tony Blair is Prime Minister and Robin Cook his Foreign Secretary. No Tory leader could commit himself in advance to policies over which we have no control.

The *Telegraph* then moves on to the question of removing hereditary peers from the House of Lords, a reform of which he was once in favour. 'Mr Hague has written that "the present composition of the House of Lords can no longer be defended" and said "it is hard to defend an assembly where the members sit through privilege or accident of birth". Hague has said he is a "radical"; is that what he means?' It continues: 'The article and the speech were made a long time ago – in 1978 and 1980 respectively. But defence of the Lords will be one of the party's main tasks in the Commons, and so the question must be asked: "Does Mr Hague believe that hereditary peers should remain in the second chamber?"' I do not believe that this particular question was put by the *Telegraph* to either Howard or Lilley.

And the questions kept coming:

Mr Hague criticised the directors of Camelot for taking their pay bonuses. 'I do not think the Conservative party should be afraid to say that some people have abused the position that we have put them in,' he said. But the bonuses could not remotely be described as an abuse of the directors' position; they were related to Camelot's excellent 1996 results. Could the ex Welsh Secretary explain what he meant?

Last Sunday Mr Hague said that he was in favour of homosexual marriages. 'When they are not causing any harm to other people, why should we object?' He emphasised that this was a personal view, and not one that he would seek to impose on the party. But does he really think that such a view could be described as Conservative?

Mr Hague is now opposed to euthanasia. It appears that he was once in favour of 'the general principle'. Why did he change his mind?

There is a time to keep silent and a time to speak. Now it is Mr Hague's time to speak . . .

This remarkable leader by a newspaper that has always supported right-wing candidates for the leadership can only help Ken Clarke. Hague is a young man, with a young man's views. Few Tories (save for me) would sympathise with his views on euthanasia; even fewer would advocate homosexual marriages. As for the future of the Lords, the important thing is its powers, not its composition. The Tory party should be prepared to embrace radical change. I think the significance of this leader is that it shows the disenchantment with the right, whose sole standard-bearer now remaining is the unelectable Redwood. Will Redwood's votes on a third ballot go to Clarke or to Hague – or to no one? The contest is still wide open.

15 June

The German poet Schiller wrote a line which aptly describes the present state of the Tory party in Westminster: 'Against stupidity even the gods struggle in vain.'

Clarke stands to win the second ballot against Hague and Redwood by perhaps six votes, with Redwood in third place, his votes coming largely from right-wingers. Unless the rump of 164 Tories wake up to what is happening, when Redwood's votes are transferred on the third ballot the result is likely to put Hague narrowly in front of Clarke. Knowing the prejudices of Tory MPs pretty well after over thirty years in the House, and having read the list of who voted for each candidate in the first round, I am fairly certain that my forecast of a likely Hague victory could be realised.

My prediction of the outcome is shared by the bulk of today's Sunday papers. What is worse, they claim that Hague will offer Clarke the deputy leadership if, and only if, he renounces support for a common currency for ten years. This would be a device deliberately designed to send Clarke to the back benches, embitter the left of the party and drive people like Michael Heseltine out of Tory politics altogether. The real winner of such an outcome would be neither Redwood nor the infant Hague but the sinister figure of an unforgiving Margaret Thatcher. In 1990 she lost the premiership; in 1997 she will revenge herself by destroying the Conservative Party.

Kenneth Clarke is far and away the best-equipped Tory to lead the party on what will inevitably be a long journey back to power. He has the support of all the party's MEPs, the overwhelming majority of Tory peers (many of whom have been in the Commons) and of most of the constituency chairmen. All of these have been ignored by the worst elements of a defeated party. That these 164 survivors should have foisted an unknown thirty-six-year-old on to the party as its leader precisely because he is neither Clarke nor Redwood can only be an act of political stupidity. Have we not troubles enough, faced with a popular Labour Prime Minister with an enormous majority, a tranquil economy and the prospect of peace? On top of it all, must we now nurse William Hague into a position where he will be taken seriously by an uncaring electorate among whom he is largely unknown?

Clarke was crucially handicapped by the size of the rump of the post-election Tory party. Had 265 Tories been returned instead of 165 he would have walked it. Sixty-two Members retired at the dissolution, and high proportion of today's MPs are new to Parliament. They are as green as so many unripe bananas. They have only heard Clarke, Redwood and Hague perform at party conferences at the seaside; they have no knowledge of how the contenders have performed in the House of Commons, and it is competence in the House that matters.

Can any rational being suppose that William Hague can dominate the House with its enormous Labour majority? He may well have obliged Mrs Thatcher to get to her feet twenty years ago to join a conference ovation given to a precocious sixteen-year-old (while many of us went outside to vomit), but what else has 'Just William' achieved? He served an unremarkable stint at the Welsh Office in John Major's government; otherwise – nowt. He is in favour of homosexual marriage and the abolition of the hereditary principle of entry into the House of Lords. Perhaps with John Redwood in mind, he has flirted with the idea of euthanasia. He should be dismissed – rightly – as Curzon – wrongly – dismissed Baldwin: 'a man of utmost insignificance'.

And what can one say about Redwood that has not been said already? A satanic figure of the kind that would put Miss Ann Widdecombe to flight; were he to become leader by some mischance, half the Tory party would get into bed with Paddy Ashdown. As it is, were Clarke forced to the back benches, Tories both within and outside the House would be bound to reconsider their position.

Clarke is a One Nation Tory in a party suffering from Thatcheritis. He is not a nationalist, as is Redwood. He stands for something, unlike Hague. And again unlike Hague, he has done more in his political life than lay down a series of markers announcing his ambition.

What an appalling mess! Only Ken Clarke can offer the party leadership from the centre, which is the ground on which elections are won and lost. Lloyd George once called the Conservatives 'the stupid party': surely he cannot still be right? If the 164 vote for Hague on Tuesday in defiance of majority opinion in the party at large, the leader of the opposition will be drawing his pension before he takes office.

16 June

I had a thought in the night. Were William Hague to win, and Clarke to return to the back benches – as he has threatened to do – the 'fall guy' must be John Redwood. Had he not resigned from the Welsh Office in 1995 to take on John Major, Hague would probably not have been promoted to Cabinet rank – or, at any rate, not soon enough to make him a credible leadership challenger this year. So one could say that, had Redwood been less ambitious in 1995, he might very well have been the favoured candidate of the right in 1997, Lilley and Howard being disqualified – or so it seems – for personal reasons.

18 June

The result of yesterday's ballot was as follows: Clarke 64; Hague 62; Redwood 38. The left is thus outnumbered by nearly forty votes and a Hague victory in the third ballot seems likely. Will Redwood prove to have been the kingmaker? If so, it can only be King Billy about to ascend the throne, having moved steadily towards a centre-right position. Most, if not all, of Redwood's 'barmy army' can now only throw themselves behind 'Just William'.

Today's *Times* leader struck a somewhat tentative note: 'Mr Hague's relatively disappointing performance shows the extent of the doubts about his candidacy. Messrs Howard and Lilley threw their weight behind him; fewer than half their supporters followed. Some were unimpressed by his performance on Monday evening, when he addressed a gathering of MPs. Even if he does win tomorrow, his victory will be a poor weak thing . . . Hague's views have seemed to move, even in the past week. If he were to win, he would start to suffer John Major's problems from day one. Both the right and the left would try to pull him in their direction, strengthened by the haziness of his opinion . . .'

This morning we drove to London. At eleven o'clock the news on the car radio told us that Clarke and Redwood had struck a deal. In return for Redwood's support, Clarke would make him shadow Chancellor. I was astounded. Is this another Hitler–Stalin pact? Is the move too clever by half? Will it swing opinion Hague's way by its very outrageousness? More to the point, can Redwood the Immaculate (from the point of view of his coterie) carry with him the bulk of his supporters in this new guise? At the end of the news it was announced that Lady Thatcher, who has never been very far from the scene of the action, has come out for Hague.

This evening we heard Peter Tapsell spluttering with rage on behalf of Puffing Billy, and Mrs Thatcher reminding the people (as if we did not know it already) that Hague was her man. 'He will govern as I did,' she proclaimed with typical vanity. Mrs Gorman, whom I have always thought daft, has come out for Clarke ('He is a big hitter') and so has the taciturn John Wilkinson. Clarke and Redwood made frequent appearances on television, claiming that they would work together, and that there would be a free vote on the common currency. What an odd couple!

The excitement in and around Westminster must be intense; how I wish I were still an MP, able to vote and to vote for Clarke.

19 June

The Clarke–Redwood pact has incurred the wrath of the combined right-wing press. Terrified at the prospect (however remote) of a Clarke victory, the editor of the *Telegraph*, Charles Moore himself, left his ivory tower to pen a major article on the op-ed page. He was beside himself with indignation. Under a somewhat fanciful heading 'A marriage made in the Tory party's hell' and a pastiche of a Low cartoon, Moore wrote of Clarke and Redwood getting wed in the registry office of politics. Clarke, were he to win, 'would impose upon the Tory party the most left-wing policies he can possibly get away with. He will make the Tory party the more high-spending and Europhile of the two social democratic parties.' Moore's anger, however, was concentrated on Redwood, who had clearly let the side down.

Moore went on: 'Westminster is a village and one so inbred that it has more than its fair share of village idiots, immemorial feuds and malicious rumours. It may be that too many of the villagers are sucked into all that. But the rest of us can at least point out how the Clarke/ Redwood deal looks from the outside. It looks, in Lady Thatcher's words, "incredible".'

All good stuff; but is not 'Fleet Street', however geographically scattered it may now be, every bit as much a village with its quota of idiots, feuds, malice and rumours?

He concluded: 'Today the Conservatives have to choose a leader, not a team, and there are only two candidates. Both are able, but neither is ideal. One leans to the left and is Europhile. The other leans to the right and is Eurosceptic. Don't you have to choose according to which of these points of view you share? I apologise if this reasoning seems too simple for "the most sophisticated electorate in the world".'

Having dismissed Hague in a leader last week, the *Telegraph* now declares itself for 'King Billy'. Such are the vagaries of both politics and journalism.

20 June

The final result was worse than I had feared: Hague 92, Clarke 70. Ken Clarke immediately and graciously stated that he would not serve on the front bench. 'For twenty-six years on the front bench I have served either in government or shadow in nearly every capacity. I fear I shall lose my appetite for politics.'

Lady Thatcher proclaimed Hague's elevation a victory for herself; and, in a sense, it was. Clarke had been her implacable enemy. 'King Billy' moved to Conservative Central Office, where he resurrected Cecil Parkinson as the new party chairman. No doubt tomorrow morning's tabloids will be reminding us all of the Parkinson *affaire* which so convulsed the 1980s – if they have any room to spare after the attention they will no doubt devote to the collapse of Jonathan Aitken's libel action, which he has abandoned on the revelation that he lied about the Ritz hotel bill. The one-time Golden Boy of the party has turned out to be cast in the mould of his wicked great-uncle, Max Beaverbrook. For his part, Cecil now has the appearance of an elderly roué.

Michael Howard has been rewarded with the post of shadow Foreign Secretary, Lilley with the shadow chancellorship. Even Redwood, whose reputation must have suffered more than any of the other contenders', was rewarded for the Clarke–Redwood pact by being made shadow industry spokesman. Of the moderates, only Dorrell was acknowledged, with education and employment. John Gummer, who had been an admirable Secretary of State for the Environment, was despatched to the back benches, where he will join Ken Clarke – who promises to behave much as Heath did in the early eighties. Hague declared that the Tories would oppose a common currency for what amounts to two parliaments. Thus we have become a fully Eurosceptic party, in one more betrayal of the European ideal for which the Conservative Party can once again plead guilty.

The return of the Bourbons: surely this is the only way to describe the Hague Shadow Cabinet and his Central Office appointments. We are in the Paris of 1816. The clock has been turned back. But it will not much matter: it will be at least ten years before the Tories can mount a serious challenge to New Labour for the centre ground which it has now occupied and fortified. When Hague made his victory speech, he included an appeal for party unity, at which point it did not go unnoticed that a wry smile appeared on John Major's face. Party unity, or rather party disunity, was what did for 'dear John'. (The cover of *Private Eye* on 27 June showed Hague saying 'I want to bring Unity to the party', and Parkinson replying, 'Good idea. She sounds like a goer'.)

The moderate pro-Europeans in the party are despondent. There is talk of a breakaway faction, to be called 'Christian Democrats'. Perhaps unity would have been out of the grasp of whoever had won. But what, frankly, does it all matter? The party was not electing a prime minister. It will be ten to twenty years before Hague can reach No. 10, and in the meantime Central Office and the parliamentary party face two mammoth tasks: the revitalisation of the party in the country, and the reform of the electoral system that made such a mockery out of this leadership contest.

The real victor has been Lady Thatcher, who had spent much of her time towards the end of the campaign hanging round the Commons tea room, making converts for Hague. She has had her revenge for 1990.

Ninety-two Tories took a gamble on William Hague to give him his prize. I hope, for the sakes of all the millions who have served, worked for and voted for the Conservative Party, that he does not make a mess of it.

PART V

The Tories and Europe: The Great Betrayal?

JULIAN CRITCHLEY

The equivocal attitude shown by both the Conservative and Labour parties to European monetary union (the common currency), and a similar equivocation shown by all the candidates for the Tory party leadership, save for Ken Clarke, prompts me to enter deeper waters than we were used to swim in during and after the general election. Throughout the campaign, 'Europe' was the one issue avoided by the leaders of the Tory and Labour parties alike. Labour politicians hostile to European integration bit their tongues; Tory Eurosceptics did their best to rock John Major's boat. They were the defeatists among Tories, interested not so much in victory as in the consequences of defeat.

It is hardly surprising that it has been difficult to conduct a rational discussion when the issues have been presented in such highly coloured and emotional terms. Margaret once said, in her speech to the College of Europe in Bruges, that 'Britain's destiny lies in Europe as part of the Community'; more recently, John Redwood and other Eurosceptics have described monetary union as a turning point in the retreat from independent nationhood, and an irrevocable step on the road to a federal European super-state. No wonder that public opinion is both confused and apathetic.

No one should be under any illusion that the EMU is essentially a political question; the economics are subordinate. Broadly speaking, those who are in favour of European integration are generally favourable to the concept of EMU, though many of them see considerable problems in its implementation. For those people who see further integration as sounding the death knell of the nation-state, the common currency is anathema. This Manichaean antithesis has produced some curious distortions in the debate as the political pundits strive to tailor their economic judgements to suit their political prejudices. Lifelong monetarists preach the need to preserve the sacred right to devalue and manipulate interest rates, while unreconstructed Keynesians praise the counter-inflationary rigour of the Bundesbank. The voters cannot be blamed for finding it hard to follow the arguments.

The economic attraction of EMU has its roots in the abiding hunger for monetary stability. Volatile exchange rates and turbulent currency markets are a twentieth-century phenomenon, born of the perception that governments can and should manipulate policy to meet the expectations of their electors in respect of improved living standards and protection from the painful consequences of adverse economic conditions. It is easy to forget that in the days of the gold standard monetary policy was largely concerned with ensuring that the national reserves were adequate to sustain confidence that government debt could be honoured; exchange rates rarely moved, and unless there was a war or another catastrophe, interest rates remained constant.

Of course, it would be absurd to suggest that in these days of a global economy and information technology so advanced that huge sums of money can be moved from one market to another at the touch of a keypad, we could somehow return to a world of fixed exchange rates, but these developments also raise questions about the credibility of independent national monetary policy. To quote Lady Thatcher, 'you can't buck the markets'. It may well be that history will see the postwar period of Keynesian-style interventionism as an interlude during which monetary management shifted from one form of external discipline to another.

While volatile exchange rates have made fortunes for currency traders such as George Soros, there is no doubt that they have been extremely bad for business. Constant change in parities across a wide spectrum of national currencies makes pricing uncertain and investment problematic. So it is not surprising that larger companies who invest and trade heavily across currency boundaries have been among the most consistent advocates of a single currency.

With stability comes the prospect of economic growth coupled with a reduction in inflationary tendencies and downward pressure on interest rates, both regarded as paramount objectives of government policy since the stagflation experienced in the 1970s. An independent central bank, bound by its statute to maintain price stability and backed by the resources of up to a dozen advanced industrial economies, is likely to be far more credible in controlling inflation than any politicians, however determined and well-intentioned. Look at the relationship between Ken Clarke and Eddie George. It is the central bank's task to stop politicians from creating artificial booms to coincide happily with the electoral cycle. It is no accident that countries such as the USA and Germany (and now, thanks to Gordon Brown, the UK), whose central banks are relatively independent, have demonstrated the best record of low inflation. With such credibility come lower interest rates as the markets no longer require a premium to compensate for the inflation risk.

Some have argued that there are ways of achieving stability without going the whole hog and creating a single currency. The experience of the European exchange rate mechanism suggests otherwise. The ERM was a sophisticated attempt to provide an area of currency stability, while leaving scope for national monetary policies to operate, through a system of fixed exchange rates with some capacity for adjustment. In the end the system proved unable to resist the power of the money markets, thus proving – at great economic and political cost – that there is no middle way between floating currencies and the irrevocable locking of exchange rates which makes speculation impossible.

'Black Wednesday', when Chancellor Lamont was forced to announce our withdrawal from the ERM, was a catastrophe from which the Major administration never recovered. The public opinion polls immediately after that episode showed how unpopular the government had become, and they told the same story right up to polling day. But one failed experiment should not preclude an attempt at another; the common currency could provide the bulwark against the currency speculation that ruined the ERM.

There should also be supply-side gains to a common currency. A single monetary unit has the major advantage of removing artificial price distortions in a single market area. At present the price of the same product can differ substantially between two national markets because it is denominated in different currencies which are subject to constant change in their relative values. In a currency union such as the United States, where the dollar is the same in New York as it is in Texas, consumers can make exact comparisons between the value

of different product offers. As a result competition is focused on the
intrinsic value of the product, making the market more efficient. Similar considerations apply to the allocation of capital resources: a single
currency would greatly facilitate cross-frontier investment transfers,
so that funds would flow naturally to those projects providing the best
return, with consequent gains in competitiveness. In both cases a
single currency seems the natural corollary of a single European
market founded on the free movement of capital, goods and services.
With 53 per cent of its total trade in goods and services being conducted with other EU countries, Britain has everything to gain from
stable and consistent growth, low inflation and competitive markets
on the European continent, and if EMU makes such things possible,
it is a major prize.

Try condensing the last paragraph into a 'soundbite' and you will
see just how hard it is to make people see sense, and how simple it
is to frighten them by a resort to cheap xenophobia. Given that the
reader has been carried thus far, the anti-EMU case can be seen as
springing from funk out of raw nationalism. How many of the Tory
candidates (over two hundred of them) who disregarded the party's
manifesto, and who were largely responsible for John Major's defeat,
understood the issues at stake? It could only have been a very few.

Let me offer several quotations. In his recent report for the Economist Intelligence Unit, Professor David Currie of the London
Business School concluded that 'with the right set of policy responses,
the EMU could ... travel towards a sustainable and well functioning
monetary union. With appropriate policies, Europe could become an
economic dynamo. Without them, it will continue to decline and lose
out to other parts of the world, particularly Asia.'

Ian Davidson, rapporteur for the Action Centre for Europe's Kingsdown inquiry, noted in his report that 'we have to keep in mind that
leading member states of the European Union, with long track records
of economic management far more successful than Britain's, are politically committed to monetary union. Are we to believe that they have
engaged themselves frivolously and ignorantly in a senseless adventure
that is bound to go wrong? Are we to suppose that, if defects arise,
they will not subsequently take steps to remedy the system in the light
of experience?'

What, then, is Britain's interest? So far I have suggested that for the EU as a whole the economic advantages of EMU significantly outweigh the disadvantages, and the risks of going ahead are less than the risks of abandonment. The Kingsdown inquiry concluded: 'On balance, the message from most of the participants was: and if it works well it is probably in Britain's interest to be part of it. But several of them added: it may not work well.' On the face of it, this seems like an endorsement of the official consensus between the two main parties on a policy of 'wait and see'. Sadly, wait and see is probably the most advanced pro-European position possible, given the prevailing state of public opinion. The United Kingdom may have the chance to join in a second wave, perhaps in 2002 when euro notes and coins become available – but we cannot take our admission then for granted.

What are the risks of staying out?

If we assume that EMU starts on schedule with a hard core of seven or eight members, Britain will be one of the outs for at least two or three years. As a result we shall be excluded from decisions on European monetary policy and will not be represented on the board of the European central bank. To that extent we will find ourselves in an outer tier, a position analogous to that of the EFTA countries: heavily dependent on our trade with the EU states but unable to take part in some decisions that vitally affect our national interest. It is a curious way of protecting our 'sovereignty'.

Companies trading across the single market would tend to use the euro instead of sterling for their major transactions, so there would be a loss of business to the banking industry and financial services in general would be disadvantaged through having to offer products denominated in a currency in which they only had limited reserves.

While the City would continue to survive and prosper outside EMU, this is not to say that not joining would be a cost-free alternative. If Britain were to opt out of the single currency it would reduce its overall participation in the European Union, and might jeopardise its position in the single market; member states that went ahead, by contrast, would tend to reinforce their economic integration, and thus become more attractive to inward investment – for example from Japan.

It is hardly surprising that neither the Blair government nor the rump of the Tory party any longer has the stomach to take decisions of such magnitude. Of the Tory leadership candidates, only Ken

Clarke was in favour of the EMU. Dorrell is full of fudge; Howard, Redwood and Lilley were all hostile, as is Hague. They are Nervous Nellies, unduly influenced by newspaper opinion (which is largely Atlanticist) and represent the worst elements in the 'stupid party'.

*

How did we reach this state of stagnation and pusillanimity? It is worth taking a look back at the evolution of Britain's, and the Tory party's, ideas about the European project in the years immediately after the Second World War. Did Britain's leaders then have a true allegiance to the vision of a united Europe, or were their rousing speeches and protestations of commitment mere window-dressing, a veil drawn over quite other priorities?

In the 1970s, as a consolation prize for lack of office, the Tory party whips appointed me as a delegate to the Council of Europe and the Western European Union: one of thirty-six MPs from the three parties who would travel to Strasbourg three times a year, and twice to Paris. I and my Conservative colleagues in the delegation were drawn from *le deuxième cru* of the party, and our expeditions, invariably by charter flight, were in marked contrast to those of the late forties and early fifties, when Winston Churchill, Duncan Sandys, Anthony Eden and Harold Macmillan, among many such others, boarded the express at La Gare de L'Est on a six-hour journey bound for the delights of Strasbourg. They would have been pulled by a great black pacific steam locomotive, which, its distinguished passengers having taken their places among the snow-white napery of the dull-green restaurant car, would have gathered speed through the darkening industrial suburbs of Paris, causing no more disturbance within than the gentle tinkling of ice on glass. And how well they must have dined, those great men, cosseted by the best chefs of the SNCF and comforted by a noble claret! They would have arrived at Strasbourg at a late hour, these mellow victors of Hitler's war, to be met by le Préfet, the Mayor and the city's band. Vive Churchill! Vive L'Angleterre! Vive la France!

In the early seventies the Council of Europe was still housed in a prefabricated two-storey building in the northern suburbs of the city, opposite a park with a sad zoo, a lake and a large building used frequently for *les vins d'honneur*. The dingy building was torn down in 1978 and replaced by a spectacular new Palais, opened by Giscard d'Estaing in a ceremony that rivalled in magnificence the opening of the Odeon, Swiss Cottage, by Merle Oberon and Alexander Korda immediately before the outbreak of the war. To the new building were ceremoniously moved the yellowing photographs of the great men of the forties: Churchill; his two sons-in-law, Sandys and Soames, standing besides the well-upholstered figure of Bob Boothby, their faces flushed by *les vins d'Alsace*. Here they stand in the congenial company of those 'fathers' of Europe Robert Schuman, Paul Henri Spaak and Alcide de Gasperi. To this day, all the photos of the forties remain hanging in the new multi-coloured building – but in remote corridors, where they serve as fading reminders of what was once a great idealism.

Were we British sincere in our much-rehearsed oratory in favour of a united Europe? That was certainly the impression given in Europe by the frequent speeches of these great men. Or was it all a genial act of deception aimed at encouraging France to make an alliance with the Federal Republic of Germany, the *rapprochement* disguised by 'European' oratory and the encouragement given to Italy and the Benelux countries to join the club? After all, the idea of a united Europe pre-dated Hitler, who had himself attempted the unification of continental Europe by force of arms. Even the German anti-Nazi conspirators, Von Stauffenberg, Beck and Von Trott, looked beyond Hitler's war to a Europe united in peace. Norman Angell advocated a united Europe before the 1939–45 war.

How genuine were Churchill, Eden and Macmillan? Was their expressed enthusiasm just 'conference oratory' designed for Blackpool and Brighton, its purpose to draw a distinction between the Tory party on the one hand and, on the other, Attlee's suspicions of a capitalist Europe and his government's refusal to join the Coal and Steel Community? It was not enough for the Foreign Secretary, Ernie Bevin, to proclaim Strasbourg the new capital of Europe. Did he not discover that its inhabitants spoke German at home, and French between nine and five? If he did, it was because Sir Frank Roberts, at that time his private secretary, had told him so.

I should perhaps quote here from the diaries of Churchill's medical man Lord Moran, which were published in the mid-1960s to the vociferous indignation of the medical profession. Whatever the ethics of the medical profession may be with regard to patients' confidences, the book is a boon to historians. My father, a neurologist, was most censorious of Moran (known in the medical profession as 'corkscrew Charlie') – but he bought the book nonetheless.

> Strasbourg, October 1 1954
> . . . the PM's fear that America might withdraw from Europe and 'go it alone' was not without reason. When the nine power conference met on Wednesday, Mr Dulles spoke of a great wave of disillusionment which had swept over America after the European Defence Community had been rejected (by France); there was a feeling, he said that 'the situation in Europe is pretty hopeless'. It was in this bleak atmosphere that the delegates were asked to find some means of re-arming Germany that would be accepted by a majority of the French Assembly. Round the table they sat, doodling, mumbling, despairing . . .
> . . . Then Mr Eden rose and told the representatives of the nine powers that if the conference were successful Britain would undertake to keep on the continent the forces now stationed there; that she would not withdraw them without the consent of a majority of the Brussels Treaty Powers, including West Germany and Italy, as well as France and the Low Countries. Mr Eden called this 'a very formidable step to take', since it committed Britain to the defence of Europe. The delegates sat dumbfounded. The silence was at last broken by M. Spaak, who, turning to M. Pierre Mendès-France, said 'you've won'. Everyone felt that the situation had been transformed and that Mr Eden's pledge saved the conference when it was bound to end in fiasco . . .

What role had the British played? Was Churchill's 'support' for a united Europe no more than a sentimental gesture towards the building of a monument to his greatness? Anthony Eden harked back to the prewar balance of power in Europe, with Britain playing its time-honoured role. He lacked both Churchill's vision and his sentimentality. Only Harold Macmillan spoke at the time with something approaching sincerity. In the 1960s, when Prime Minister, he was to become a convert to the idea of Britain in Europe. In the late 1940s, Boothby would have had Britain join, but he carried little weight. Soames and Sandys were in general sympathetic to Britain's entry. The bulk of the Tory party was not. It considered the idea outrageous.

But, before reaching any conclusions, we must first examine the record.

In Harold Macmillan's *Tides of Fortune*, the future Prime Minister quotes from a speech he made in the Commons on the future of Germany. It was 1949. Paper guarantees were useless, thought Macmillan. 'The only guarantee is if the soul of the German people is won for the West. If Germany enters a Western European system, as a free and equal member, then indeed German heavy industry can be subjected to control; but not an individual control directed against Germany alone, but to exactly the same regulations as to quantity, planning, development and so forth, as the coal, iron and steel industries of Belgium, Holland, Luxembourg, France, Italy and Britain.'

Let us return for a moment to Moran's diaries. Immediately after the passage quoted above, the good doctor continues: 'I brought him [Churchill] back to Anthony's [Eden's] pledge. "It can be cancelled at any time," he went on with a mischievous smile. "It does not mean anything. All words. Of course, I shall not say that," he added hastily. "But what is all the fuss about? No one in their senses thought we would bring our forces back from the Continent." He paused, spoke of the Russian threat and concluded: "Now they are going to do exactly what I suggested at Strasbourg in August 1950. Never", he said, smiling broadly "was the leadership of Europe so easily won."'

England (I make no apologies for using the proper term) has, since the end of the war, aspired 'to lead Europe', regardless of the fact that we refused to join the Treaty of Rome in 1957, strove to build up EFTA, a rival trading organisation without political content, and dismissed out of hand the notion of a British contribution to the European Defence Community, which is, today, forty years on, symbolised by a common Franco-German brigade. The younger Tories of the 1950s were reminded of the three interlocking circles, with Britain at the centre of each: the Atlantic Alliance, the Commonwealth and Europe. Three horses but only one fit to ride. How ridiculous we were!

The truth was that the British Labour Party (with the exception of Ernie Bevin) was insular and reluctant to join a 'capitalists' club'. Its concern was to build the welfare state. Churchill, whose reputation stood higher in Europe than that of any other political leader, in or out of office, was a Liberal Unionist with Imperialist leanings. He was a Victorian, determined to preserve what was left of England's greatness. He deplored the two European civil wars of the twentieth century and was determined to avoid a third. But he was a nationalist who saw a united Europe in terms of British leadership. Hence his short-lived glee before Moran. If England 'led' Europe in 1954, it has not done so since.

The same was true of Anthony Eden, for whom European relationships were bilateral, as at Suez when he connived with the French and Israelis against Nasser. He was also a believer in the 'special relationship' with America, which revisionist historians like John Charmley have argued never existed, and which, if it ever did, was swiftly destroyed by Eden's Suez adventure. Neither Churchill nor Eden saw clearly the hostility with which Americans like Roosevelt, Dulles and Kennedy regarded 'British Imperialism'.

In 1951, when Churchill, old and sick, returned to Downing Street, the Empire had vanished with Indian independence, and the Commonwealth, which was to take its place, had little influence or power. Canada was bound closely to the United States. Australia was, however, still pro-British, the idea of a Republic of Oz unthinkable. New Zealand sent us its soldiers (the best in the world) and its lamb (frozen stiff). The African territories, including South Africa, were awaiting Harold Macmillan's 'wind of change' and Iain Macleod's act of liberation. The choice became increasingly obvious to those who could see it: isolation or Europe? Macmillan set out to convert his party to the latter option. But what kind of Europe was on offer?

'Europe' has long meant different things to different peoples. The Dutch had outlived their period of greatness, and Dutch 'nationalism' was long since dead. They were content to ally themselves closely with their neighbours. Belgium was a relatively modern state, the Walloons being pro-French, the Flemish, or many of them, pro-German. (A Flemish SS division had been raised during the war.) But there was no such thing as Belgian nationalism – in fact, the opposite was true: there was a desire for internal harmony and external friendship. Together with Luxembourg, they made up a community of their own, Benelux, and were at the van of progress towards European unity.

France was still deeply nationalistic, despite its defeats, and the corruption and inefficiency of the Fourth Republic. Its principal aim was to bring about a friendship with the now divided Germany, a duality of powers roughly equal in strength and population. France had the bomb; Germany, the industrial potential and the distant prospect of reunification. France, too, wished 'to lead Europe' – and has, in many ways, succeeded in doing so. For the Elysée, the key was the Franco-German alliance; for de Gaulle, it was the exclusion of England.

Italy, a relatively recent creation of the 1860s, had rejected the Roman ambitions of Mussolini and was content to play host to the signatories of the Treaty of Rome. Agriculturally and industrially, it had much to gain. An independent Italian foreign policy smacked of Fascist illusions of grandeur, of Ethiopia, Tripoli and the unhappy invasion of Greece. A country that had lost the war and changed sides, besides fighting a civil war, had had its fill of nationalism. It was enough to have invented the Vespa scooter and set up fashion and film industries to rival those of France.

West Germany under Adenauer was eager to bury the past. German nationalism had died in the fires of 1918 and 1945, and politicians of all parties used West Germany's place in a new Europe as a substitute for reunification and nuclear rearmament. In the years 1945–51 Adenauer sought the goodwill of the rest of Europe, together with the creation of the Bundeswehr as the substitute for the European Defence Community, which was to be rejected by the Gaullist right in France. Germany was to be the good neighbour and the powerhouse of Europe, its economic miracle the envy of its neighbours. The closeness of its relations with France under the Fifth Republic went a long way towards limiting the effect of France's withdrawal from the military side of NATO in the early sixties.

Thus England was, with France, the only European country to preserve its nationalism. Had we not emerged victorious from two world wars? Were we willing to sacrifice our sovereignty and lose our identity to a bunch of unreliable foreigners? Everyone thought not, save for some of the far-seeing younger members of the Tory party. The British monarchy served as the symbol of our national independence, and the acquisition of nuclear weapons by Attlee served to disguise our decline in power relative to both friend and foe. Our coal was as cheap as our fish, and we had no wish to share either commodity with our continental neighbours.

The Euro-optimists of the late forties might well have read Duff

Cooper's famous paper to the Foreign Office, delivered in 1944. In the months leading up to D-Day, Eden and Cooper quarrelled bitterly with Churchill over the course of postwar British foreign policy. Eden, the heir apparent, was obsessed with detail, Churchill with the larger picture; Cooper was, of the three, by a long way the most far-sighted. A career diplomat with the rank of ambassador, Cooper argued strongly for a united Europe as a bloc between American power and Russian imperialism. Churchill, who disliked de Gaulle intensely, took sides with Roosevelt, and would do nothing that might increase Soviet suspicions. De Gaulle and Churchill met in a stationary train on the south coast where the British Prime Minister made it plain to the Free French leader that were Britain faced with a choice between an alliance with America and some rival European arrangement, Britain would always choose America. So dogmatic a statement made a great impression on de Gaulle (who had also quarrelled with Roosevelt), and was to be returned with interest in 1963 when de Gaulle exercised his veto against Harold Macmillan's attempt to take this country into Europe. It was that veto, not Profumo's love affairs, that brought about the fall of the Macmillan government in 1963.

The Attlee government of 1945–51 was a government of national reconstruction. Labour had adopted Lord Beveridge's plan for a welfare state, and the country was on the verge of bankruptcy. Attlee looked to Truman to save Britain as Churchill had to Roosevelt, and General Marshall duly obliged. The thrust of British policy was aimed at 'low' rather than 'high' politics. Aneurin Bevan was against rearmament and in favour of the National Health Service, which he regarded as his creation, brought about despite the opposition of the doctors. Ernie Bevin was a patriot and a great Foreign Secretary. He recognised Soviet ambition for what it was, and was determined to see western Europe rearm. But the idea of a united Europe, however vague, was left to the Tories, and to a lesser extent to the Liberals, as their particular province. Hence the importance given by people living on the continent of Europe to speeches such as Churchill's in 1949 when he filled La Place Kleber in Strasbourg with 20,000 people. Every hotel window was full – save for Ernie Bevin's. But Eden never shared Churchill's transitory enthusiasm for a united Europe, and it was left to less senior Tories like Macmillan, Boothby, Sandys and Soames to march behind the blue, starred banner.

Also in 1949, towards the end of the summer, I was invited by the London Young Conservatives to visit a European Movement camp at the Lorelei on the Rhine. It had no especial significance, save that I was eighteen, waiting to do my National Service in the Rifle Brigade, and interested in a political career. A hundred or so young people of both sexes and from all the countries of western Europe were put under canvas on the cliff overlooking the castle-studded Rhine. The indoctrination was moderate, which could not be said for the consumption of Rhenish wine in green goblets. The neighbouring tent was filled by a party of British ATS whose language and sexual conversation were something of an eye-opener to a well-brought-up public school boy. It was all great fun, and I returned to England with a sympathy for the European ideal that I have retained ever since. The London Young Conservatives, financed by Conservative Central Office, continued these annual visits for ten years or more, and by so doing coloured the viewpoint of a generation of Young Tories.

If the bulk of the postwar adult Tory party held no view about Europe, the handful of enthusiasts were balanced by a group of antis that included Lord Hinchinbroke, Angus Maude and Sir Derek Walker Smith. The traditional right of the party were suspicious of Winston Churchill, whom they regarded as a Liberal Unionist at heart. His acknowledged heir, Eden, was no friend of integration with the continent. Butler was regarded as 'wet' and devious, while Harold Macmillan was thought of as 'pink' (did not Attlee once say before the war that he would one day lead the Labour Party?), and more liable than any of his peers to adopt unsound policies. In terms of their own definition of soundness, they were quite correct: by 1957 Macmillan, having restored the country's fortunes after Suez, was moving towards Europe and colonial independence. But by this stage the bulk of the party were concentrating their fire upon the Labour government, whose social revolution was running out of puff and whose majority had shrunk drastically in the election of 1950. Only the Tory 'Young Turks' were in favour of closer ties with Europe, and they were, not unreasonably, all Macmillanites.

The visits to Strasbourg, Luxembourg and Brussels had a great effect upon those MPs of both parties who were lucky enough to be included as delegates to the Council of Europe and the Western European Union. Strasbourg was the most beautiful of the three rival cities. The black and white heart of Strasbourg, with its single-spired cathedral, carefully re-created after the ravages of the wars, and encircled by canals connected to the Rhine, was surrounded by suburbs: French-looking towards the railway station, German in the administrative and university quarter built under the Kaisers. The food, to those more used to England's postwar privations, was unbelievably good: French in flavour; German in quantity; the cafés and *Bierstube* were packed by the Strasbourgeois eating quiche Lorraine, onion tart, knuckle of pork and river fish served in a cream sauce. The wines were a discovery in themselves: Riesling that had none of the cloying effect of the German equivalent, Tokay (Pinot Gris) and the ubiquitous Gewürztraminer with its scented sweetness. The delegates to the Council of Europe would spend evenings during the spring and autumn sessions sitting with a bottle of Gewürz, an admirable aperitif, outside cafés, gazing towards the blue line of the Vosges like so many Frenchmen deprived of their two provinces after Prussia's victory in 1870. 'Speak of it rarely; think of it often' had been their watchword. In 1945 Strasbourg was once again French; and, what was more, the putative capital, if the French government had its way, of the new Europe.

Conservative MPs were not alone in becoming enamoured of Strasbourg, *les routes des vins* and the black and white villages of the Vosges which looked so much like parts of Herefordshire. Roy Jenkins returned from the city to make a series of compelling speeches in favour of Europe to MPs of all parties and influential opinion beyond Westminster. He certainly converted me when I was elected to the House in October 1959. Maurice Edelman, the suave Labour MP of Jewish origins with a penchant for writing novels in which every minister had his mistress, became a 'European'. So, too, did Shirley Williams, and many other Labour politicians who were later to form the SDP. We were romantic idealists who, en route for Strasbourg by car, had viewed the battlefields of the Franco-Prussian War, Mars la Tour and Vionville, with Michael Howard's book in hand, pausing at Verdun where we gazed through the dusty windows of L'Ossuaire, surely the most ugly building in the world: a long, low, lizard-like edifice with a stump of a tower inside which were piled the bones of 200,000 French and German soldiers who had no known grave. 'Europe' was about putting an end to the civil wars that had devastated the continent and cut down the flower of German, French and British manhood; it was not, as it was later to become at the prompting of obscurantist Tory MPs like William Cash, Christopher Gill, Teresa Gorman and Sir Teddy Taylor, a matter of the straightness of bananas. God preserve us from those who cannot see beyond the end of their long noses!

Immediately after the Second World War, the British Labour Party was alone among European parties of the democratic left to take an anti-European, nationalist stance: the French, Dutch, German and Italian socialist parties were all pro-European. Communists of every nationality, however, were opposed to a movement that could only serve to create a European identity and recruit the power of the Federal Republic to the defence of the continent against Soviet ambition. The British Tory party contained the highest cards: its leaders had defied Hitler and Churchill had 'won the war'; but its attitude towards Europe was equivocal. Did it go much beyond dinners with de Gasperi, Schuman (a Lorrainer who had fought for the Germans in the Kaiser's war and for France in Hitler's), Adenauer and Monnet? How perfidious was Albion? Was British oratory fuelled only by *les vins d'Alsace* and the genius of the head chef of Le Crocodile? There were many abroad who feared so.

The concept of a united Europe was almost as old as Europe itself. For many centuries, statesmen and philosophers have dreamed of the day when the countries of the continent, conscious of their common heritage, could forget their animosities and rivalries and join together in peace and prosperity. The Roman Empire, the Roman Catholic Church and Charlemagne had shown the way. The barbarian invasions from the east, Luther and the rise of nationalism with Napoleon the Great had cast obstacles in the path.

How strange it is to read a statement made by Lord Salisbury, Tory Prime Minister in 1897 at the time of Queen Victoria's jubilee – the apogee of British Imperialism. Surveying the European scene, he declared: 'The federated action of Europe, if we can maintain it, is our sole hope of escaping from the constant terror and calamity of war, the constant pressure of the burdens of an armed peace, which weigh down the spirits and darken the prospect of every nation in this part of the world. The Federation of Europe is the only hope we have.'

Macmillan in *Tides of Fortune* quotes from a response he made to a questionnaire on war aims in October 1939. He wrote: 'Many people are asking what kind of Europe one could hope to emerge out of the chaos of today. The picture could only be painted in the broadest colours. But if Western civilisation is to survive, we must look forward to an organisation, economic, cultural and perhaps even political, comprising all the countries of Western Europe.'

In the autumn of 1942, a few days before the battle of El Alamein, Churchill wrote a minute to Eden of extraordinary foresight. 'I must admit', he said, 'that my thoughts rest primarily in Europe – the revival of the glory of Europe, the parent continent of the modern nations and civilisation. It would be a measureless disaster if Russian barbarism overlaid the culture and independence of the ancient States of Europe. Hard as it is to say now, I trust that the European family must act unitedly as one under a Council of Europe.' Churchill continued: 'I look forward to a United States of Europe in which the barriers between the nations will be greatly minimised and unrestricted travel will be possible. I hope to see the economy of Europe studied as a whole.'

The Council of Europe which Churchill foresaw came into being (despite Bevin's resistance) with the signature of its Statute on 5 May 1949. The first meeting of the Council proper was held in Strasbourg in September 1949, attended by 101 individuals from twelve countries (all democracies). The British delegation consisted of eleven socialists, six Conservatives and one Liberal. The socialists included Hugh Dalton and Herbert Morrison (both ministers), William Whiteley, the government chief whip, Edelman and Mackay, both ardent Europeans, Fred Lee and Lynn Ungoed Thomas. The Tory team consisted of Churchill, David Maxwell Fyfe, David Eccles, Boothby, Ronald Ross and Harold Macmillan. Duncan Sandys took part in his capacity as chairman of the European Movement. (Sandys was still a prominent member of the British delegation when I became a member in the 1970s.)

The city of Strasbourg felt a particular loyalty to Churchill. In the winter of 1944, at the time of the German offensive in the Ardennes, Eisenhower wanted to pull back the American and French troops covering Strasbourg, which had been recently liberated. Churchill persuaded Eisenhower to stand firm, and the Strasbourgeois were saved from Nazi retribution. Thus, holding no political office, Churchill lived off his reputation, and in Strasbourg he clearly dominated events. A villa was put at his disposal, amply stocked with food and drink by a grateful populace.

High water for the Council of Europe lay between 1949 and the signing of the Treaty of Rome in 1957: the days when Churchill pressed for the admittance of West Germany, Herbert Morrison treated the assembly as if it were an extension of the London County Council, and Harold Macmillan pressed most strongly of all for the unity of Europe. After Britain's entry into the Community in 1973 under the premiership of Edward Heath (Harold Macmillan's confidant), the European Parliament came gradually to replace the Council of Europe in power and influence. Even in its first, unelected, incarnation as an 'assembly', the Parliament attracted the more able among the European politicians; when it was transformed into an elected body, the process continued at a faster rate, although the national parliaments resisted any transfer of power to it. The two bodies shared the same buildings in Strasbourg and Luxembourg, but the European Parliament looked increasing towards Brussels, home of the Council of Ministers and the Commission – the two bodies over which the European Parliament strove to win control.

When the Tories were returned to power in Britain in October 1951, Churchill, no longer the man he was, re-entered No. 10 Downing Street with his attentions absorbed by the Cold War, the conflict in Korea and the rebuilding, as he saw it, of the 'special relationship' with the United States. Anthony Eden, brittle and impatiently waiting for the Old Man to retire, shared the Eurosceptic views of the Foreign Office. Sir David Maxwell Fyfe, who had spoken up for Europe at Strasbourg, was given the Home Office. Harold Macmillan was given the choice between the Board of Trade and minister for housing, responsible for fulfilling the party conference pledge of building 300,000 houses a year, something the economists claimed could not be done without a serious dislocation of resources. They were right. Macmillan was removed from the international scene and spent his time, helped by Ernie Marples, building housing estates upon windswept northern hillsides at the end of bus routes; the kind of housing Philip Larkin described as 'where only relatives go'. Macmillan was bitterly disappointed, but his radicalism encouraged him in the project of building houses – albeit unfit for a nation to live in, and involving the destruction of long-established and generally law-abiding communities. Duncan Sandys and Soames were given junior office, and the Conservative element of the delegation to Strasbourg was drawn increasingly from the *deuxième cru* of its MPs. In my day the delegates came to be led by Sir John Rodgers, who never missed a party; Sir Simon Wingfield Digby, whose idea of Europe was Antibes; and Sir Frederic Bennett, who collected foreign decorations. Europe was put on the back burner.

In *Tides of Fortune* Macmillan wrote:

> The return of Churchill to power was hailed throughout Europe and America as likely to mark a wholly new approach towards the question of European Unity. His great prestige, unrivalled since the days of Marlborough, and the energy with which he had thrown himself into the founding and promotion of the European Movement, not unnaturally served to raise widespread hopes. Now, at last, after so many hesitations, Britain might be expected to give a definite lead. If what followed was to prove a sad disillusionment – almost a betrayal – it is right to recall some of the difficulties, internal and external, with which Churchill was faced.

But a 'betrayal' it most certainly was.

The external factors such as Soviet ambition, Korea and then Suez, were all eventually to solve themselves. Britain's economic problems waxed and waned, with a more general prosperity replacing the days of Labour austerity. But in respect of the internal factors which curbed any enthusiasm Churchill might have had for a diminution of our sovereignty and closer European integration, the situation remains much the same today. Macmillan described it as 'an ambivalence if not a division within the ranks of the Conservative Party over Europe'. The traditional right of the party, imperialist in tone, who rebelled against the government over Suez, were – with the possible exception of Julian Amery – every bit as keen to defend concepts such as 'identity', and 'sovereignty', as Mr James Cran *et al.* are today. The party's 'ballast', the so-called 'knights of the shires', were more inclined towards loyalty than are their equivalents today, the 'knights of the suburbs'.

In 1951 Labour lost power after six years in which a social revolution had taken place; today the Tory party has endured eighteen years of power, during which the wear and tear of the Thatcher years, her overthrow, and the unsuccessful attack on the premiership of John Major by the right (aided and abetted by Messrs Murdoch and Black) have combined to increase the fragility of the party. The Eurosceptics include several from among the cleverer of the new Tories, and their numbers, combined with the narrowness of John Major's majority, severely restricted the Prime Minister's freedom of action. In the more than forty years that have elapsed since the return of Churchill to Downing Street, great progress has been made towards a more united Europe. Yet Labour has been converted to a kind of Europeanism which governance must sorely test; the Liberal Democrats are still in favour of Europe, but count for little; and the Tory party is wracked by its internal divisions. We are paying the price of progress: the inevitable reaction against change, the growing influence of the third-rate. How can Britain adopt a policy of isolation in a world dominated by the United States, the Russian Federation, China, the European Union and the countries of the Pacific rim? Are we to be crippled by the policies of despair?

By the 1997 election, the two main parties had both moved steadily towards Euroscepticism. The newspapers, save possibly for the *Independent*, were hostile to further integration. It was the age of 'straight banana' stories. The Tories and Labour alike poured cold water on the starting date for a common currency (January 1999), which had been agreed at the Treaty of Maastricht. John Major's cry that 'Britain must be at the heart of Europe' seemed vulnerable to his divided Cabinet and party. Ironically, Britain looked like achieving the convergence criteria, while Germany, partially crippled by the cost of reunification, and France, bedevilled by unemployment, seemed less likely to do so. Only the Liberal Democrats remained the party of Europe, and at general elections their fate is to be marginalised.

In a nod towards even-handedness, Conrad Black's *Telegraph* printed at the end of March an article by Klaus Kinkel in which the German foreign minister spelled out once again the case for European integration. Kinkel reminded his readers that Europe was a new model for international relations, replacing the old balance of power which had led remorselessly to two world wars. In answer to the question 'what kind of Europe?', he suggested that the debate continues between advocates of a United States of Europe, a Europe of nation-states, and a partnership of nations. He claimed that European integration is an evolving process in response to changing political and economic challenges. He wrote that subsidiarity means that every public task should be assigned to the lowest possible level of public authority – whether a local council, a *Land* government, a member state or the EU itself – thus ruling out automatic centralisation. 'Less, but better, regulation' is Commission President Santer's prescription. Kinkel asserted, somewhat optimistically, that the intergovernmental conference in June would lead to substantial progress on issues such as majority voting, internal security in a border-free union, the free movement of goods within a single market and environmental protection. Europe will be heard in the world, he concluded, 'if it speaks with one voice'.

Europe is more than a high-class free trade zone. The authors of the Treaty of Rome had a vision, that of overcoming the spiritual, political and economic consequences of the Second World War, and they created a successful model for peace and prosperity. Did John Major take this on board? And, if he did, would his atavistic party have permitted him to take advantage of it? The same goes for Tony Blair. Of recent Tory prime ministers only Harold Macmillan and Edward Heath have glimpsed the future as it might, and should, be. On 10 April 1997 Lady Thatcher went to my old constituency of Aldershot (I had succeeded in keeping her out for twenty-seven years) only to warn of an inevitable loss of sovereignty in June. The press described Lady T as 'a big gun'; I would prefer the description 'loose cannon'.

It gives me no pleasure to write this piece. It is not I who has changed; it is the party. I put on record before the election that I would not vote for the obscurantist Tory in Ludlow, Chris Gill. My disillusionment with my old party runs even deeper. I am afraid that yet once more in the long story of Britain and Europe we will once again miss the bus. If we are so foolish to do so, there will be nothing splendid in our isolation.

Epilogue

JULIAN CRITCHLEY

What were the most important elements in determining the fate of the Tory party after its election defeat? The first must be the stupidity of John Major in declaring his immediate relinquishment of the leadership in the wake of his crushing defeat – for which others should take much of the responsibility. Had he soldiered on until November and only then called an election for the leadership, he would have permitted the party to recover from its collective nervous breakdown. In the meantime, in the Commons Clarke would have shone; Hague would have had a chance to show his mettle.

Secondly, the choice facing the party was greatly impoverished by Michael Heseltine's angina attack which compelled him to abandon his remaining hopes of leading the party. Would he have fared better than Clarke in the contest? Who knows? I doubt that he would have made the error of entering into a pact with Redwood. But he would have been in his seventies before the Tories would have been likely to win a general election. Along with F. E. Smith, Curzon and Iain Macleod, he ranks among the greatest Tories never to have achieved supreme office.

Thirdly, the outcome of the leadership election was dictated by the nature of the electorate – the rump of a defeated party. One hundred and sixty-four MPs disregarded the views of the rest of the Conservative Party and picked an unknown and untried candidate as their – and our – leader. Had John MacGregor gained the chairmanship of the 1922 Committee, he might have tried to widen the franchise, perhaps to include the Tories in the Lords who had formerly served in the Commons. But Archie Hamilton, never the cleverest of men, obstinately refused to make any changes. Had the electorate been 264 Tories and not 164, Blair would still be Prime Minister, but Clarke would be leader of the opposition.

And what of Hague? Is his age of any advantage? I very much doubt it. His career so far has not been remarkable: junior office followed by two years as Secretary of State for Wales, the least important of positions of Cabinet rank. He has neither the brains of Lilley, the experience of Howard, nor even the messianic qualities of Redwood. As the leadership campaign progressed, he continually shifted his opinions, earning first the contempt of the *Telegraph*, eventually a relieved acknowledgement: at least, said that great newspaper, he was not Ken Clarke. Knowing the fickleness of the party activists as I do, I expect him to be greeted with enthusiasm at some seaside resort in the autumn. But it is in the House that he will be judged.

The Tory party does not always plump for mediocrity; but it did in 1990 and in 1923 (though Baldwin is still under-rated), and it has a taste for it. The party preferred Neville to Winston until the eleventh hour. As for Margaret Thatcher, the jury is still out. Would Whitelaw have done better, and lasted longer?

Kenneth Clarke was, sadly, 'yesterday's man'. He stood for the Macmillanite tradition, the last flowering of which occurred in the early years of Ted Heath's government. He eschewed ideology, favoured greater European integration and, when he was not introducing Thatcherite policies, as he did as health secretary, was a staunch believer in the One Nation tradition. He was an excellent Chancellor of the Exchequer, in the mould of Roy Jenkins. But the Tory party had changed beneath him. Thanks to Margaret Thatcher and, more recently, to Dame Angela Rumbold after she had foolishly been put in charge of candidate selection at Central Office, it had become narrow, bigoted and nationalistic. It had lost its idealism, its sense of vision.

John Major, it must be admitted, was weak and vacillating; but the party never gave him half a chance. He, too, admired Iain Macleod, but he let the Thatcherites get the better of him. Major's gift to us is William Jefferson Hague. I can only hope that he will prove able to restore the fortunes – and change the policies – of what was once the most successful political party of them all. Only time will tell.

BIRKBECK COLLEGE

1 1149235 7

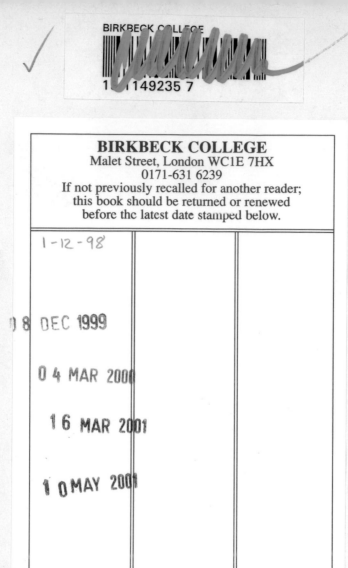

BIRKBECK COLLEGE
Malet Street, London WC1E 7HX
0171-631 6239
If not previously recalled for another reader;
this book should be returned or renewed
before the latest date stamped below.

1 - 12 - 98

0 8 DEC 1999

0 4 MAR 2000

1 6 MAR 2001

1 0 MAY 2001